THE volumes of the University of Michigan Studies and Publications are published by authority of the Board of Regents under the direction of the University of Michigan Press. The contributors are chiefly, but not exclusively, members of the faculties or graduates of the University. The expense is borne in part by gifts, in part by appropriations of the Board of Regents.

A list of the volumes in this series is given at the end of this book. Orders and requests for detailed book lists should be directed to the University of Michigan Press.

University of Michigan Publications

LANGUAGE AND LITERATURE

VOLUME XX

WORDSWORTH'S FORMATIVE YEARS

WORDSWORTH'S FORMATIVE YEARS

BY GEORGE WILBUR MEYER

ANN ARBOR · THE UNIVERSITY OF MICHIGAN PRESS
LONDON   ·   HUMPHREY MILFORD, OXFORD UNIVERSITY PRESS
1943

COPYRIGHT, 1943
BY THE UNIVERSITY OF MICHIGAN

Paperback ISBN: 978-0-472-75183-9

Preface

THIS volume, the first of a projected series to be devoted to the reinterpretation of Wordsworth's complete work, is an attempt to throw new light on the poet's early development by an examination of the poetry and prose which he wrote in the first twenty-eight years of his life. My study differs from previous descriptions of this period in that I have not used *The Prelude* as a primary source of information about Wordsworth's formative years. I have worked from the assumption that the best evidence of the growth of Wordsworth's philosophical and artistic power from 1787 to 1798 is found not in *The Prelude*, which, save for a few lines, was composed after the period in question, but in the poems and letters that Wordsworth wrote between 1787 and 1798. This procedure would not have been possible, however, had it not been for the admirable investigations of my predecessors—particularly Legouis, Harper, Garrod, Beatty, Campbell, and Mueschke—and for Ernest de Selincourt's excellent new edition of the Wordsworth correspondence and his recent publication of previously unknown manuscript versions of Wordsworth's most important early poems.

I wish to take this opportunity to thank all those who have helped me in this work. My greatest debt is to Professor Paul Mueschke, of the University of Michigan, under whose direction my study of Wordsworth's youth began. Credit for whatever virtues my book may possess belongs in large part to him. For their reading and criticism of the manuscript I am grateful to Professor Oscar James Campbell, of Columbia University, who first excited my interest in the poetry of Wordsworth, and to Professors Louis I. Bredvold, Clarence

WORDSWORTH'S FORMATIVE YEARS

DeWitt Thorpe, Henry W. Nordmeyer, and Hayward Keniston, of the University of Michigan. I owe sincere thanks, finally, to Miss Grace E. Potter and to Dr. Eugene S. McCartney, of the University of Michigan Press, for their sympathetic interest and expert criticism in the editing of my book.

G. W. M.

SHAKER HEIGHTS, OHIO
February 10, 1943

Contents

CHAPTER	PAGE
Preface	v
I Biography, 1770-95	3
II The Early Poems	37
III "The Letter to the Bishop of Llandaff"	88
IV "Guilt and Sorrow"	110
V "The Borderers"	153
VI The Naturalism of 1798	220
Bibliography	255
Index	259

NOTE

The few citations from Wordsworth's poetry not otherwise indicated are from *The Poetical Works of William Wordsworth,* eight volumes, edited by William Knight (London and New York, 1896). Quotations from the poems of *Lyrical Ballads* are from the text of the first (1798) edition. All references to *The Prelude,* unless otherwise noted, are to Ernest de Selincourt's edition (Oxford, 1926) of the version of 1805–6.

WORDSWORTH'S FORMATIVE YEARS

CHAPTER I

Biography, 1770-95

I

ONE night in the summer of 1788, when he was merely a young Englishman on his first long vacation from Cambridge, William Wordsworth took part in a country revel that lasted well into the morning hours. Many years later, after he had achieved fame as a poet, he wrote into the fourth book of *The Prelude*—his long autobiographical poem, addressed to his friend and collaborator, Samuel Taylor Coleridge—this description of his return from the festivities:

> Two miles I had to walk along the fields
> Before I reached my home. Magnificent
> The morning was, in memorable pomp,
> More glorious than I ever had beheld.
> The Sea was laughing at a distance; all
> The solid Mountains were as bright as clouds,
> Grain-tinctured, drench'd in empyrean light;
> And, in the meadows and the lower grounds,
> Was all the sweetness of a common dawn,
> Dews, vapours, and the melody of birds,
> And Labourers going forth into the fields.
> —Ah! need I say, dear Friend, that to the brim
> My heart was full; I made no vows, but vows
> Were then made for me; bond unknown to me
> Was given, that I should be, else sinning greatly,
> A dedicated Spirit. On I walk'd
> In blessedness, which even yet remains.
>   (Vv. 329–345)[1]

This is excellent poetry. But it is misleading and therefore bad autobiography. One might suppose, at first glance,

[1] P. 124.

that Wordsworth on this gorgeous morning had been consciously inspired to devote his life to poetry. Close scrutiny of the lines reveals, however, that they merely reflect Wordsworth's later conviction that on a particular morning in his nineteenth year his progress and development in poetry were guaranteed by the intelligent intervention of some friendly power outside himself. Wordsworth does not explain just how or when he learned that this was the particular day on which God or nature began to act in his behalf, but his admission that the "bond" was *unknown* to him makes it plain that this information was not forthcoming until sometime after the event described.

Like most successful egoists, Wordsworth came in later life to regard his personal history as a miracle wrought by mysterious powers whose ways are dark and hidden from all but favored eyes. The passage cited above is only one of many distributed throughout *The Prelude* in which Wordsworth gives the impression that all his youthful thoughts and experiences were portentous preparation for hard and high poetic duties soon to follow. But not even Wordsworth, able rationalizer that he was, could make all the facts of his youth fit this attractive mystical hypothesis. Some of these facts he chose to omit from *The Prelude;* others he mentioned with a brevity quite unwarranted by their true significance. Yet biographers have accepted without remarkable question or consistent protest this inaccurate, romanticized version of Wordsworth's youth for so long that it has hardened into convention and acquired the unmistakable odor of sanctity. Consequently, events and circumstances of prime importance to Wordsworth's development in this critical early period have been seriously neglected when they have not been entirely overlooked. The result is that we now have only the most confused and cursory understanding of what actually happened in Wordsworth's formative years.

The letters written by William and Dorothy Wordsworth in the years 1787–95 reveal that the young Wordsworth, far from being a "dedicated Spirit" receiving regular and salutary impulses from intelligent tutelary powers, was in truth a rather unengaging victim of what modern psychologists would probably describe as maladjustment and emotional immaturity. The history of his life from his matriculation at Cambridge in 1787 to his settlement at Racedown in 1795 is the history of a long and painful effort to adjust unruly emotions and presuppositions to a world which he found to be more hostile than friendly. To understand this period of Wordsworth's life, and the emotional and intellectual origins of his mature work, we must first take brief notice of the idealistic view of the world which he formed as a child. Then we must study those events and circumstances which, by clashing with and contradicting the illusions of his childhood, caused Wordsworth to feel ill at ease in the world and dissatisfied with his environment. Finally, we must observe the effects of this conflict between the real and the ideal upon Wordsworth's personal behavior and, in the following chapters, upon the direction of his literary efforts.

II

"Fair seed-time had my soul," wrote Wordsworth in middle age of his childhood days of carefree familiarity with the objects of external nature, of his life at home under his mother's loving and indulgent care, and of his happy schooltime, after his mother's death, at Hawkshead. His idyllic situation among the hills and lakes of northern England and the liberal methods of education employed by his early teachers prompted him to form an ideal and dreamlike conception of the world which he found difficult to reconcile in later years with the reality of his personal experience. Indeed, almost every circumstance and adventure of his early life, according to *The Prelude*, served to convince Wordsworth of the excellence of the created universe and of the innate goodness and perfectibility of man. Nowhere does he express this high estimate of his youthful experience more impressively than in the ninth book of *The Prelude*, where he explains to Coleridge how and why he was predisposed to favor the principles and doctrines of the French Revolution:

> For, born in a poor District, and which yet
> Retaineth more of ancient homeliness,
> Manners erect, and frank simplicity,
> Than any other nook of English Land,
> It was my fortune scarcely to have seen
> Through the whole tenor of my School-day time
> The face of one, who, whether Boy or Man,
> Was vested with attention or respect
> Through claims of wealth or blood; nor was it least
> Of many debts which afterwards I owed
> To Cambridge, and an academic life
> That something there was holden up to view
> Of a Republic, where all stood thus far
> Upon equal ground, that they were brothers all
> In honour, as in one community,
> Scholars and Gentlemen, where, furthermore,
> Distinction lay open to all that came,
> And wealth and titles were in less esteem
> Than talents and successful industry.
> Add unto this, subservience from the first
> To God and Nature's single sovereignty,
> Familiar presences of awful Power
> And fellowship with venerable books
> To sanction the proud workings of the soul,
> And mountain liberty.   It could not be
> But that one tutor'd thus, who had been form'd
> To thought and moral feeling in the way
> This story hath described, should look with awe
> Upon the faculties of Man, receive
> Gladly the highest promises, and hail
> As best the government of equal rights
> And individual worth.   (Vv. 217–248)[2]

This retrospective account of the origins and causes of Wordsworth's faith in the ideals which he pursued throughout the years of his significant poetic activity suggests that his youth was unmarked by any collision with what we may call the more unpleasant realities of human existence. Social justice and equality, the reward of men for true merit and accomplishment rather than for inherited wealth and the accident of birth, the narrowing of the gap between the extremes of poverty and riches—all those things for which the French were fighting—Wordsworth, so he tells us, regarded

[2] P. 320.

as fixed properties of the natural order and took for granted because they were characteristic of the "poor District" where he was born and bred. God, nature, "venerable books," the simple rural virtues and obvious natural dignity of the "Statesmen" of Cumberland and Westmorland, "the proud workings of the soul, And mountain liberty," all combined, as Wordsworth saw it later, to inform him that the world and man were good.

Whether or not Wordsworth is accurate in thus describing the roots of his mature social optimism, he misleads us when he suggests that none of his experience prior to his sojourn in France in 1791-92 might have excused a somewhat less sanguine view of life's possibilities. Perhaps the events of his boyhood were so consistently fortunate and happy that he then had no occasion to suspect the presence of evil in the world. Certain it is, however, that he had felt the presence of evil at least as early as 1787, and that his adolescent optimism was challenged by his personal experience long before his ill-starred affair with Annette Vallon, and long before his acute distress in 1793 at the declaration of war between France and England—the events usually supposed by his biographers to have precipitated the first of the various "crises" with which Wordsworth's life is conveniently punctuated.[3]

Wordsworth's mother died when he was seven years old. His father followed her to the grave five years later. No record exists of Wordsworth's reaction to his mother's death, but in "The Vale of Esthwaite," a poem written by Wordsworth in 1787, there are some twenty-odd lines in which he reflects on the death of his father:

> One Evening when the wintry blast
> Through the sharp Hawthorn whistling pass'd
> And the poor flocks, all pinch'd with cold

---

[3] See, for example, Émile Legouis, *The Early Life of William Wordsworth, 1770-1798*, tr. by J. W. Matthews (New York, 1918), pp. 234-235; George McLean Harper, *William Wordsworth, His Life, Works, and Influence* (New York, 1929), pp. 148-149; and H. W. Garrod, *Wordsworth: Lectures and Essays* (Oxford, 1923), p. 60. Wordsworth himself provided the basis for this interpretation in *The Prelude*, X, 230-275.

> Sad-drooping sought the mountain fold
> Long, long, upon yon naked rock
> Alone, I bore the bitter shock;
> Long, long, my swimming eyes did roam
> For little Horse to bear me home,
> To bear me—what avails my tear?
> To sorrow o'er a Father's bier.
> Flow on, in vain thou hast not flow'd,
> But eased me of a heavy load;
> For much it gives my heart relief
> To pay the mighty debt of grief,
> With sighs repeated o'er and o'er,
> I mourn because I mourned no more.
> Nor did my little heart foresee
> She lost a home in losing thee.
> Nor did it know, of thee bereft,
> That little more than Heaven was left.
>   (Vv. 418–437)[4]

These sentimental lines reveal that Wordsworth felt appropriate sorrow at the loss of his father, but they do not suggest that he was deeply moved by the experience. "The mighty debt of grief" was paid apparently out of fondness for eighteenth-century sentiment and a becoming respect for filial obligation. But the concluding couplets, in which Wordsworth declares that he did not foresee what later years were to reveal—that Dorothy and he lost a home when they lost their father—contain matter of high importance. They suggest the gravity of the consequences for the Wordsworth children of the death of their parents, particularly that of the father, and direct attention to a phase of Wordsworth's biography that has never received the attention and emphasis its significance merits.

The death of Wordsworth's father was the immediate cause of a lengthy chain of circumstances which brought his children face to face with various unpleasant aspects of reality. The megalomaniacal Earl of Lonsdale, in whose employ the elder Wordsworth had served as a law agent, refused to discharge his obligation in the amount of £4,700 to the

---

[4] *The Poetical Works of William Wordsworth: Poems Written in Youth, Poems Referring to the Period of Childhood*, ed. by Ernest de Selincourt (Oxford, 1940) (hereafter referred to as *The Poetical Works*), pp. 279–280.

BIOGRAPHY, 1770-95

Wordsworth estate, and the five Wordsworth orphans soon found that they could gain no satisfaction in the corrupt courts of late eighteenth-century England. The consequent economic insecurity made the future ever uncertain, and forced the children into irksome dependence upon well-meaning but cantankerous and conservative relatives. This situation had a profound effect upon the development of William.

Probably Wordsworth's first conscious encounter with social evil and injustice came when he and his brothers and sister were engaged against the Earl of Lonsdale in the English courts of law. George McLean Harper has given the best account of this proceeding and its unfortunate results: "The family estate," he writes,

consisted chiefly of claims, amounting to about £4,700, on the Earl of Lonsdale, who had withheld money due to his agent, and even forced from him considerable loans. He held himself superior to the law, and when subsequently the case came up for trial, he retained all the best counsel, and succeeded in thwarting justice during the rest of his life. Meanwhile, for nineteen years, the Wordsworth children lived on prospects, which would not have carried them far had not their relatives come to their assistance. The children were put in charge of their father's brother Richard and their mother's uncle Christopher Crackanthorpe Cookson. Upon the earl's death, in 1802, their property was paid to them with interest by his successor.[5]

The young Wordsworths unfortunately had no way of knowing in advance that the affair would have a satisfactory ending, and Dorothy's letters to Jane Pollard, her closest friend and correspondent, reveal that she and William were fully conscious of the wrong and injustice which the criminal power and inclination of the noble Lonsdale forced them to endure.

Dorothy mentions the Lonsdale affair in at least eight letters to Jane; quotations from four of them suffice to establish the fact that the young Wordsworths were aware not only of the details of Lonsdale's iniquity, but also of the disloyalty and dishonesty of all those quondam friends who

[5] *Op. cit.*, p. 16.

owed them money. In a letter dated the summer of 1787 Dorothy wrote to Jane:

> Our fortunes will I fear be very small as Lord Lonsdale will most likely only pay a very small part of his debt which is 4700 pound. My uncle Kit (who is our Guardian) having said many disrespectful things of him and having always espoused the cause of the Duke of Norfolk, has incensed him so much that I fear we shall feel through life the effects of his imprudence.[6]

On August 5 or 6 of the same year Dorothy complained to her friend:

> ... it is indeed mortifying to my Brothers and me to find that amongst all those who visited at my father's house he had not one real friend; ... a gentleman of my father's intimate acquaintance, who is not worth less than two or three thousand a year, and who always professed himself to be the real friend of my father refused to pay a bill of seven hundred pound to his children without considerable deductions: when my Father died his affairs were in a very unsettled way and Lord Lonsdale does not owe us less than 4 thousand 7 hundred pounds of which I daresay we shall never receive a farthing ... .[7]

On June 26, 1791, Dorothy reported:

> When I last wrote to you I told you that our affairs wore a promising aspect; they are now in a very critical state; our trial is to come on at the next Carlisle assizes, where we hope the justice of our cause will carry us through. Lord Lonsdale has retained all the best counsel, who except one, are engaged to serve him upon all occasions, and that one he had just engaged the moment before my brother went to him. We have got a very clever man on our side but as he is young he will not have much authority ... .[8]

And on February 16, 1793, Dorothy was forced to write that she and her brothers were still being "deprived of our patrimony by the cruel Hand of lordly Tyranny."[9]

Wordsworth in these early years seems to have had nothing to say concerning the Lonsdale case—at least no record of any remarks of his upon the matter has been preserved.[10]

---

[6] *The Early Letters of William and Dorothy Wordsworth (1787–1805)*, ed. by Ernest de Selincourt (Oxford, 1935) (hereafter referred to as *The Early Letters*), pp. 3–4.
[7] *Ibid.*, pp. 6–7. [8] *Ibid.*, p. 52. [9] *Ibid.*, p. 84.
[10] Unfortunately, only eight of the letters written by Wordsworth before 1794 are extant.

But he expressed himself at least once upon the subject of the British courts of law, and the unequivocal sarcasm of his reflection betrays the bitterness of the feelings from which it sprang. In his *Letter to the Bishop of Llandaff,* 1793, Wordsworth wrote with the authority and conviction of personal experience when he referred to the Bishop's declared admiration for the administration of English law:

> I congratulate your Lordship upon your enthusiastic fondness for the judicial proceedings of this country. I am happy to find you have passed through life without having your fleece torn from your back in the thorny labyrinth of litigation. But you have not lived always in colleges, and must have passed by some victims, whom it cannot be supposed, without a reflection on your heart, that you have forgotten.[11]

The Lonsdale business revealed to Wordsworth that there was evil in England, that virtue and right were by no means consistently triumphant, and that the principles of justice and equality which governed life among the "Statesmen" of the northern hills were sometimes forgotten in the larger world of affairs. But Lonsdale's shameless refusal to meet his obligations did more than introduce the Wordsworth children to the injustice and inconveniences long suffered by the middle and lower classes in the almost feudal society of England; it forced them to be dependent upon guardian relatives, and necessitated a domestic experience that proved particularly distasteful and humiliating to Dorothy and William.

Biographers have hitherto supposed that the displeasure with England voiced by Wordsworth in 1793 in his *Letter to the Bishop of Llandaff* and in *Guilt and Sorrow* was the result of his newly acquired allegiance to the principles of the French Revolution and his misguided enthusiasm for the shocking radical philosophy and social criticism of William Godwin. After his return from France in the winter of 1792/93 Wordsworth endorsed the popular French republican belief that a monarchical form of government inevitably caused the degeneration of the population, and that the inequitable distribution of property and wealth obtaining

---

[11] *The Prose Works of William Wordsworth,* ed. by Alexander B. Grosart (London, 1876), I, 20.

under a monarchy tended to stifle and destroy the mild virtues of friendliness and love that are the natural inheritance of noble man. Indeed, the disintegration of the family and the decay of the domestic virtues, owing to the economic calamities frequent in monarchical England, were abiding themes in Wordsworth's poetry until at least as late as 1800. The truth is, however, that Wordsworth's general dissatisfaction with England was based in part upon personal experience which antedated both his zeal for the French Revolution and his knowledge of Godwin, and that his special interest in the fate of the English family unit was first aroused by his distress at the fate of his own family and by his and Dorothy's relationship with guardian relatives whom they found to be unfriendly and exacting.

The record of the slights and humiliations suffered by the Wordsworth children under the care of their guardians is preserved in the extensive correspondence between Dorothy and Jane Pollard. In the summer of 1787, after apologizing for tardiness in writing, Dorothy forwarded the following pathetic information to her confidante:

Do, pray do forgive me and write to me at the appointed time. I might perhaps have employed an hour or two in writing to you but I have so few, so very few to pass with my Brothers that I could not leave them. You know not how happy I am in their company. I do not now want a friend who will share with me my distresses. I do not now pass half my time alone. I can bear the ill-nature of all my relations, for the affection of my Brothers consoles me in all my griefs, but how soon alas! shall I be deprived of this consolation! and how soon shall I again become melancholy, even more melancholy than before. They are just the boys I could wish them, they are so affectionate and so kind to me as makes me love them more and more every day. . . . Many a time have Wm, Jn, C, and myself shed tears together, tears of the bitterest sorrow, we all of us, each day, feel more sensibly the loss we sustained when we were deprived of our parents, and each day do we receive fresh insults. You will wonder of what sort; believe me of the most mortifying kind, the insults of servants, but I will give you the particulars of our distresses as far as my paper will allow . . . . I was for a whole week kept in expectation of my Brothers, who staid at school all that time after the vacation began owing to the ill-nature of my Uncle who would not send horses for them because when they wrote they did not happen to mention them, and only said when they should break up which was always before sufficient. This was the beginning of my mortifications for I felt that if they had had another home to go to, they would have been behaved to in a very different manner, and received with more chearful countenances, indeed nobody but myself expressed one wish to see them. At last however they were sent for, but not till my Brother Wm had hired a horse for himself and came over because he thought someone must be ill; the servants are every one of them so insolent to us as makes the kitchen as well as the parlour quite insupportable. James has even gone so far as to tell us that we had nobody to depend upon but my Grandfr, for that our fortunes we[re] but v[ery sma]ll, and my Brs can not even get a pair of shoes cleaned without James's telling them they require as much waiting upon as any *gentlemen,* nor can I get a thing done for myself without absolutely entreating it as a [fav]our. James happens to be a particular favorite [with] my Uncle Kit, who has taken a dislike to my Br [and] never takes any notice of any of us, so that he thinks [whi]le my Uncle behaves in this way to us he may do anything. We are found fault with every hour of the day both by the servants and my Grandfr and Grandmr, the former of whom never speaks to us but when he scolds, which is not seldom. I daresay our fortunes have been weighed thousands of times at the tea table in the kitchen and I have no doubt but they always conclude their conversations with "they have nothing to be proud of"....

Oh Jane! when they have left me I shall be quite unhappy, I shall long more ardently than ever for you my dearest, dearest friend. We have been told thousands of times that we were liars but we treat such behaviour with the contempt it deserves. [We] always finish our conversations which generally take a melancholy turn, with [w]ishing we had a father and a home.[12]

Obviously the young Wordsworths believed themselves to be ill treated, unappreciated, and misunderstood, and apparently their belief was not without foundation. In the situation described by Dorothy, and conscious as they were of the improbability of a just resolution of the Lonsdale case, they naturally despaired of soon regaining the delights of a congenial home and of enjoying the normal exercise of the domestic affections. For such loss and frustration William, as we shall see, found compensation in his poetry, especially in *An Evening Walk,* where—after sharing vicariously the perfect bliss and felicity of a family of swans whose domestic situation is ideal—he envisions a future day when he and Dorothy will be happily established in a cottage of their own. Dorothy it was, of course, who suffered most, for she

[12] *The Early Letters,* pp. 2-4.

alone was in continuous residence with the guardians. Her letters to Jane Pollard in these years are full of melancholy complaints similar to those expressed above. But if Dorothy, living as she did in the household of her Uncle Kit, was the one who suffered most from proximity to the insolent James, it was William who incurred Uncle Kit's special and concentrated disfavor.

The brother to whom Uncle Kit had "taken a dislike" was William. In her letter to Jane of August 5 or 6, 1787, Dorothy makes this clear assertion: "I absolutely dislike my Uncle Kit who never speaks a pleasant word to one, and behaves to my Br Wm in a particularly ungenerous manner."[13] And on July 10, 1793, Dorothy revealed to Jane that the passage of six years had not improved William's position in the circle of the family:

> You must know that this favorite brother of mine happens to be no favorite with any of his *near* relations except his Brothers by whom he is adored. I mean by John and Christopher, for Richard's disposition and his are totally different, and though they never have any quarrels yet there is not that friendship between them which can only exist where there is some similarity of taste, or sentiment or where two hearts are found to sympathize with each other in all their griefs and joys.[14]

But William's fall from grace in 1793 is matter for a later page.

Wordsworth's unpleasant experiences with the Earl of Lonsdale and with his guardians enabled him to understand that the world of reality did not coincide at every point with the attractive world of fancy which the limited knowledge of his childhood had permitted him to create. Near the conclusion of "The Vale of Esthwaite" Wordsworth acknowledged his consciousness of the discrepancy between the real and the ideal by admitting that he soon would have to abandon the idle carefree ways of his youth, "To delve in Mammon's joyless mine."[15] But Wordsworth persistently refused to delve in any such mine. So powerful and compelling were the illusions and presuppositions Wordsworth brought from childhood to the problems of his later life that he refused for

---

[13] *The Early Letters*, p. 7.   [14] *Ibid.*, p. 97.
[15] *The Poetical Works*, pp. 282–283.

years to recognize reality and to take the steps necessary to cope successfully with its existence. This was maladjustment. This was what his guardians could not understand. This, finally, is the most striking feature of the history of Wordsworth's activity from his matriculation at Cambridge in 1787 to his establishment with Dorothy at Racedown in 1795. A study of his behavior in these years reveals that Wordsworth's guardians and his brother Richard had good reason to regard their charge with particular disfavor.

In the first place, William had but very little money. This we learn from Dorothy's letter to Jane of December 7, 1791, which describes in detail the Wordsworth children's financial outlook for the future, and enables us to estimate with fair accuracy William's economic status. "My Grandmother," writes Dorothy,

has had possession of a very handsome estate about a year. She has shown us great kindness, and if her life be prolonged for a few years will have it in her power to do something handsome for us, and I am very sure she will not neglect the opportunity. She has promised to give us five hundred pounds (a hundred a piece) the first time she receives her rents, which will be very soon. . . . I must not omit to tell you, as an instance of my Grandmother's particular goodness to me, that she sent me five guineas as a present in the summer along with a new gown. I fear that when at last our affairs with Lord Lonsdale (the greatest of tyrants) are settled, that the deductions must be very considerable, £5000 was the sum agreed to be due to us at Carlisle but I shall be quite happy if I can call £1000 my own, when all our possessions are collected and divided. Our several resources are these: The £500 which my Gmr is to give us, £500 which is due on account of my mother's fortune, about £200 which my uncle Kitt owes us, and a thousand pounds at present in the hands of our guardians; and about a hundred and fifty pounds which we are to receive out of the Newbiggin estate, with what may be adjudged to us as due from Ld L. My Brother Richard has about £100 per annum, and William has received his education, for which a deduction will be made, so that I hope, unless we are treated in the most unjust manner possible, my three younger Brothers and I will have 1000£ a piece, deducting in William's share the expenses of his education.[16]

Émile Legouis concluded from this that Wordsworth "possessed about £1000, less the expense of his education."[17]

[16] *The Early Letters*, pp. 63–64.   [17] *Op. cit.*, p. 191.

Careful examination of the evidence, however, shows that he possessed nowhere near this sum. Dorothy reached the figure of £1,000 only after adding into her column £500 *promised* by their grandmother, £500 *due* them from their mother's estate, £200 *owed* them by their Uncle Kit, £150 *expected* out of the Newbiggin estate, and an unmentioned figure, which simple arithmetic proves to have been about £2,650, that Lonsdale probably would pay. No more than £1,000 in cash seems to have been in the hands of the guardians; all other assets were at least temporarily frozen. This means that William had back of him in 1791 his fifth of the £1,000, about £200. And from his £200 his guardians were to deduct the cost of his education at Cambridge, as well as his share of the legal expenses incurred by the proceedings against Lonsdale. We do not know the amount of these expenses in 1791, but they came to £972 3s. 7d. in May, 1794.[18] It is quite clear from this that the young Wordsworth, if not indeed a pauper, had very little money of his own.

When these cold economic facts are borne in mind, a review of Wordsworth's attitudes and behavior during the trying years from 1787 to 1795 clarifies the nature of the antagonism between him and his uncles, and enables us to understand more properly than has been hitherto possible his enthusiasm for French republican principles and his criticism of the social, economic, and political structure of England as these are expressed in *Descriptive Sketches,* the *Letter to the Bishop of Llandaff,* and *Guilt and Sorrow.* For the sake of accuracy, we shall be concerned here only with facts presented in letters contemporaneous with the events in question and not with Wordsworth's romantic interpretation of the facts after they had been made attractive by the wonderful alchemy of his memory.

Wordsworth entered St. John's College, Cambridge, in October, 1787. Evidently he intended to prepare himself for the legal profession, for in the summer of that year Dorothy wrote Jane that William "has a wish to be a Lawyer if his health will permit, and it will be very expensive";[19] and again,

---

[18] See de Selincourt in *The Early Letters,* p. 4 n.
[19] *The Early Letters,* p. 4.

BIOGRAPHY, 1770-95

in August: "My Br Wm goes to Cambridge in October . . . he wishes very much to be a Lawyer if his health will permit, but he is troubled with violent head-aches and a pain in his side, but I hope they will leave him in a little time."[20] Except to tell her friend that he had read Burns's *Poems, Chiefly in the Scottish Dialect,* Dorothy does not again refer to William's ambitions or accomplishments until the spring of 1790, one year before he was to complete his undergraduate education. By that time the intention and desire to become a lawyer had been discarded, and Wordsworth had not as yet fixed definitely upon any other profession or occupation as likely to engage his interest. We may easily imagine the concern felt by Wordsworth's guardians at his failure to choose a means of supporting himself when we note that even his sympathetic sister, whose faith in his integrity and ability was never shaken, was disturbed about his future:

I long to have an opportunity of introducing you to my dear Wm. I am very anxious about him just now, as he will shortly have to provide for himself: next year he takes his degree; when he will go into orders I do not know, nor how he will employ himself, he must, when he is three and twenty either go into orders or take pupils; he will be twenty in April.[21]

That Wordsworth himself was neither upset by the uncertainty of the future nor considerate of the anxiety of his sister and his guardians is revealed by the fact that he employed the summer vacation of his third year at Cambridge to go off on a walking tour on the Continent with Robert Jones, whose acquaintance he had made at the university. Professor Harper has commented pertinently on this adventure, but has rather understated its significance. "The academic year," he writes,

or at least that part of it in which residence was required, being only about half the calendar year, students who expected to distinguish themselves in the examinations were accustomed to spend their final long vacation in hard study, either at Cambridge or in some quieter place. Wordsworth's relatives, therefore, were disappointed when he decided to make use of the summer and early autumn of 1790 in a way which

[20] *Ibid.,* p. 7.
[21] *Ibid.,* p. 28.

apparently would not lead to academic honours nor to a profession nor to pecuniary profit.[22]

Wordsworth's relatives were not only disappointed at his decision to throw away his long vacation on a walking tour; they were annoyed that he should embark upon a scheme that was likely to prove expensive. From Switzerland, on September 6, 1790, Wordsworth wrote his sister a letter in which he was pointedly careful to emphasize the low cost of living on the Continent. After assuring Dorothy that he was in excellent health and having a wonderful time, he continued:

> ... you will be surprised when I assure you that our united expenses since we quitted Calais, which was on the evening of the 14th of July, have not amounted to more than twelve pounds. Never was there a more excellent school for frugality than that in which we are receiving instructions at present. I am half afraid of getting a slight touch of avarice from it.[23]

This message, with its touch of roguish irony, was calculated to throw into confusion all those who had objected to the tour on the ground of extravagance. The conclusion of the letter contains a sentence clearly designed to meet the argument that the youthful traveler might better have spent his time in study: "You will remember me affectionately to my uncle and aunt: as he was acquainted with my having given up all thoughts of a fellowship, he may, perhaps, not be so much displeased at this journey. I should be sorry if I have offended him by it."[24]

This makes it fairly clear that Wordsworth had not troubled to consult his uncle concerning the practicability of his visit to the Continent, and it is to be feared that his uncle was offended. Wordsworth, moreover, tells us here that as early as 1790 he himself had "given up all thoughts of a fellowship." His guardians, however, did not give up hope for this possible and convenient solution of the problem of the young man's immediate future until the results of his examinations were made known, just before his graduation on January 21, 1791. Dorothy's account of this lost cause, written on June 26, 1791, to Jane Pollard, indicates that the point

[22] *Op. cit.*, p. 56.   [23] *The Early Letters*, p. 31.   [24] *Ibid.*, p. 37.

was a sore one in family circles for months after the original disappointment:

> William you may have heard lost the chance, indeed the certainty of a fellowship by not combating his inclinations, he gave way to his natural dislike of studies so dry as many parts of the mathematics, consequently could not succeed at Cambridge. He reads Italian, Spanish, French, Greek and Latin, and English, but never opens a mathematical book. We promise ourselves much pleasure from reading Italian together at some time, he wishes that I was acquainted with the Italian poets, but how much have I to learn which plain English will teach me. William has a great attachment to poetry; indeed so has Kitt, but William particularly, which is not the most likely thing to produce his advancement in the world . . . .[25]

The events of the next two years doubtless convinced the guardians that William, if not actually dangerous, was at least an irresponsible, headstrong, and idle young man who deliberately and consistently refused to prepare himself for the normal responsibilities of maturity. There is no evidence suggesting that he gave a serious thought to the choice of a profession in 1791 after his graduation. On May 23, 1791, when Dorothy writes again to Jane Pollard, it is only to disclose that her brother's ardor for rambling about the country has once again triumphed over his better judgment: ". . . he is now in Wales where he intends making a pedestrian tour along with his old friend and companion Jones, at whose [house h]e is at present staying."[26] And two letters written by Wordsworth himself from Plas-yn-llan, Jones's home in Wales, to his friend William Mathews express a devil-may-care frame of mind that was certain to drive almost to distraction anyone seriously interested in his future. In the first, dated June 17, 1791, Wordsworth confessed with a rather impudent pride that he failed to detect in himself that intellectual progress for which he had some vague desire:

> I have often [wished], when I have found upon reflection how much of my time has lately passed unconnected with reading, that I could perceive in myself a small share of that improvement, which from your necessary engagements every day must render you more and more conscious of. All the conclusion that this reflection has ever been able to

[25] *Ibid.*, pp. 51–52.   [26] *Ibid.*, p. 45.

lead me to is how desirable an attainment would learning be, if the time exacted for it were not so great. Miserable weakness![27]

And in the second, dated August 13, 1791, he describes with an air of feigned indifference his continued listlessness and intellectual inactivity:

> You desire me to communicate to you copiously my observations on modern literature, and transmit to you a cup replete with the waters of that fountain. You might as well have solicited me to send you an account of the tribes inhabiting the central regions of the African Continent. God knows my incursions into the fields of modern literature—excepting in our own language three volumes of *Tristram Shandy*, and two or three papers of the *Spectator*, half subdued—are absolutely nothing. Were I furnished with a dictionary and a grammar, and other requisites, I might perhaps make an attack upon Italy, an attack valiant; but probably my expedition, like a redoubted one of Caligula's of old, though of another kind, might terminate in gathering shells out of Petrarch, or seaweed from Marino. The truth of the matter is that when in Town I did *little*,[28] and since I came here I have done nothing. A miserable account! However I have not in addition to all this to complain of bad spirits. That would be the devil indeed. I rather think that this gaiety increases with my ignorance, as a spendthrift grows more extravagant, the nearer he approximates to a final dissipation of his property. I was obliged to leave all my books but one or two behind me. I regret much not having brought my Spanish grammar along with me. By peeping into it occasionally I might perhaps have contrived to keep the little Spanish or some part of it, that I was master of. I am prodigiously incensed at those rascal creditors of yours. What do they not deserve? Pains, stripes, imprisonments, &c, &c.[29]

Wordsworth's indignation with Mathews' creditors, jesting though it be, is curious. Surely this was not the Wordsworth who was

> born in a poor District, and which yet
> Retaineth more of ancient homeliness,
> Manners erect, and frank simplicity,
> Than any other nook of English Land,

or the Wordsworth who was to look upon the French Revolution as "nothing out of nature's certain course" and champion

---

[27] *The Early Letters*, p. 49.

[28] This is a reference to a three- or four-month sojourn in London made by Wordsworth just after his graduation from Cambridge. In *The Prelude*, IX, 18–31, he claims inaccurately to have spent a year in London at this time.

[29] *The Early Letters*, pp. 55–56.

the republican principle of equality in his *Letter to the Bishop of Llandaff* in 1793. This was a young man rather whose collegiate experience and brief acquaintance with Continental life had made of him something of a poseur and pretender. The studied indifference to significant intellectual employment and the deliberately manufactured attitude of genteel scorn here betrayed are striking in their similarity to characteristics of the traveled Englishman of the Renaissance who was ridiculed for decades in Elizabethan and Jacobean satiric literature.

The next communication to Mathews, dated September 23, 1791, shows, however, that Wordsworth was at least developing a social conscience, even though he contemplated no immediate steps toward establishing his own social independence and identity. Evidently Mathews had suggested that they throw themselves together upon the land and eke out some kind of existence as practicing vagrants. Wordsworth's reply is interesting:

I cannot look with much satisfaction on your present situation, yet still I think you ought to be dissuaded from attempting to put in practice the plan you speak of. I do not think you could ever be happy while you were conscious that you were a cause of such sorrow to your parents, as they must undoubtedly be oppressed with; when all that they will know of you is that you are wandering about the world, without perhaps a house to your head. I cannot deny that were I so situated, as to be without relations, to whom I were accountable for my actions, I should perhaps prefer your idea to your present situation, or to vegetating on a paltry curacy. Yet still there is another objection which would have influence upon me which is this. I should not be able to reconcile to my ideas of right, the thought of wandering about a country, without a certainty of being able to maintain my self [ ] being indebted for my existence to those charities of which the acceptance might rob people not half so able to support themselves as myself. It is evident there are a thousand ways in which a person of your education might get his bread, as a recompence for his labour, and while that continues to be the case, for my own part I confess I should be unwilling to accept it on any other conditions. I see many charms in the idea of travelling, much to be enjoyed and much to be learnt, so many that were we in possession of perhaps even less than a hundred a year apiece, which would amply obviate the objection I have just made, and without any relations to whom we were accountable, I would set out with you this moment with all my heart, not entertaining a doubt but that by some means or other we should be soon able to secure ourselves that independence you so ardently pant after, and what is more with minds furnished with such a store of ideas as would enable us to enjoy it. But this is not the case; therefore, for my own part, I resign the idea. I would wish you to do the same.

What then is to be done? Hope and industry are to be your watchwords and I warrant you their influence will secure you the victory."[30]

This same letter reveals that Wordsworth had virtually abandoned any idea of entering the church. His visit in Wales, he wrote to Mathews, had been terminated by "a summons from Mr. Robinson, a gentleman you most likely have heard me speak of, respecting my going into orders, and taking a curacy at Harwich where his interest chiefly lies, which curacy he considered as introductory to the living. I thought it was best to pay my respects to him [in] person, to inform him that I was not of age."[31] Mr. Robinson was distantly related to the Wordsworths and, according to Professor de Selincourt, was "a great favorite of George III . . . well known for his zeal and success in obtaining posts for his relatives and friends. Both the cousin and the brother of W. W. owed their captaincies in the East India Service to him."[32] Wordsworth's guardians were no doubt behind the summons which he sent to the young man at Plas-yn-llan, and they cannot have been pleased when their indolent charge dismissed the matter so easily.

Failing to detect in his nephew any inclination whatever to settle down and select a profession, Wordsworth's Uncle William recommended that he undertake a course of study in the Oriental languages by way of preparation for going into orders.[33] This plan, however, did not meet with Wordsworth's complete approval. When he was next heard of—on

[30] *The Early Letters*, pp. 58–59. It is difficult to resist the suspicion that Wordsworth, in the last sentences of this passage, was mocking the pithy unctuous language frequently directed at him by his righteous guardians.
[31] *Ibid.*, p. 57.
[32] *Ibid.*, p. 57 n. Mr. Robinson evidently had followed Wordsworth's progress with interest; in 1788, according to de Selincourt, he wrote Wordsworth "An affectionate letter . . . urging him to 'stick close to College for the first 2 or 3 years,' and hoping to 'hear him go out Senior Wrangler'" (*ibid.*).
[33] See Dorothy's letter to Jane Pollard, October 9, 1791 (*ibid.*, p. 60).

BIOGRAPHY, 1770-95

November 23, 1791, again in a letter to Mathews—he was not studying Oriental languages or the law; nor was he preparing in any way to enter the church. He was at Brighton, waiting for favorable winds to carry him over the Channel to France and the Revolution! Whatever his guardians may have thought, Wordsworth was not worried. His letter conveys only the same self-conscious insouciance that characterizes his other communications to Mathews:

> I am doomed to be an idler through my whole life. I have read nothing this age, nor indeed did I ever. Yet with all this I am tolerably happy. Do you think this ought to be a matter of congratulation to me, or no? For my own part I think certainly not. My uncle, the clergyman, proposed to me a short time ago to begin a course of Oriental literature, thinking that that was the best field for a person to distinguish himself in, as a man of letters. To oblige him I consented to pursue the plan upon my return from the continent. But what must I do amongst that immense wilderness, I who have no resolution, and who have not prepared myself for the enterprise by any sort of discipline amongst the Western languages? who know little of Latin, and scarce anything of Greek. A pretty confession for a young gentleman whose whole life ought to have been devoted to study. And thus the world wags.[34]

Precisely what Wordsworth's motives were for going into France at this time we cannot be sure. Professor Harper has considered the problem, but his conclusions savor too much of the romantic hindsight of *The Prelude* to be completely satisfactory:

> Why did Wordsworth make choice of France? No doubt the agreeable impression produced by the French whom he had met on his long foot-tour had something to do with it. They had charmed him by their manners, their alertness, and their speech. He knew the language fairly well by this time. And there was no doubt a more significant reason, in his sympathy with the Revolutionary spirit, now at its height. Love of adventure, a desire to be near the scene of great events, a feeling that the air of France would be good for him at that particular time when he was hesitating and France was rushing confidently forward—all these elements were doubtless present in his mind as motives.[35]

These considerations may have influenced Wordsworth, but there surely was another motive, not mentioned by Professor

[34] *Ibid.*, p. 61.   [35] *Op. cit.*, p. 80.

Harper, which was foremost in his mind. Wordsworth's Uncle William, as we have seen, had been forcing the issue of a profession and had been urging unattractive plans for his nephew's future. By so doing, he provided Wordsworth with his most compelling motive for a second excursion into France—the motive of escape.

The guardians probably made the same objections to William's going to France in 1791 that they had made the year before to his walking tour with Robert Jones. They no doubt protested that it would be a waste of time and money. William, however, countered their arguments by suggesting optimistically that further residence in France would prepare him to shoulder the responsibilities of tutor and professional traveling companion to some hypothetical rich young man. Dorothy reveals this much to Jane Pollard on December 7, 1791:

> William is, I hope, by this time arrived at Orleans, where he means to pass the winter for the purpose of learning the French Language which will qualify him for the office of travelling companion to some young gentleman if he can get recommended; it will at any rate be very useful to him, and as he can live at as little expense in France as in England (or nearly so), the scheme is not an ineligible one. He is at the same time engaged in the study of the Spanish language, and if he settles in England at his return, (I mean if he has not the opportunity of becom[ing] travelling tutor) he [w]ill begin t[he] study of the oriental Languages.[36]

There seems to have been concern in the family about the economic practicability of the scheme, however, even after William's departure for French shores. At least he felt obliged, shortly after his arrival at Orleans, to reassure his brother Richard, the businessman of the family, that his plan for living in France was really feasible financially. On December 19, 1791, Wordsworth wrote his brother the following account of his affairs:

> I will now give you a criterion by which you may judge of my expenses here. I had in Paris six hundred and forty three livres for 20 £—I give for my Lodging which is a very handsome apartment on the first floor, 30 Livres per month if I stay only three months, 27 if I

[36] *The Early Letters*, pp. 64–65.

BIOGRAPHY, 1770-95

stay six, and 24 and ten sous, viz halfpence, if I stay 8 months—My board . . . costs me fifty Livres per month breakfast excluded. There are other little expenses which it would not be easy to sum up. But this as you will perceive is the bulk, and I think extremely reasonable considering the comfortable manner in which I live. . . .

I have as yet no acquaintance but in the house, the young Parisian and the rest of the tables, and one Family which I find very agreeable, and with which I became acquainted by the circumstance of going to look at their Lodgings, which I should have liked extremely to have taken, but I found them too dear for me . . . . I am not yet able to speak French with decent accuracy but must of course improve very rapidly. I do not intend to take a master. I think I can do really as well without one, and it would be a very considerable augmentation of my expenses.[37]

The practical-minded Richard was doubtless pleased to learn that William was getting his room and board, "breakfast excluded," for about two and a half pounds a month, and that he had had shrewdness enough to forego taking rooms that were "too dear." One wonders, however, what emotions were generated in Richard's breast when he, remembering that the sole justification for these expenditures was William's desire to learn the French language, received the information that his lazy younger brother had neglected—in the name of economy—to engage a French teacher.

Wordsworth evidently had wheedled his guardians into sanctioning his year in France by agreeing to study Oriental languages and eventually take orders if he were unable, on his return to England, to find the imaginary "young gentleman" anxious to travel with a companion equipped with facility in the French tongue. Little hope was held at home of Wordsworth's success in the field of his choice, and preparations went on against his return. Dorothy, writing to Richard in the spring of 1792, informed him of the most recent developments:

. . . my Uncle and I have had some conversation about William. He said he wondered whether Mr Robinson had any Design of placing him at Harwich, and that he wished much to know; for if it would be any object for him to get ordained immediately he would keep his Title open for him, though at the same time it would be very inconvenient

[37] *Ibid.*, pp. 66–67.

> for him, as he wishes to keep a Curate, and not to leave his Churches in the manner he has hitherto done to the care of the neighbouring Clergymen during his short absences from Forncett—I told him I thought Captain Wordsworth would perhaps be able to give him Information about it if he were in Town, he replied that he would make enquiry some way or other, and he also said that he conceived it would be Mr Robinson's wish to get Mr Cowper to resign the Living, as it is impossible he can ever return to Harwich. It would be a charming thing if William could be placed there, as, though till Mr Cowper's Debts are paid, he could only enjoy the Profits as of a Curacy, yet it would in the end be a certain Provision—I imagine if he goes to Harwich my Uncle's Title would be unnecessary as he would most likely get one from thence.[38]

That some kind of agreement had been reached between Wordsworth and his Uncle William before he went to the Continent seems evident, moreover, when we read his letter to Mathews of May 17, 1792:

> You have still the hope that we may be connected in some method of obtaining an independence. I assure you I wish it as much as yourself. Nothing but resolution is necessary. The field of Letters is very extensive, and it is astonishing if we cannot find some little corner, which with a little tillage will produce us enough for the necessities, nay even the comforts of life. Your residence in London gives you if you look abroad, an excellent opportunity of starting something or other. Pray be particular in your answer upon this subject. It is at present my intention to take orders, in the approaching winter or spring. My uncle the clergyman will furnish me with a title. Had it been in my power, I certainly should have wished to defer the moment. But though I may not be resident in London, I need not therefore be prevented from engaging in any literary plan, which may have the appearance of producing a decent harvest. I assure you again and again that nothing but confidence and resolution is necessary. Fluency in writing will tread fast upon the heels of practice, and elegance and strength will not be far behind. I hope you will have the goodness to write to me soon, when you will enlarge upon this head. You say you have many schemes. Submit at least a few of them to my examination. Would it not be possible for you to form an acquaintance with some of the publishing booksellers of London, from whom you might get some hints of what sort of works would be the most likely to answer?[39]

It appears certain from this that there were circumstances which Wordsworth thought would force him into orders on his return from France. He deplored the idea, as we have

[38] *The Early Letters*, pp. 69–70.   [39] *Ibid.*, pp. 74–75.

seen, of "vegetating on a paltry curacy," but it seems that no choice remained to him. It is significant that he writes, "Had it been in my power," not "Were it in my power," suggesting, it would seem, that before he left England in November, 1791, his promise to take orders had been given to his uncle. The plans that were on foot at home for him to acquire the curacy at Harwich tend to confirm this view, as does Dorothy's invitation to Jane Pollard, extended February 16, 1793, to come and spend "at least a year" with her and William at their "little Parsonage."[40]

The letter to Mathews is of further interest to us because it reveals the stiffening of Wordsworth's hitherto vague desire to enter the literary profession. He had been writing poetry in France, and it is quite probable that he determined some time in the summer of 1792 not to go into orders after all, but to take his chances with literature instead. On September 3, 1792, at any rate, he had decided to publish the poems now known to the world as *An Evening Walk* and *Descriptive Sketches,* for on that date he wrote the following to his brother Richard in London: "I am very happy you have got into Chambers, as I shall perhaps be obliged to stay a few weeks in town about my publication—you will I hope with Wilkinson's permission find me a place for a bed . . . I shall be in town during the course of the month of October . . . ."[41]

The climax of this chapter of his life is well known to all students of Wordsworth. Events made his return to England in October, 1792, inadvisable. On December 15, Annette Vallon, his mistress, bore him a daughter—Anne Caroline. Presumably Wordsworth felt obliged to remain with Annette as long as possible; and, although he was not present at his daughter's birth, he delayed his return home until later in the month, possibly until January, 1793—we know only that he was back in England before January 21, the date of the execution of Louis XVI.

All the details of what happened in England between Wordsworth and his relatives after his return we shall never know. Such records of the episode as family correspondence

[40] *Ibid.,* p. 84.   [41] *Ibid.,* p. 77.

may have contained have apparently been destroyed. Of this much, however, we are certain: instead of taking orders, Wordsworth published *Descriptive Sketches* and *An Evening Walk,* composed the *Letter to the Bishop of Llandaff*—a sarcastic and effective republican harangue so revolutionary in nature as to be offensive in the extreme to respectable society in general and to his guardians in particular—and turned over to his sister Dorothy the difficult task of divulging to the family the awkward consequences of his relationship with Annette Vallon.[42] When next we hear of him, on June 16, 1793, Dorothy is ". . . very anxious about him just now as he has not yet got any settled employment. He is looking out and wishing for the opportunity of engaging himself as tutor to some young gentleman, an office for which even friends less partial than I am, allow him to be particularly well qualified."[43] And a month later, on July 10, 1793, we find the young poet once more on tour:

> He is now going upon a tour to the West of England along with a gentleman who was formerly a schoolfellow,[44] a man of fortune, and who is to bear all the expenses of the journey and only requests the favour of William's company as he is averse to the idea of going alone. As William has not the prospect of any immediate employment I think he cannot pursue a better scheme, as his expenses will be reduced to the articles of cloaths and washing, and he is perfectly at liberty to quit his companion as soon as anything more advantageous shall offer.[45]

In the light of these circumstances—of Wordsworth's continuous indecision, vacillation, indifference for the future, and apparent lack of stability—it is not surprising that Dorothy, in her letter to Jane Pollard of July 10, 1793, must write:

> If my Brother makes an engagement which will take him out of England or confine him to one spot for any length of time, then he is determined to come and see me at Forncett, if it be but for one day, though he has never received an invitation from my Uncle and though he can have no possible inducement but the pleasure of seeing me. You must know that this favorite brother of mine happens to be no favorite with

---

[42] For a more detailed discussion of Wordsworth's behavior in the early months of 1793 see below, pp. 88–95.
[43] *The Early Letters,* p. 92.
[44] The gentleman was William Calvert.
[45] *The Early Letters,* p. 94.

any of his *near* relations .... I have not time or room to explain to you the foundation of the prejudices of my two Uncles against my dear William; the subject is an unpleasant one for a letter, it will employ us more agreeably in conversation, then, though I must confess that he has been somewhat to blame, yet I think I shall prove to you that the excuse might have been found in his natural disposition. "In truth he was a strange and wayward wight fond of each gentle etc., etc. That verse of Beattie's *Minstrel* always reminds me of him . . . ."[46]

None of Wordsworth's accomplishments or activities in the following months were calculated to raise him in the estimation of his alienated uncles. In the late summer and early fall he wrote the first draft of *Guilt and Sorrow*, but we may be sure that he took especial pains to keep the nature of its contents, and probably the fact of its existence, from his conservative relatives, for the political implications of *Guilt and Sorrow* would have proved most repugnant to his guardians. Meanwhile, in direct and deliberate opposition to the wishes of their Uncle William, the two young Wordsworths plotted an early clandestine reunion.[47] Although its execution was long delayed, this plan was crowned with success in the winter of 1794.

William and Dorothy enjoyed one another's company for several months in the late winter and spring of 1794, and for a while lived alone together in a cottage at Windy Brow, half a mile from Keswick. The cottage belonged to William's friends, Raisley and William Calvert. To reach it, William and Dorothy walked from Kendal to Keswick—thirty-three miles—in two days.[48] Such a combination of circumstances— Dorothy's walking over thirty miles of English roads to live unchaperoned in the lodging of young gentlemen with a brother whose character had clearly been corrupted by his long residence with the immoral and revolutionary French— at least one member of the family could not accept with equanimity. Mrs. Crackanthorpe, when she learned of the shocking state of affairs at Windy Brow, no doubt expressed

[46] *Ibid.*, pp. 97–98.
[47] *Ibid.*, pp. 94, 96–99, 105, 107 (Dorothy to Jane Pollard, July 10, 1793, and August 30, 1793). Jane Pollard was informed in advance of this dark scheme, but was pledged to closest secrecy.
[48] *Ibid.*, p. 110 (Dorothy to ?).

the emotions felt by other representatives of her generation when she called her niece to account in a letter which Dorothy, on April 21, 1793, answered thus:

My dear Aunt,

I should have answered your letter immediately after the receipt of it, if I had not been upon the point of setting forward to Mrs. Spedding's of Armathwaite where I have been spending three days. I am much obliged to you for the frankness with which you have expressed your sentiments upon my conduct and am at the same time extremely sorry that you should think it so severely to be condemned. As you have not sufficiently developed the reasons of your censure I have endeavoured to discover them, and I confess no other possible objections against my continuing here a few weeks longer suggest themselves, except the *expence* and that you may suppose me to be in an unprotected situation. As to the former of these objections I reply that I drink no tea, that my supper and breakfast are of bread and milk and my dinner chiefly of potatoes from choice. In answer to the second of these suggestions, namely, that I may be supposed to be in an unprotected situation, I affirm that I consider the character and virtues of my brother as a sufficient protection, and besides I am convinced that there is no place in the world in which a good and virtuous young woman would be more likely to continue good and virtuous than under the roof of these honest, worthy, uncorrupted people so that any guardianship beyond theirs, I should think altogether unnecessary.

I cannot pass unnoticed that part of your letter in which you speak of my "rambling about the country on foot." So far from considering this as a matter of condemnation, I rather thought it would have given my friends pleasure to hear that I had courage to make use of the strength with which nature has endowed me, when it not only procured me infinitely more pleasure than I should have received from sitting in a post chaise—but was also the means of saving me at least thirty shillings.[49]

There is no record of Mrs. Crackanthorpe's ever again having presumed to correct the independent Dorothy; but neither is there any evidence to suggest that Dorothy's lofty opinion of her brother's "character and virtues" made the slightest altera-

---

[49] *The Early Letters*, pp. 113–114. In concluding her letter, Dorothy made it quite clear that she intended to remain at Windy Brow for several more weeks. Her brother's society, she added, was both a pleasure and a profit: "I have regained all the knowledge I had of the French language some years ago, and have added considerably to it, and I have now begun reading Italian, of which I expect to have soon gained a sufficient knowledge to receive much entertainment and advantage from it" (*ibid.*, p. 114).

tion in the regard of her Uncles William and Christopher for their wayward and intractable nephew.

By May 28, 1794, the brief against Wordsworth was complete, for by that time his willingness to espouse and expound dangerous and subversive political principles was known within the family circle. On this date Dorothy found it necessary to write to Richard and reassure him of William's prudence about giving voice to his revolutionary ideas: "I think I can answer for William's caution about expressing his political opinions. He is very cautious and seems well aware of the dangers of a contrary conduct."[50] This, we are informed by Professor de Selincourt, was "In answer to a letter from R. to W., urging W. to 'be cautious in writing or expressing your political opinions. By the suspension of the Habeas Corpus Acts the Ministers have great powers.' "[51] Richard evidently was worried not only by the possibility of William's running afoul of ministerial power, but also by the chance that his younger brother's rash and radical utterances might have an adverse effect upon their case against the Earl of Lonsdale, for he remarked further in his letter: "I see no end to the business. I have always avoided writing and speaking upon this subject, because his lordship has so many spies in every part of the country. You may read this letter to Dolly, afterwards it may be as well to burn it."[52]

Within a month, however, the anguish and concern which Wordsworth had caused his guardians and his brother Richard were relieved, for in June, 1794, he could write to Mathews—"I have a friend in the country who has offered me a share of his income."[53] This friend was Raisley Calvert. For a little more than six months Wordsworth lived with Calvert at Windy Brow and Penrith, and the last weeks of this period he spent painfully and faithfully, though impatiently, waiting for his friend to die of tuberculosis.[54] And then, on January 16, 1795, Dorothy wrote laconically to Richard: "No doubt William has informed you of the death

[50] *Ibid.*, p. 117. [51] *Ibid.*, p. 117 n.
[52] *Ibid.* [53] *Ibid.*, p. 123.
[54] See Wordsworth's letters to Mathews, November 7 and December, 1794 (*ibid.*, pp. 126–131).

of his poor friend Raisley Calvert, and that he has made an alteration in his will by which he bequeathed to him the sum of nine hundred pounds."[55] Only at the end of his twenty-fourth year and in such a way did Wordsworth gain economic independence.

After Calvert's death Wordsworth lost no time in getting to London, where he expected to find employment through the good offices of William Mathews. Almost a year before he had written to Mathews and informed him that his attitude toward the professions remained unchanged, despite the increasing pressure which the events of 1792 and 1793 had brought to bear upon him: "I have done nothing and still continue to do nothing," he wrote, on February 17, 1794. "What is to become of me I know not. I cannot bow down my mind to take orders, and as for the law I have neither strength of mind, purse, or constitution, to engage in that pursuit."[56] Mathews replied cordially with an invitation for Wordsworth to come to London, where they might try their luck at publishing "a monthly Miscellany from which some emolument might be drawn."[57] Journalism appealed to Wordsworth, and for a while in the summer of 1794 he and Mathews planned to launch *The Philanthropist, a Monthly Miscellany*,[58] in which was to appear, among other things, "an accurate account of the Polish Revolution . . . ."[59] But lack of capital and Wordsworth's inability to go to London while Raisley Calvert's fate was undetermined combined to kill this noble scheme. Wordsworth's wish to go to London, however, and Mathews' desire to have him there did not abate. Mathews apparently had outlined for Wordsworth the various possibilities of employment open in the field of journalism and, it would seem, had suggested that Wordsworth's best chance might be as a reporter of parliamentary debates. At

---

[55] *The Early Letters*, p. 131. In October, 1794, Raisley Calvert's intention was to leave Wordsworth £600 (see Wordsworth's letter to William Calvert [*ibid.*, p. 126]).

[56] *Ibid.*, p. 109. [57] See Wordsworth to Mathews, May 23, 1794 (*ibid.*, p. 115).

[58] See Wordsworth to Mathews, June, 1794 (*ibid.*, p. 121).

[59] *Ibid.*, p. 125. So enthusiastic was Wordsworth over this idea that he offered to undertake a voyage to Dublin with a view to stimulating the circulation of *The Philanthropist* (*ibid.*, p. 124).

any rate, Wordsworth, late in December, felt obliged to give his agent the following information:

> I must premise . . . that I have neither strength of memory, quickness of penmanship, nor rapidity of composition, to enable me to report any part of the parliamentary debates. I am not conscious of any want of ability for translating from the French or Italian Gazettes; and with two or three weeks reading I think I could engage for the Spanish. . . . I could furnish . . . remarks upon measures and events as they pass, and now and then an essay upon general Politics. I should prefer, notwithstanding, confining myself to the two former employments; at least till I had a little more experience. . . .
>
> There is still a further circumstance which disqualifies me for the office of parliamentary reporter, viz. my being subject to nervous headaches, which invariably attack me when exposed to a heated atmosphere, or to loud noises; and that with such an excess of pain as to deprive me of all recollection. I was aware of the objection drawn from the company one must partly be forced into; but this, when a man has his bread to earn, may be easily surmounted. . . . This post however at all events I must decline from the reasons already stated. I should be happy to hear that you could give me grounds to suppose you could find employment for me in any other part of a newspaper, for which you think me qualified.[60]

Of Wordsworth's activities in London for the seven or eight months that were to pass before he went to Racedown we know very little. He had not been there long, however, before he succeeded once again in disturbing the calm of the family elders. On March 11, 1795, Mrs. Rawson—one of the few members of the family who recognized Wordsworth after his French disgrace—wrote:

> Dorothy and Wm. have now a scheme of living together in London, and maintaining themselves by their literary talents, writing and translating; not that they are altogether without other means of support, as he has had a legacy of £900, but the interest will not go far towards keeping house, and the rest they mean to procure by their pens. We think it a very bad wild scheme.[61]

Dorothy, needless to say, was not permitted to go to London, and this was just as well, for it was not long before William was eager to escape from the city life which he was to disparage for years in his poetry.

[60] *Ibid.*, pp. 129–130.
[61] Cited by Ernest de Selincourt in *Dorothy Wordsworth: A Biography* (Oxford, 1933), pp. 58–59.

WORDSWORTH'S FORMATIVE YEARS

Fortune smiled upon him for the second time within a year, and by the end of September, 1795, he and Dorothy were established in a cottage—given to them rent-free by John Frederick Pinney—at Racedown, with the expectation of an annual income of £170 in addition to whatever William could earn by his pen.[62] During his brief sojourn in London, Wordsworth had made new and valuable friends; it is to be feared, however, that he lost an old one, for—so far as we know—he heard no more than once or twice again from William Mathews.

III

So much then for the salient facts of Wordsworth's youth. The record does not suggest a "dedicated Spirit" who "walk'd In blessedness." We have rather the picture of a youth whose childhood training and experience provided him with optimistic presuppositions which he refused to surrender in the face of the distressing and contradictory events and circumstances whose first cause was the death of his father. Wordsworth's refusal to recognize the implications of his personal experience, his refusal to admit the validity of reality, made him, in all outward appearances at least, lazy, shiftless, and stubborn. Like most maladjusted young men, Wordsworth showed no inclination whatever to prepare himself to meet with the demands of life. Before settling down to literary pursuits he dallied with the possibility of becoming a lawyer; he considered going into orders, studying Oriental languages, and Romance languages; he entertained notions of running off to Barbados with his brother John, or of becoming a general in the army, or of discovering some rich young gentleman to whom he would be tutor and traveling companion. Meanwhile he was going through his all too meager funds, wasting his time on walking tours, and exposing himself to the radical ideas of the day. Little wonder is it, therefore, that his conservative and parsimonious uncles were apprehensive lest they be forced to support indefinitely a

[62] For a complete account of the details of the Racedown establishment see Dorothy's letter to Jane Marshall [nee Pollard], September 2, 1795 (*The Early Letters*, pp. 137–142).

BIOGRAPHY, 1770-95

worthless and revolutionary ne'er-do-well who had recklessly squandered his patrimony, refused to try for a Cambridge fellowship, turned down a curacy, and prepared himself only to fulminate dangerously against the officers of the Established Church and the symbol of the best of all Anglo-Saxon genius and experience—the Constitution of Great Britain.

When he was thirty-five years old and a great poet, Wordsworth could look back upon his youth with satisfaction and with little or no self-reproach. From the vantage point of 1805 his early years assumed the bright and glorious aspect of a miracle. His choices, he thought, had been inspired by a benevolent, omnipotent, and omniscient power whose plan was good. His failure to meet responsibility he could regard as noble nonconformity; his opposition to his guardians he might interpret as evidence of strength of character and stout fixity of high and virtuous purpose. His sister Dorothy and his friend Samuel Taylor Coleridge, he could imagine, were angels sent from above to guide and light his way through the wilderness of the 1790's. But there would have been no miracle, Wordsworth's youthful course would not have seemed a wise one, he could not have settled with Dorothy at Racedown in 1795, and he might never have known Samuel Taylor Coleridge, had it not been for the generosity of Raisley Calvert. In *The Prelude,* where he chose to single out Dorothy and Coleridge as deserving of the greatest praise for having contributed to his success, Wordsworth acknowledged a debt to Calvert:

> A Youth (he bore
> The name of Calvert; it shall live, if words
> Of mine can give it life,) without respect
> To prejudice or custom, having hope
> That I had some endowments by which good
> Might be promoted, in his last decay
> From his own Family withdrawing part
> Of no redundant Patrimony, did
> By a Bequest sufficient for my needs
> Enable me to pause for choice, and walk
> At large and unrestrain'd, nor damp'd too soon
> By mortal cares. Himself no Poet, yet

> Far less a common Spirit of the world,
> He deem'd that my pursuits and labours lay
> Apart from all that leads to wealth, or even
> Perhaps to necessary maintenance,
> Without some hazard to the finer sense;
> He clear'd a passage for me, and the stream
> Flow'd in the bent of Nature. (XIII, 349–367)

But the fullness of his appreciation for the part played in his development by this ill-fated young philanthropist was not expressed in verse until 1806, when Wordsworth wrote his sonnet—now too little known—"To the Memory of Raisley Calvert":

> Calvert! it must not be unheard by them
> Who may respect my name, that I to thee
> Owed many years of early liberty.
> This care was thine when sickness did condemn
> Thy youth to hopeless wasting, root and stem—
> That I, if frugal and severe, might stray
> Where'er I liked; and finally array
> My temples with the Muse's diadem.
> Hence, if in freedom I have loved the truth;
> If there be aught of pure, or good, or great,
> In my past verse; or shall be, in the lays
> Of higher mood, which now I meditate;—
> It gladdens me, O worthy, short-lived, Youth!
> To think how much of this will be thy praise.

CHAPTER II

The Early Poems

I

WORDSWORTH's first published poems of any length,[1] *An Evening Walk* and *Descriptive Sketches*, were intended to demonstrate to the world in general and to his guardians in particular what William Wordsworth, Cambridge B.A., could do. "It was with great reluctance," wrote Wordsworth to William Mathews on May 23, 1794, "I huddled up those two little works, and sent them into the world in so imperfect a state. But as I had done nothing by which to distinguish myself at the University, I thought these little things might shew that I could do something."[2] With this purpose firmly in mind the young writer brought all he possessed of literary ability and knowledge of popular authors, ancient and modern, English and French, to the composition of *An Evening Walk* and *Descriptive Sketches*. In an effort to impress the reading public, and to make certain that his poems would suffer from no lack of dignity, Wordsworth embellished them with gems of imagery and wisdom—many of which he "improved" upon—culled from the works of his distinguished predecessors.[3] He also discarded the octosyllabic couplet, the

---

[1] His "Sonnet on Seeing Miss Helen Maria Williams Weep at a Tale of Distress" had appeared in *The European Magazine* in 1787 (see Émile Legouis, *The Early Life of William Wordsworth, 1770–1798*, tr. by J. W. Matthews [New York, 1918], pp. 153–154).

[2] *The Early Letters of William and Dorothy Wordsworth (1787–1805)*, ed. by Ernest de Selincourt (Oxford, 1935) (hereafter referred to as *The Early Letters*), p. 116.

[3] For a truly remarkable account of Wordsworth's borrowings from earlier poets see Legouis, *op. cit.*, pp. 139–145.

easy and familiar verse medium which he had used in most of his juvenile poetry,[4] in favor of the more elegant and stately heroic couplet. And though he had already tried his hand at the sentimental and Gothic horror modes currently popular,[5] the ambitious youth determined to spurn these faddish methods and win distinction in a poetic genre that had stood the test of time. Robert A. Aubin, in his elaborate study of English "topographical poetry,"[6] reveals that *An Evening Walk* is a "region poem" and discloses that it could boast of more than ninety poetic forebears, the first of which is dated 1652.[7] And *Descriptive Sketches,* it appears, is a "journey poem" whose lineage, though not so imposing as that of its companion piece, is by no means despicable.[8]

Wordsworth was willing to admit in 1794 that his poems were "imperfect" as they first appeared, but he was disposed to believe that they had merit nevertheless. That he had surpassed his many predecessors in fidelity to nature, in the all-important matter of keeping the eye on the object and describing with accuracy the wonders and beauties of his beloved Lake District, Wordsworth was certain. In 1843, when he was dictating the notes on his poems to Isabella Fenwick, he declared of *An Evening Walk,* "There is not an image in it which I have not observed . . . ," and the moment described in the lines,

> And, fronting the bright west, yon oak entwines
> Its darkening boughs and leaves, in stronger lines,

he recalled, "was important in my poetical history; for I date from it my consciousness of the infinite variety of natural appearances which had been unnoticed by the poets of any age or country, so far as I was acquainted with them; and I made a resolution to supply, in some degree, the deficiency."

Critics have agreed that Wordsworth succeeded in his

[4] See Ernest de Selincourt, *The Early Wordsworth,* Presidential Address to the English Association (Oxford, 1936), p. 8.
[5] *Ibid.,* pp. 7, 10–12, 26.
[6] *Topographical Poetry in XVIII-Century England* (New York, 1936).
[7] *Ibid.,* pp. 365–369.
[8] *Ibid.,* pp. 385–389. More than sixty "journey poems," the first of which was written in 1641, preceded *Descriptive Sketches.*

THE EARLY POEMS

first efforts to record in poetry "the infinite variety of natural appearances." *An Evening Walk* was greeted by the following remarks in the *Critical Review:*

> Our northern lakes have of late years attracted the attention of the public in a variety of ways. They have been visited by the idle, described by the curious, and delineated by the artist; their beauties, however, are not exhausted, and this little poem is a proof of it. Local description is seldom without a degree of obscurity, which is here increased by a harshness both in the construction and the versification; but we are compensated by that merit which a poetical taste most values, new and picturesque imagery.[9]

And Émile Legouis more than a century later described *An Evening Walk* as "a compact collection of images mostly derived from personal observation,"[10] and went on to utter these words of high praise for Wordsworth's performance:

> Never perhaps had any English poet paid such close and loving attention to the most insignificant sights and sounds of the country; not even Milton in his *L'Allegro* and *Il Penseroso*, which, if they had more of subtle human interest, were less accurate; not Thomson, more vague if more majestic; nor even Cowper, who, although his touch was more distinct, was too much given to moralising.[11]

Finally, *Descriptive Sketches* caused Coleridge later to remark that "seldom, if ever, was the emergence of an original poetic genius above the literary horizon more evidently announced."[12]

Critics have been content for the most part, however, to regard *An Evening Walk* and *Descriptive Sketches* only as evidence of the young Wordsworth's indebtedness to eighteenth-century authors and literary conventions, and as works which reveal the minor improvements made by his budding genius upon the imagery and observations of his predecessors. Legouis, for example, whose study of these poems has never been surpassed, was satisfied to track down verbal borrowings, to describe the enormities and eccentricities of Words-

---

[9] Cited by Aubin, *op. cit.*, p. 218.
[10] *Op. cit.*, p. 148.
[11] *Ibid.*
[12] Samuel Taylor Coleridge, *Biographia Literaria*, ed. by J. Shawcross (Oxford: At the Clarendon Press, 1907), I, 56.

worth's derivative style, to provide the poems with an elaborate eighteenth-century pedigree, and to admire whatever felicities of expression and descriptive notation he could find within their eleven-hundred-odd lines.[13] Some efforts, it is true, have been directed toward relating these verses of Wordsworth's apprenticeship to his personal experience and to his subsequent work: Professor Harper notes that *Descriptive Sketches* "contains a distinct confession of religious unbelief,"[14] and that, in the latter part of the poem, "Humane aspirations begin to crowd upon the images of nature with which till now he has been content."[15] H. W. Garrod concerns himself with the political implications of *Descriptive Sketches*,[16] and hazards the conjecture that the melancholy of the poem reflects not "the fashionable Welt-Schmerz" of *An Evening Walk,* but the painful emotions roused in Wordsworth's breast by his affair with Annette Vallon.[17] But these efforts have been cursory and unsustained. This chapter subjects the contents of *An Evening Walk* and *Descriptive Sketches* to close examination from the point of view afforded by our knowledge of Wordsworth's early experience. Such a study reveals the peculiar personal values and emotions which prompted Wordsworth to compose the poems, enhances our understanding and appreciation of them, and establishes the basis for a larger conception of Wordsworth's poetic development.

II

The impulse to publish is not the impulse to write. Wordsworth's letter to Mathews, cited above, suggests that a sense of shame or guilt, caused by his persistent refusal to take advantage of the various opportunities provided by his own native ability and his anxious guardians, prompted Wordsworth to publish *An Evening Walk* and *Descriptive*

---

[13] *Op. cit.,* pp. 120–160.
[14] George McLean Harper, *William Wordsworth, His Life, Works, and Influence* (New York, 1929), p. 138.
[15] *Ibid.,* p. 139.
[16] *Wordsworth: Lectures and Essays* (Oxford, 1923), pp. 40–41, 53–54.
[17] *Ibid.,* p. 48.

THE EARLY POEMS

Sketches. But if we are to discover the impulse responsible for the creation of the poems—a subject of which the letter tells us nothing—we must look further into Wordsworth's biography and the poems themselves.

An Evening Walk and *Descriptive Sketches* proceeded from the unhappiness felt by William and Dorothy Wordsworth at having no normal domestic existence. We have seen how the death of their parents and the injustice of the Earl of Lonsdale reduced the Wordsworth children to a state of dependence upon guardian relatives who were not entirely sympathetic, and we have noticed the pathetic complaints registered by Dorothy in her letters to Jane Pollard against the humiliation suffered by her and her brothers at the hands of the insolent James. These circumstances caused William and Dorothy to despair of ever enjoying the normal pleasures and comforts of a proper home, and forced them to seek compensation for their loss in self-pity and in the fanciful creation of an ideal home in an ideal world. Such a home in such a world is bodied forth in great detail in William's two early poems and is frequently described by Dorothy in letters written to Jane Pollard both before and after the publication of *An Evening Walk* and *Descriptive Sketches.* A study of the pertinent passages of Dorothy's correspondence with Jane and of a letter written to Dorothy by William from Switzerland in 1790 discovers those attractions of life which the young Wordsworths held most dear, and serves as an illuminating introduction to *An Evening Walk* and *Descriptive Sketches.*

There is ample evidence in her letters to prove that, so far as Dorothy Wordsworth was concerned, living parents were the first requirement for domestic bliss. Dorothy placed particular emphasis upon this when she wrote to Miss Pollard in the summer of 1787:

[We] always finish our conversations which generally take a melancholy turn, with [w]ishing we had a father and a home. Oh! Jane, I hope it may be long ere you experience the loss of your parents, but till you feel that loss you will never know how dear to you your sisters are; till you feel that loss! do I say? I almost wish you may never feel it, for 'tis the greatest misfortune that can befal one but 'tis what in the course of nature one must expect; but I shall be making you as melancholy as myself and am distressing both you and myself with thinking of an event that I hope will not happen these many, many years, during which time I hope my dear Jane will never experience any of the mortifications to which her friend is continually subject, and that the domestick happiness which now reigns in your family may never once be interrupted.[18]

Two years later Jane's "domestick happiness" had been seriously threatened, for on January 25, 1790, Dorothy wrote: "I rejoice with you on the prospect of your dear Father's perfect recovery. I did indeed sympathize with you in your distress for I too well know how irreparable is the loss of an indulgent parent."[19] But the elder Pollard's recovery, contrary to expectations, was incomplete after more than a year. Jane's continued felicity was therefore uncertain, so that Dorothy again had occasion to touch upon one of her favorite subjects:

I am very happy to hear that your father's health continues to improve, and that your mother (of whom I heard by my aunt) continues to preserve her health and evenness of spirits. Long may you enjoy that domestic comfort uninterrupted for which your family is so remarkable, and which is in fact the only thing which deserves the name of happiness.[20]

Her father and mother being dead, Dorothy of course could not expect to know again the utmost possible measure of happiness. She found it necessary to adjust her dreams and expectations to the facts with which she was faced. In her visions of future bliss, therefore, Dorothy wisely substituted for the unattainable joys and comforts of an unbroken and congenial family circle the pleasures to be derived from the company of her brothers—particularly William—and close friends, and from the wonders of external nature. The ideal life, according to her conception of it, must be shared with a kindred spirit and could be found only in the country, where morning and evening walks were possible, where splendid views and sublime prospects lay on every hand, and where

[18] *The Early Letters*, pp. 4–5.
[19] *Ibid.*, p. 23.
[20] *Ibid.*, p. 50.

THE EARLY POEMS

the beauties of nature inevitably contributed to the dignity and improvement of human conduct. Hence, when she was on her way to Forncett with her Uncle William and his bride toward the end of 1788, Dorothy could write with rejoicing to Jane: "You know how partial I always was to a country life but I almost despaired of ever enjoying it; but to live in the country and with such kind friends! have I not every reason to be thankful? My happiness was very unexpected for I knew nothing of it ten days before; when my Uncle told me I was almost mad with joy . . . ."[21]

Dorothy was excited at the prospect of living with her aunt and uncle not only because of the opportunity to commune with nature which the country would afford, but also because of the habits of plain living and high thinking which, it was agreed, were to prevail in moments of leisure at Forncett:

We have sketched out a plan of the manner in which we are to spend our time, which I will give you that you may have some idea of my situation. We are to have prayers at nine oclock (you will observe it is *winter*) after breakfast is over we are to read, write, and I am to improve myself in French till twelve oclock, when we are to walk or visit our sick and poor neighbours till three, which is our dining hour; and after tea my Uncle will sit with us and either read to us or not as he and we find ourselves inclined.[22]

Three weeks later, on December 28, parts of this admirable program had been put to the test of actual practice, and the humanitarian impulse extended not merely to the poor but to the neighborhood birds as well. "I think I have not told you of one of my amusements," Dorothy remarks to Jane,

it is feeding the Robin redbreasts; there are at present two in the room which are gone to rest; you may imagine how tame they are when I tell you that they hop about the room where we sit, without shewing the least appearance of fear.

We have, I think, visited most of the poor people in the parish—my Uncle will I am sure do a great deal of good in the place.[23]

This situation was almost ideal, and Dorothy could regret only that Jane was not with her to share her delight:

[21] *Ibid.*, p. 17. [22] *Ibid.*, p. 18. [23] *Ibid.*, p. 22.

You would laugh to see us wading through the snow in our half boots and spatterdashes; we never go out without them for we find them not only very *comfortable* but *necessary*. Oh! my dear friend if you were with me how happy we should be! I often wish for you to walk with me in the garden. My room is one of the pleasantest in the house. I wish you were here to share it with me; some of the views are beautiful and I frequently wish that you were with me when I am admiring them: —but all this is very foolish as I know it is impossible and as I have so great reason to be contented it is wrong, yet still it cannot be very blamable to wish to see one's friends and that they could be partakers of one's pleasures.[24]

That William's conception of the good life was essentially the same as Dorothy's we know from the evidence contained

[24] *The Early Letters*, pp. 20–21. How sure Dorothy was of the final excellence of this plan of life is revealed in passages from her letters written to Jane Pollard in 1793. In February of that year, when she was expecting to be mistress of William's parsonage and hostess to Jane, she wrote: "I have laid the particular scheme of happiness for each Season. When I think of winter I hasten to furnish our little Parlour, I close the Shutters, set out the Tea-table, brighten the Fire. When our Refreshment is ended I produce our Work, and William brings his book to our Table and contributes at once to our instruction and amusement, and at intervals we lay aside the Book and each hazard our observations upon what has been read without the fear of Ridicule or Censure. We talk over past days, we do not sigh for any Pleasures beyond our humble Habitation . . ." (*ibid.*, p. 84). Five months later, when there was no longer a chance of bliss in the parsonage, Dorothy's hopes were unchanged and undimmed: "The evening is a lovely one, and I have strolled into a neighbouring meadow where I am enjoying the melody of birds and the busy sounds of a fine summer's evening, while my eye is gratified by a smiling prospect of cultivated fields richly wooded, our own church, and the parsonage house. But oh how imperfect is my pleasure! I am *alone;* why are not you seated with me? and my dear William why is not he here also? I could almost fancy that I see you both near me. I have chosen a bank where I have room to spare for a resting-place for each of you. I hear *you* point out a spot where, if we could erect a little cottage and call it *our own* we should be the happiest of human beings. I see my Brother fired with the idea of leading his sister to such a retreat as Fancy ever ready at our call hastens to assist us in painting; our parlour is in a moment furnished; our garden is adorned by magic; the roses and honeysuckles spring at our command, the wood behind the house lifts at once its head and furnishes us with a winter's shelter, and a summer's noon-day shade" (*ibid.*, pp. 93–94). Not having quite exhausted the subject, Dorothy added in a later passage of the same letter: ". . . think of our moonlight walks attended by my own dear William, think of our morning rambles when we shall—after having passed the night together and talked over the pleasures of the preceding evening, steal from our lodging-room, perhaps before William rises, and walk alone enjoying all the sweets of female friendship. Think of our mornings, we will work, William shall read to us. Oh my dear friend how happy we shall be!" (*ibid.*, p. 100).

THE EARLY POEMS

in a letter that he wrote her when he had almost completed his Alpine tour. This letter of September 6, 1790, in which Wordsworth naturally spoke of those aspects of his Continental experience which were likely to prove most engaging to Dorothy, provides us with a convenient catalogue of his early interests and values, and enables us to comprehend the basis of the deep sympathy and understanding which he shared with his sister. After assuring her that his health was excellent and that the trip was costing little money, William casually outlined his itinerary for Dorothy, pausing frequently to describe in detail the outstanding prospects and beautiful objects of nature that had caught his attention. A small footpath on the banks of Lake Como had proved particularly attractive because of the rich variety of views it afforded. Wordsworth described these delightful pictures at some length,[25] and then continued in a vein calculated to give the keenest pleasure to Dorothy:

> It was impossible not to contrast that repose, that complacency of spirit, produced by these lovely scenes, with the sensations I had experienced two or three days before, in passing the Alps. At the lake of Como, my mind ran through a thousand dreams of happiness, which might be enjoyed upon its banks, if heightened by conversation and the exercise of the social affections. Among the more awful scenes of the Alps, I had not a thought of man, or a single created being; my whole soul was turned to him who produced the terrible majesty before me.[26]

So great was Wordsworth's satisfaction amid these lovely scenes that his only regret, except of course the necessity of soon returning to home and college, was his inability to share his pleasures with his sister:

> I have thought of you perpetually; and never have my eyes burst upon a scene of particular loveliness but I have almost instantly wished that you could for a moment be transported to the place where I stood to enjoy it. I have been more particularly induced to form those wishes, because the scenes of Switzerland have no resemblance to any I have found in England; and consequently it may probably never be in your power to form an idea of them. We are now, as I observed above, upon the point of quitting the most sublime and beautiful parts; and

---

[25] For this description see below, p. 66.
[26] *The Early Letters*, pp. 32-33.

you cannot imagine the melancholy regret which I feel at the idea. I am a perfect enthusiast in my admiration of Nature in all her various forms; and I have looked upon, and as it were conversed with, the objects which this country has presented to my view so long, and with such increasing pleasure, that the idea of parting from them oppresses me with a sadness similar to what I have always felt in quitting a beloved friend.[27]

These two passages show that there was little difference between Dorothy's conception of the ideal existence and that of her brother. Of the things which were dear to her he also was fond. William, like Dorothy, was convinced that the greatest happiness was to be found in nature, that "conversation and the exercise of the social affections" were necessary for such happiness, and that it was pleasant and good to cherish a desire to share one's joys with one's dearest friends. William probably did not pray at nine in the morning, as did Dorothy and the Cooksons at Forncett, but he did permit his soul to turn "to him who produced the terrible majesty" of the higher Alps. And a third passage of this letter discloses his interest in the domestic customs of the Swiss and the Italians, and reveals that he had hoped to find in them the same habits of simple, virtuous, and enlightened living as prevailed at Forncett:

With regard to the manners of the inhabitants of this singular country, the impression which we have had often occasion to receive has been unfavourable; but it must be remembered that we have had little to do but with innkeepers, and those corrupted by perpetual intercourse with strangers. Had we been able to speak the language, which is German, and had time to insinuate ourselves into their cottages, we should probably have had as much occasion to admire the simplicity of their lives as the beauties of their country. My partiality to Switzerland, excited by its natural charms, induces me to hope that the manners of the inhabitants are amiable.... It was with pleasure I observed, at a small inn on the lake of Como, the master of it playing upon his harpsichord, with a large collection of Italian music about him. The outside of the instrument was such that it would not much have graced an English drawing-room; but the tones that he drew from it were by no means contemptible.[28]

Not very long after his return from Switzerland, probably just before his graduation from Cambridge, William spent

[27] *The Early Letters*, p. 34.   [28] *Ibid.*, pp. 35-36.

THE EARLY POEMS

six weeks at Forncett with his sister. The two kindred souls were united in the country and could at last share with one another the pleasures to be derived from close attention to natural beauty. Dorothy's letter to Jane of May 23, 1791, suggests that they exhausted their leisure, if not their enthusiasm for nature, walking in their uncle's garden:

> My brother William was with us six weeks in the depth of winter. You may recollect that at that time the weather was uncommonly mild; we used to walk every morning about two hours, and every evening we went into the garden at four or half past four and used to pace backwards and forwards till six. Unless you have accustomed yourself to this kind of walking you will have no idea that it can be pleasant, but I assure you it is most delightful, and if you and I happen to be together in the country, as we probably may at Mr. Rawson's, we will try how you like my plan if you are not afraid of the evening air.[29]

Dorothy places such emphasis upon walking in the "evening air" because, as she has confessed in the sentence immediately preceding this passage, "I am particularly fond of a moon-light or twilight walk—it is at this time that I think most of my absent friends."[30]

Dorothy's preference for a "moon-light or twilight walk" no doubt had been influenced by William's similar predilection, and by his as yet unpublished poem, *An Evening Walk*.[31] We may suppose, moreover, that the thoughts of absent friends evoked in Dorothy's memory by twilight were more often than not thoughts of William, who had taught her to understand why the finest walks of all were those taken in the evening and who had already developed in her that sensitiveness to natural objects which was to make her an ideal companion in later years for himself and Samuel Taylor Coleridge. At least these suppositions find support in Dorothy's letter to Jane of May 6, 1792, wherein Dorothy yields to Jane's request that she send her one of William's poems. "I take the first that offers," writes Dorothy with poorly dissembled nonchalance and modesty; "It is only valuable and dear to me

---

[29] *Ibid.*, p. 46.
[30] *Ibid.*
[31] Professor de Selincourt, who has seen the manuscripts of this early work, declares that it was "the work of his [Wordsworth's] first two long vacations" (*The Early Wordsworth*, p. 27).

because the lane which gave birth to it was the favourite evening walk of my dear William and me—":

> Sweet was the walk along the narrow lane
> At noon, the bank an[d] hedge-rows all the way
> Shaggd with wild pale green tufts of fragrant hay,
> Caught by the hawthorns from the loaded wain,
> Which Age with many a slow stoop strove to gain;
> And Childhood, seeming still most busy, took
> His little rake; with cunning side-long look,
> Sauntering to pluck the strawberries wild, unseen.
> *Now,* too on melancholy's idol dreams
> Musing, the lone spot with my soul agrees,
> Quiet and dark; for (through) the thick wove trees
> Scarce peeps the curious star till solemn gleams
> The clouded moon, and calls me forth to stray
> Thro' tall, green, silent woods and ruins gray.[32]

These facts concerning Dorothy's partiality for twilight walks, and this sonnet—which we shall soon recognize as *An Evening Walk* in miniature—have a double significance. They give us specific information about William and Dorothy's favorite diversion, and they suggest that the principle of association and the high value of memory were understood by the young Wordsworths long before William discovered the psychology of David Hartley.[33] The sonnet which she sent to Jane was cherished by Dorothy because it was conceived, and probably composed, in the lane which was associated with William and the great pleasure they shared on their favorite evening walk. The lane and the sonnet were especially dear because of the memories and emotions she associated with them. They were objects valued by Dorothy in the same way that the cornerstone of the unfinished sheepfold, to choose an example from Wordsworth's later work, was valued by Michael, and by Luke—until "ignominy and shame Fell on him." We shall see in the analysis of *An*

---

[32] *The Early Letters,* pp. 72–73.

[33] The most complete discussion of the influence of David Hartley's *Observations on Man, His Frame, His Duty, and His Expectations* on Wordsworth is Arthur Beatty's *William Wordsworth: His Doctrine and Art in Their Historical Relations,* University of Wisconsin Studies in Language and Literature, No. 24 (Madison, 1927). Professor Beatty dates this influence from 1795 and Wordsworth's acquaintance with Coleridge (*op. cit.,* pp. 99–102).

THE EARLY POEMS

Evening Walk that William, no less than Dorothy, was aware of the pleasures, slightly melancholy pleasures, to be derived from memory and association.

III

The close relationship between these letters which we have just reviewed and *An Evening Walk* is unmistakable. A study of the poem reveals that Wordsworth was therein attempting to glorify the emotions, attitudes, and values essential to the ideal life which he and his sister hoped to share at some hypothetical point in the future. In *An Evening Walk* Wordsworth is preoccupied with the soft affections that exist between parent and child, with the various and innumerable joys available in the world of nature, and with those habits of plain living which were characteristic of the lake and hill people among whom his boyhood had been spent, and which he hoped to find among the Swiss. He expresses, moreover, a humanitarian interest in the sufferings of the poor which parallels that of his Uncle William and his sister, and he betrays an impulse to share with his sister—his "dearest Friend" —all the comforts and delightful experiences allotted to him. He confesses that the troubles of the world weigh heavily upon him, causing him to regret the passing of his youth and the advent of the cares and responsibilities of maturity. He suggests, furthermore, that of all the multifarious pleasures to be gained from the observation of external nature, those afforded by an evening walk are supreme. Finally, he declares unequivocally that the "sole object" of his life is to secure the cottage home and domestic felicity whose specifications had long existed in his and Dorothy's imagination.

The opening lines of *An Evening Walk* describe Wordsworth's unenviable situation far from his sister, to whom the poem is addressed, alone as he is among the beauties of the Lake District, which, it is important to note, are endeared to him by "twilight glens" and the "memory of departed pleasures":

> Far from my dearest Friend, 'tis mine to rove
> Thro' bare grey dell, high wood, and pastoral cove;
> His wizard course where hoary Derwent takes

> Thro' craggs, and forest glooms, and opening lakes,
> Staying his silent waves, to hear the roar
> That stuns the tremulous cliffs of high Lodore:
> Where silver rocks the savage prospect chear
> Of giant yews that frown on Rydal's mere;
> Where peace to Grasmere's lonely island leads,
> To willowy hedgerows, and to emerald meads;
> Leads to her bridge, rude church, and cottag'd grounds,
> Her rocky sheepwalks, and her woodland bounds;
> Where, bosom'd deep, the shy Winander peeps
> 'Mid clust'ring isles, and holly-sprinkl'd steeps;
> Where twilight glens endear my Esthwaite's shore,
> And memory of departed pleasures, more.

The years have bowed his head, it seems, but he can still recall the happy days of his childhood, when the charms of the region filled him with a joy that needed no support from melancholy:

> Fair scenes! with other eyes, than once, I gaze,
> The ever-varying charm your round displays,
> Than when, ere-while, I taught, "a happy child,"
> The echoes of your rocks my carols wild:
> Then did no ebb of chearfulness demand
> Sad tides of joy from Melancholy's hand;
> In youth's wild eye the livelong day was bright,
> The sun at morning, and the stars of night,
> Alike, when first the vales the bittern fills,
> Or the first woodcocks roam'd the moonlight hills.

Those happy days, however, are gone beyond recall, and Wordsworth's pleasures are now the pleasures of melancholy. Memory accompanies him on his lonely way, and he perforce experiences the sad joys of association which Dorothy felt on her twilight walks in their favorite lane:

> While, Memory at my side, I wander here,
> Starts at the simplest sight th'unbidden tear,
> A form discover'd at the well-known seat,
> A spot, that angles at the riv'let's feet,
> The ray the cot of morning trav'ling nigh,
> And sail that glides the well-known alders by.

These introductory passages, their extraordinary awkwardness notwithstanding, demand careful attention because they clearly establish the fact that Wordsworth possessed and em-

THE EARLY POEMS

ployed in poetry his peculiar retrospective attitude probably as early as 1788 or 1789, when *An Evening Walk* was written, and certainly as early as 1793, the year in which the poem was published.[34] A mere glance at the verses wherein Wordsworth compares his present situation to that of an earlier period suffices to show that they constitute a definite anticipation of a famous passage of "Lines Written a Few Miles above Tintern Abbey." In "Tintern Abbey," of course, Wordsworth, from the awful perspective of his twenty-eight years, looked back upon his youth, and marveled at the change which had come over him. He had first visited the banks of the Wye in 1793, and his memory told him in 1798 that he was

> changed, no doubt, from what I was, when first
> I came among these hills; when like a roe
> I bounded o'er the mountains, by the sides
> Of the deep rivers, and the lonely streams,
> Wherever nature led; more like a man
> Flying from something that he dreads, than one
> Who sought the thing he loved. For nature then
> (The coarser pleasures of my boyish days,
> And their glad animal movements all gone by,)
> To me was all in all.—I cannot paint
> What then I was. The sounding cataract
> Haunted me like a passion: the tall rock,
> The mountain, and the deep and gloomy wood,
> Their colours and their forms, were then to me
> An appetite: a feeling and a love,

---

[34] Indeed, vv. 478–497 of the recently published "The Vale of Esthwaite" (*The Poetical Works of William Wordsworth: Poems Written in Youth, Poems Referring to the Period of Childhood*, ed. by Ernest de Selincourt [Oxford, 1940] [hereafter referred to as *The Poetical Works*], p. 281) show Wordsworth in 1787, at the ripe age of eighteen, looking back with melancholy fondness upon the road that he has traveled. Professor Beatty dates Wordsworth's retrospective attitude from "Tintern Abbey," 1798 (*op. cit.*, pp. 71–75), and suggests that Wordsworth's habit of contrasting various periods of his life and marveling at the change was the result of the influence of David Hartley. But it is a work of supererogation to consult Hartley's psychology for the source of Wordsworth's interest in the retrospective comparison of the several periods of his life, or for the source of his consciousness of the activity of memory or the principle of association. In his youth Wordsworth of course had no understanding of the mechanical subtleties of association, as Hartley described them, but it is safe to say that he understood all that was necessary for his artistic purposes.

> That had no need of a remoter charm,
> By thought supplied, or any interest
> Unborrowed from the eye.

And a comparison of these two passages reveals, moreover, that both describe the same period of Wordsworth's life, and that the lines from "Tintern Abbey" are autobiographically inaccurate. They purport to describe the Wordsworth of 1793, and they tell us that in 1793 Wordsworth's joy in nature "had no need of a remoter charm, By thought supplied." But the verses of *An Evening Walk* make it clear that Wordsworth's demands for joy in 1793, when *An Evening Walk* was published, were not satisfied by nature alone. They suggest, on the contrary, that as early as 1788 and 1789, when the poem was written, Wordsworth sought a "remoter charm" supplied by melancholy.

Wordsworth's purpose in *An Evening Walk*, however, is not to dwell at length upon his melancholy. He is mindful of the fact that he is addressing his sister. Knowing that she already has her share of troubles, and fearful lest he cause her further distress, he resists the temptation to describe his woes in full detail, and characteristically asks:

> But why, ungrateful, dwell on idle pain?
> To shew her yet some joys to me remain,
> Say, will my Friend, with soft affection's ear,
> The history of a poet's ev'ning hear?

In such a manner does Wordsworth disclose his intentions in *An Evening Walk*. Despite the fact that he is separated from Dorothy and despite the fact that the years are bringing with them mundane responsibilities deleterious to the happiness which he knew as a child, some joys remain to him. In a poem for Dorothy he will list and describe these joys and thus demonstrate his ability to discover and appreciate them. He will look ahead, in conclusion, to the day when he and Dorothy will be reunited and will share once again and to the end of life the pleasures available in nature and the delights engendered by the exercise of humanitarian feelings.

An Evening Walk, like the sonnet which Dorothy forwarded to Jane Pollard, begins with a description of the few

THE EARLY POEMS

sights which charm the poet's eye at noon. He observes the vapor that encircles the surrounding hills, the contrast of light and shadow produced by "deep embattl'd clouds," and the efforts of cattle to cool themselves in the shallows of the river. Then, after remarking the leisure of schoolboys stretched out upon the grass, the restless movements of a herd of deer, and the vain attempt of horses to follow a master who has shut the gate upon them and disappeared down a shaded pathway by the river, Wordsworth permits the "Quiet" of the hour to lead him to a secluded brookside nook where

> The eye reposes on a secret bridge
> Half grey, half shagg'd with ivy to its ridge,[35]

and where the illusion of twilight is produced by the deep shade. Here Wordsworth, quite obviously a student of Milton's *Il Penseroso*, remains until the sun declines.

Only when "eve's mild hour" invites his steps abroad does it become completely clear why Wordsworth is partial to an evening walk. Noon is characterized by inactivity and quiet; it affords but little stimulation to the powers of the descriptive poet. Evening, on the other hand, offers to his keenly receptive eye and ear a symphony of sight and sound. "The silver'd kite" whistles on the wing, and the slanting rays of the setting sun disclose gray lichens, moss, the foxglove, and the thistle's beard—noteworthy objects hidden by day in the shadow of a precipice at whose base they lurk. The evening sun transforms the stems of birch trees and the boughs of weeping willows into gold, while through the shade appear the naked masts of skiffs at anchor. The sound of "woodman's echo'd stroke," and the sight of cottage smoke curling through the trees enrich and humanize the hour with their suggestion of the presence and activity of man. Potters goad "Their pannier'd train" along a steep and winding road; a peasant "down the headlong pathway darts his sledge"; a team of horses struggles against the weight of a "pond'rous timberwain." All this and more the poet sees while his ear is en-

---

[35] This "secret bridge Half grey, half shagg'd with ivy" no doubt evoked a melancholy similar to that stimulated in Dorothy's favorite sonnet by "tall, green, silent woods and ruins gray."

gaged by the "rustic chime" of chapel bells, the sound of a hammer on the side of a boat, and the muffled thunder of blasting in a remote quarry.

Such are the pleasures available to the sensitive observer in the early evening. Having thus generally described them, Wordsworth proceeds to give *An Evening Walk* special distinction by embellishing it with a ten-line mock-serious description of the purple-crested barnyard cock, in imitation of a passage from *L'Agriculture* by the French poet, P. F. Rosset:[36]

> Sweetly ferocious, round his native walks,
> Gazed by his sister-wives, the monarch stalks;
> Spur-clad his nervous feet, and firm his tread;
> A crest of purple tops his warrior head.
> Bright sparks his black and haggard eye-ball hurls
> Afar, his tail he closes and unfurls;
> Whose state, like pine-trees, waving to and fro,
> Droops, and o'er canopies his regal brow,
> On tiptoe reared, he blows his clarion throat,
> Threatened by faintly-answering farms remote.

Then, by describing in some detail the sights and sounds afforded by men at work in a quarry, Wordsworth identifies himself with a very small number of eighteenth- and late seventeenth-century poets who cultivated an esoteric interest in mines, coalpits, caves, and quarries,[37] and thus assures his poem of a place above that of the average topographical poem:

> I love to mark the quarry's moving trains,
> Dwarf pannier'd steeds, and men, and numerous wains:
> How busy the enormous hive within,
> While Echo dallies with the various din!
> Some, hardly heard their chissel's clinking sound,
> Toil, small as pigmies, in the gulf profound;
> Some, dim between th'aëreal cliffs descry'd,
> O'erwalk the viewless plank from side to side;

---

[36] For the passage Wordsworth imitated, and for a discussion of Wordsworth's debt to Rosset, see Legouis, *op. cit.*, p. 143, and Arthur Beatty, *Wordsworth: Representative Poems* (Garden City [New York], 1937), pp. 17–18 n.

[37] See Aubin, *op. cit.*, pp. 283, 314.

THE EARLY POEMS

> These, by the pale-blue rocks that ceaseless ring,
> Glad from their airy baskets hang and sing.

After marking the appearance of the sun, whose broadening orb is split by a long blue cloud, and pausing to describe the evening operations of a shepherd and his dog in rounding up their scattered flock, Wordsworth contributes to the current stock of curious regional information with a brief comment upon some neighborhood stones which he believes to be of Druidic origin,[38] and devotes sixteen lines to an account of a particularly quaint evening superstition of the locality:

> In these lone vales, if aught of faith may claim,
> Thin silver hairs, and ancient hamlet fame;
> When up the hills, as now, retreats the light,
> Strange apparitions mock the village sight.
>   A desperate form appears, that spurs his steed,
> Along the midway cliffs with violent speed;
> Unhurt pursues his lengthen'd flight, while all
> Attend, at every stretch, his headlong fall.
>   Anon, in order mounts a gorgeous show
> Of horsemen shadows winding to and fro;
> And now the van is gilt with evening's beam,
> The rear through iron brown betrays a sullen gleam.
> Lost gradual o'er the heights in pomp they go,
> While silent stands th'admiring vale below;
> Till, but the lonely beacon all is fled,
> That tips with eve's last gleam his spiry head.

With the shadows of dusk falling fast about him, Wordsworth strays along a winding road beside the shore of the lake and discovers a family of swans whose graceful appearance and felicitous situation inspire the most lengthy and, to this study, most interesting interlude in *An Evening Walk*. Wordsworth gives half a dozen lines to an account of the grace and pride of the male, but it is obvious that his interest

---

[38] That Wordsworth was especially proud of his comment upon these "Druid-stones" is clear from the note that he appended to line 171 of *An Evening Walk:* "Not far from Broughton," he wrote, "is a Druid monument, of which I do not recollect that any tour descriptive of this country makes mention. Perhaps this poem may fall into the hands of some curious traveller, who may thank me for informing him, that up the Duddon, the river which forms the aestuary at Broughton, may be found some of the most romantic scenery of these mountains."

in the swans is great only because they symbolize perfectly the domestic bliss and security of which he and his sister had been deprived and for which they ceaselessly yearned. Death has not broken the family circle of the swans; the parents live, and Wordsworth has occasion to describe in detail the sweet maternal affection lavished upon the young:

> While tender Cares and mild domestic Loves,
> With furtive watch pursue her as she moves;
> The female with a meeker charm succeeds,
> And her brown little ones around her leads,
> Nibbling the water lilies as they pass,
> Or playing wanton with the floating grass;
> She, in a mother's care, her beauty's pride
> Forgets, unweary'd watching every side,
> She calls them near, and with affection sweet
> Alternately relieves their weary feet;
> Alternately they mount her back, and rest
> Close by her mantling wings' embraces prest.[39]

So great is the vicarious joy which he experiences at the sight of such maternal devotion that Wordsworth cannot but hope that the domestic felicity enjoyed by the swans may endure for a long time to come, just as his sister, inspired by the domestic bliss enjoyed by Jane Pollard, wished for a long continuation of that happiness whose existence depended entirely upon the good health of the elder Pollards.

Only Wordsworth's admiration for the environment in

[39] The value of living and affectionate parents was understood and appreciated by William as much as by Dorothy. This we know from the passage, cited above (pp. 7-8), from "The Vale of Esthwaite," in which Wordsworth describes his reaction to the death of his father, and his understanding of the consequences of that catastrophe for Dorothy's happiness. And Wordsworth's respect for the maternal instinct in particular is evident in an earlier poem which mourns the death of a "lovely Starling." After lamenting the situation, Wordsworth addresses the dead bird and observes with feeling:

> Yet art thou happier far than she
> Who felt a mother's love for thee.
> For while her days are days of weeping,
> Thou, in peace, in silence sleeping
> In some still world, unknown, remote
> The mighty Parent's care hast found,
> Without whose tender guardian thought
> No Sparrow falleth to the ground.

For this poem, unpublished before 1936, see *The Poetical Works*, p. 263.

which she lives with her family equals the esteem in which he holds the motherly virtues of the female swan. The cygnets are unusually fortunate in that they enjoy not only the blessings of a loving and protecting mother, but also the security and numerous advantages of a home ideally situated amidst the wonders of nature. "Long may ye roam," exclaims Wordsworth to the swans,

> these hermit waves that sleep,
> In birch-besprinkl'd cliffs embosom'd deep;
> These fairy holms untrodden, still, and green,
> Whose shades protect the hidden wave serene;
> Whence fragrance scents the water's desart gale,
> The violet, and the lily of the vale;
> Where, tho' her far-off twilight ditty steal,
> They not the trip of harmless milkmaid feel.
>
> Yon tuft conceals your home, your cottage bow'r,
> Fresh water rushes strew the verdant floor;
> Long grass and willows form the woven wall,
> And swings above the roof the poplar tall.
> Thence issuing oft, unwieldy as ye stalk,
> Ye crush with broad black feet your flow'ry walk;
> Safe from your door ye hear at breezy morn,
> The hound, the horse's tread, and mellow horn;
> At peace inverted your lithe necks ye lave,
> With the green bottom strewing o'er the wave;
> No ruder sound your desart haunts invades,
> Than waters dashing wild, or rocking shades.
> Ye ne'er, like hapless human wanderers, throw
> Your young on winter's winding sheet of snow.

How different is the plight of the human mother whom Wordsworth's humanitarian interests and sympathies impel him to introduce in the poem after this description of the "cottage bow'r" which the swans are fortunate enough to enjoy! The swan mother is blessed "by all a mother's joys," but the poor beggar woman, despite the fact that she exercises all the care and devotion in her attention to her young that Wordsworth deems desirable and fitting in a mother, knows only sore distress. When her babes are weary from tramping "the burning road" and from long exposure to "summer's breathless ray," she carries them until, "With backward gaze, lock'd joints, and step of pain," her arm grows numb and "slumbers with its weight." This woman's only pleasure lies in the willing assumption of her maternal responsibilities. Whatever else of domestic bliss she may have known in happier days has been destroyed by war, a source of human suffering which Wordsworth was to condemn at length in *Guilt and Sorrow*. Her husband is dead, and as she surveys the unshaded mountain road which she must travel, she

>bids her soldier come her woes to share,
>Asleep on Bunker's charnel hill afar.

Nature, who combines her rushes, flowers, and willows for the comfort and security of the swans, is less kind to the human mother, and provides only an occasional trick or two by which she may divert the attention of her suffering children from their misfortune. "I see her now," writes Wordsworth,

>deny'd to lay her head,
>On cold blue nights, in hut or straw-built shed;
>Turn to a silent smile their sleepy cry,
>By pointing to a shooting star on high:
>I hear, while in the forest depth he sees,
>The Moon's fix'd gaze between the opening trees,
>In broken sounds her elder grief demand,
>And skyward lift, like one that prays, his hand,
>If, in that country, where he dwells afar,
>His father views that good, that kindly star;
>. . . . .
>—When low-hung clouds each star of summer hide,
>And fireless are the valleys far and wide,
>Where the brook brawls along the painful road,
>Dark with bat-haunted ashes stretching broad,
>The distant clock forgot, and chilling dew,
>Pleas'd thro' the dusk their breaking smiles to view,
>Oft has she taught them on her lap to play
>Delighted, with the glow-worm's harmless ray
>Toss'd light from hand to hand; while on the ground
>Small circles of green radiance gleam around.

The lack of a husband and a home, however, and the manifest unfriendliness of nature do not cause the mother's care and affection for her children to diminish. The maternal instinct is true to the end. When wintry storms assail

THE EARLY POEMS

the unhappy family, the mother attempts to warm her children's fingers with her breath and shelter them from the cold with her almost frozen body. Lightning at length reveals that merciful death has intervened and relieved their undeserved suffering:

> Press the sad kiss, fond mother! vainly fears
> Thy flooded cheek to wet them with its tears;
> Soon shall the Light'ning hold before thy head
> His torch, and shew them slumbering in their bed,
> No tears can chill them, and no bosom warms,
> Thy breast their death-bed, coffin'd in thine arms.

In this manner does Wordsworth show in *An Evening Walk* not only his early consciousness of a vast discrepancy between the world of nature and the world of man, but also his firm faith in the excellence and integrity of the maternal instinct.

Having disclosed his humanitarianism and the essential purity of his feelings by this show of admiration for the tender passion of a mother and of gentle sympathy for innocence in distress, Wordsworth returns to his description of the charms of evening with a catalogue of sounds that constitutes the best passage in the poem:

> Sweet are the sounds that mingle from afar,
> Heard by calm lakes, as peeps the folding-star,
> Where the duck dabbles 'mid the rustling sedge,
> And feeding pike starts from the water's edge,
> Or the swan stirs the reeds, his neck and bill
> Wetting, that drip upon the water still;
> And heron, as resounds the trodden shore,
> Shoots upward, darting his long neck before.
> While, by the scene compos'd, the breast subsides,
> Nought wakens or disturbs it's tranquil tides;
> Nought but the char that for the may-fly leaps,
> And breaks the mirror of the circling deeps;
> Or clock, that blind against the wanderer born
> Drops at his feet, and stills his droning horn.
> —The whistling swain that plods his ringing way
> Where the slow waggon winds along the bay;
> The sugh of swallow flocks that twittering sweep,
> The solemn curfew swinging long and deep;
> The talking boat that moves with pensive sound,
> Or drops his anchor down with plunge profound;

> Of boys that bathe remote the faint uproar,
> And restless piper wearying out the shore;
> These all to swell the village murmurs blend,
> That soften'd from the water-head descend.
> While in sweet cadence rising small and still
> The far-off minstrels of the haunted hill,
> As the last bleating of the fold expires,
> Tune in the mountain dells their water lyres.

Night comes on apace, bringing with it noteworthy changes in light and shadow and a cessation of the sounds of evening:

> —'Tis restless magic all; at once the bright
> Breaks on the shade, the shade upon the light,
> Fair Spirits are abroad; in sportive chase
> Brushing with lucid wands the water's face,
> While music stealing round the glimmering deeps
> Charms the tall circle of th'enchanted steeps.
> —As thro' th'astonish'd woods the notes ascend,
> The mountain streams their rising song suspend;
> Below Eve's listening Star the sheep walk stills
> It's drowsy tinklings on th'attentive hills;
> The milkmaid stops her ballad, and her pail
> Stays it's low murmur in th'unbreathing vale;
> No night-duck clamours for his wilder'd mate,
> Aw'd, while below the Genii hold their state.

The disappearance of the "pageant scene" which so long has held his attention leads Wordsworth to make a heavy moral observation, part of which was borrowed with acknowledgment from Young's *Night Thoughts:*

> So vanish those fair Shadows, human Joys,
> But Death alone their vain regret destroys.

The "purple prospects" and "pensive, sadly-pleasing visions" upon which Wordsworth's eye has been focused are no longer visible; the memory of them, however, lingers on, and the result is melancholy:

> Yet still the tender, vacant gloom remains,
> Still the cold cheek its shuddering tear retains.

But this interval of retrospective melancholy musing is short-lived, for several features of the later evening remain to be noticed before Wordsworth is content to bring his poem to a close. The night bird whistles a greeting to the rising

THE EARLY POEMS

moon, who "lifts in silence up her lovely face" in an effort to dispel the darkness of night. The moon's attempt to brighten all the landscape is not immediately successful; at first only those favored hillsides which receive her rays directly are illuminated. So is it, Wordsworth observes, with "Hope":

> Thus Hope, first pouring from her blessed horn
> Her dawn, far lovelier than the moon's own morn,
> 'Till higher mounted, strives in vain to cheer
> The weary hills, impervious, blackening near;
> Yet does she still, undaunted, throw the while
> On darling spots remote her tempting smile.

"Hope," so far as Wordsworth is concerned, is young and in the early morn of her career, but already she has cast upon him the benefits of her revealing rays: "Ev'n now," he writes, addressing Dorothy directly,

> she decks for me a distant scene,
> (For dark and broad the gulf of time between)
> Gilding that cottage with her fondest ray,
> (Sole bourn, sole wish, sole object of my way;
> How fair its lawn and silvery woods appear!
> How sweet its streamlet murmurs in mine ear!)
> Where we, my Friend, to golden days shall rise,
> Till our small share of hardly-paining sighs
> (For sighs will ever trouble human breath)
> Creep hush'd into the tranquil breast of Death.

The importance of these verses—the last in *An Evening Walk* save twenty-odd lines in which Wordsworth describes the sights and sounds that greet his eye and ear as he finds his way homeward in the moon's full light—to an understanding of the poem and of Wordsworth's early life cannot be overestimated. We have seen already that Wordsworth's purpose in *An Evening Walk* was to describe for Dorothy the joys which remained to him in spite of the painful aspects of his situation—his lack of any proper home, his separation from his sister, his consciousness of the fact that increasing years bring irksome responsibilities which render life less pleasant. We have seen, moreover, that the joys which Wordsworth describes for Dorothy are those that come from close attention to the sights and sounds in nature, from the exercise of memory and the generation of sweet melancholy, and from humanitarianism—joys which Dorothy herself pursued and described in her letters to Jane Pollard. Finally, in the lines just quoted, we have Wordsworth's plain and candid declaration that the "Sole bourn, sole wish, sole object" of his way was a small cottage with a lawn, "silvery woods," and murmuring streamlet, where he and Dorothy might rise to "golden days" and the realization of their dream of the ideal existence.

In the light of these facts, we must regard *An Evening Walk* as essentially the product of Wordsworth's dissatisfaction with the circumstances into which he was plunged by the untimely death of his father. Wordsworth's primary ambition in his youth was to secure such an ideal domestic situation as the one variously described above in his own and his sister's correspondence; and it is clear that *An Evening Walk* is little more than the compensatory expression of this paramount desire and the sundry emotions and attitudes associated with it. Contrary to the traditional view of this poem, therefore, we must conclude that the value which Wordsworth here attaches to nature, to memory, to melancholy, and to humanitarianism was the result not so much of his extensive acquaintance with the traditions of eighteenth-century poetry, as of his firm conviction in the excellence of a mode of life which his partially starved emotions urgently demanded, and whose worth, to a considerable extent at least, had already been tried, tested, and confirmed by his and Dorothy's personal experience. Although the extensive influence of his predecessors upon him is unmistakable in the form and style of *An Evening Walk,* it is equally certain that Wordsworth had discovered sometime before 1793 that he must search within his own proper being for the inspiration and the content of his poetry.

IV

Descriptive Sketches, published in 1793 as a companion piece to *An Evening Walk,* combines the impressions and observations gathered by Wordsworth on his tour of the Swiss and Italian Alps in 1790 with the expression of miscellaneous

THE EARLY POEMS

political sentiments which he acquired during his residence in revolutionary France in 1791 and 1792. Earlier critics have pointed out that *Descriptive Sketches,* in so far as it reflects its author's later French experience, goes beyond *An Evening Walk* and is, therefore, of some significance as a transitional document in the history of his development. But their accounts of Wordsworth's intellectual and artistic progress from the period represented by *An Evening Walk* to that reflected in *Descriptive Sketches* have been superficial and unsatisfactory. They have observed, to be sure, that these two early poems both were written in heroic couplets and were full of verbal borrowings from earlier eighteenth-century poets, and they have noted that the glaring stylistic faults of *An Evening Walk* are even more obvious and exaggerated in *Descriptive Sketches.* They have failed, however, to discover the close and significant relationship of the two poems to one another, both in content and inspiration. In consequence, their descriptions of Wordsworth's development as it is recorded in *Descriptive Sketches* are lacking in both precision and completeness. The immediate purpose, therefore, is an examination of those elements of *Descriptive Sketches* which connect it closely and unmistakably with *An Evening Walk.* Such a study reveals still more conclusively the strength and persistence of Wordsworth's impulse to describe in verse the ideal situation and existence which he and Dorothy hoped one day to achieve, and enables us to distinguish clearly between the old and the new elements in *Descriptive Sketches.*

In the opening paragraphs of the poem Wordsworth presents two ideas for his reader's consideration and edification. He first suggests that if happiness is to be found anywhere in this pain-racked world, it will be found in natural surroundings. Then he declares that of all men the pedestrian traveler is the one most likely to discover and enjoy true happiness. This is true, he argues, because nature is particularly kind to and solicitous of him who deliberately and day after day seeks out and appreciates her various charms. His intention in *Descriptive Sketches* is to describe in detail the beauties of Switzerland and the virtues of her people, and he wishes the reader to understand that these virtues and charms are available to any appreciative soul who troubles to walk through the Swiss Alps:

> Were there, below, a spot of holy ground,
> By Pain and her sad family unfound,
> Sure, Nature's GOD that spot to man had giv'n,
> Where murmuring rivers join the song of ev'n;
> Where falls the purple morning far and wide
> In flakes of light upon the mountain-side;
> Where summer Suns in ocean sink to rest,
> Or moonlight Upland lifts her hoary breast;
> Where Silence, on her wing of night, o'er-broods
> Unfathom'd dells and undiscover'd woods;
> Where rocks and groves the power of waters shakes
> In cataracts, or sleeps in quiet lakes.
>   But doubly pitying Nature loves to show'r
> Soft on his wounded heart her healing pow'r,
> Who plods o'er hills and vales his road forlorn,
> Wooing her varying charms from eve to morn.
> No sad vacuities his heart annoy,
> Blows not a Zephyr but it whispers joy;
> For him lost flowers their idle sweets exhale;
> He tastes the meanest note that swells the gale;
> For him sod-seats the cottage-door adorn,
> And peeps the far-off spire, his evening bourn!
> Dear is the forest frowning o'er his head,
> And dear the green-sward to his velvet tread;
> Moves there a cloud o'er mid-day's flaming eye?
> Upward he looks—and calls it luxury;
> Kind Nature's charities his steps attend,
> In every babbling brook he finds a friend,
> While chast'ning thoughts of sweetest use, bestow'd
> By Wisdom, moralize his pensive road.
> Host of his welcome inn, the noon-tide bow'r,
> To his spare meal he calls the passing poor;
> He views the Sun uprear his golden fire,
> Or sink, with heart alive like Memnon's lyre;
> Blesses the Moon that comes with kindest ray
> To light him shaken by his viewless way.
> With bashful fear no cottage children steal
> From him, a brother at the cottage meal,
> His humble looks no shy restraint impart,
> Around him plays at will the virgin heart.
> While unsuspended wheels the village dance,
> The maidens eye him with inquiring glance,

THE EARLY POEMS

> Much wondering what sad stroke of crazing Care
> Or desperate Love could lead a wanderer there.[40]

A glance at the first twelve lines of the poem reveals that the characteristics of the "spot of holy ground" whereon true happiness is likely to be discovered are the characteristics of the English Lake District, already celebrated in *An Evening Walk*, and suggests that the impulse which caused Wordsworth to describe his native region in the earlier poem persists and accounts at least in part for his enthusiasm for Switzerland. What is more, we notice immediately that the pleasures of the pedestrian traveler are essentially the same as those experienced by Wordsworth in *An Evening Walk*. Each enjoys the sights and sounds of nature; each treads a "pensive road" with a mind full of "chast'ning thoughts of sweetest use, bestow'd By Wisdom";[41] neither is unresponsive to encounters with human suffering—Wordsworth, we have seen, was highly sympathetic toward the unfortunate beggar mother, and the foot traveler, no mean humanitarian himself, gladly shares his bread with the "passing poor." Indeed, the only true advantage which the pedestrian traveler has over the Wordsworth of *An Evening Walk* is that derived from "conversation and the exercise of the social affections." He is permitted to occupy sod seats by cottage doors; he enjoys the company of itinerant beggars at his meager lunch; he is a "brother at the cottage meal"; so friendly and inoffensive is his mien that children do not fear him, while village virgins feel free to glance at him and wonder at his presence. Such pleasures as these Wordsworth lacked in *An Evening Walk*, where he was forced to satisfy vicariously his appetite for domestic bliss and social intercourse by the studious observation of a family of swans.

[40] There can be no doubt that this emphatic and extensive praise of pedestrian traveling was Wordsworth's answer to those members of the family who had objected to his tour with Jones in 1790, and who perhaps were skeptical of the wisdom of his second trip to France. It is a clear case of special pleading.

[41] It is perhaps worth noting that the heart of the pedestrian traveler is annoyed by "no sad vacuities," whereas Wordsworth, in *An Evening Walk*, seems to suffer such a "vacuity" for a brief period between the arrival of darkness and the rise of the moon.

WORDSWORTH'S FORMATIVE YEARS

The first of the series of pictures which Wordsworth presents in *Descriptive Sketches* is one to be seen on the shores of the Lake of Como, and the details of the scene prove to be those with which Wordsworth was preoccupied in *An Evening Walk*. Most of these details Wordsworth recorded when they were fresh in his memory, in the letter which he sent to Dorothy in 1790 from Switzerland:

> A more charming path was scarce ever travelled over than we had along the banks of Como. The banks of many of the Italian and Swiss lakes are so steep and rocky, as not to admit of roads; that of Como is partly of this character. A small foot-path is all the communication by land between one village and another, on the side along which we passed, for upwards of thirty miles. We entered upon this path about noon, and, owing to the steepness of the banks, were soon unmolested by the sun, which illuminated the woods, rocks, and villages of the opposite shore. The lake is narrow, and the shadows of the mountains were early thrown across it. It was beautiful to watch them travelling up the side of the hills for several hours, to remark one half of a village covered with shade, and the other bright with the strongest sunshine.
>
> It was with regret that we passed every turn of this charming path, where every new picture was purchased by the loss of another which we would never have been tired of gazing at. The shores of the lake consist of steeps, covered with large sweeping woods of chestnut, spotted with villages; some clinging from the summits of the advancing rocks, and others hiding themselves within their recesses. Nor was the surface of the lake less interesting than its shores; part of it glowing with the richest green and gold, the reflection of the illuminated woods and part shaded with a soft blue tint. The picture was still further diversified by the number of sails which stole lazily by us as we paused in the woods above them. After all this we had the moon.[42]

For his account of Lake Como in *Descriptive Sketches*[43] Wordsworth merely paraphrased in heroic couplets this passage from his letter to Dorothy, added a few details, and arranged his materials according to the general pattern he had already used in *An Evening Walk*. As in the earlier poem, Wordsworth makes few observations before the approach of evening. He notes that the shores of the lake are steep, and wooded where they are not bare and rocky. There are many towns, some at the water's edge, others lurking in "woody sunless glens profound" or clinging obtrusively from "bend-

[42] *The Early Letters*, p. 32. [43] Vv. 80–147.

THE EARLY POEMS

ing rocks." These towns are fortunate in being free of the rude noises of the day, particularly the sounds of the "ringing team" and the "grating wain." And Wordsworth suggests that the path which "twines" along Como's "hidden margin" owes its extraordinary daytime charm to the circumstance that "Silence loves its purple roof of vines." Evening increases the attractiveness of the situation by bringing a medley of sights and sounds curiously similar to those seen and heard in *An Evening Walk*. Wordsworth peeps through the trees which shade his path and espies sails on the water, maidens at work in gardens, and villagers tripping in a "ringlet-tossing Dance," while his keen ear catches the sound of a "Lip-dewing Song" and of music made by lyres in the neighborhood cabins. After thus attending to the available evidence of human activity and amusement detected by his eye and ear, Wordsworth gives his consideration to the colors and shifting lights and shadows brought by evening: he

> stops the solemn mountain-shades to view
> Stretch, o'er their pictur'd mirror, broad and blue,
> Tracking the yellow sun from steep to steep,
> As up th'opposing hills, with tortoise foot, they creep.
> Here half a village shines, in gold array'd,
> Bright as the moon, half hides itself in shade.
> From the dark sylvan roofs the restless spire,[44]
> Inconstant glancing, mounts like springing fire.
> There, all unshaded, blazing forests throw
> Rich golden verdure on the waves below.

It is no wonder that Wordsworth was impressed by the picture of evening on the shores of Lake Como, for almost none of the details which gave him joy on the banks of Esthwaite or Winander, in *An Evening Walk*, are lacking here. As the English twilight was brightened by the reflection of light from "skiffs with naked masts at anchor laid," so is twilight on Lake Como enlivened by the

---

[44] Wordsworth seems to have taken particular care to comment upon the reflection of light from spires, and the like. In *An Evening Walk*, for instance, he pointed out that the Penrith Border Beacon was the last source of light by day. As the sun declined its reflected rays gradually disappeared,

> Till, but the lonely beacon all is fled,
> That tips with eve's last gleam his spiry head.

>   household boat beside the door,
>   Whose flaccid sails in forms fantastic droop,
>   Bright'ning the gloom where thick the forests stoop.

As the moon in *An Evening Walk* frosted "with hoary light the pearly ground," so do the stars in *Descriptive Sketches* cause the towns on the edge of Como to "glimmer hoar in eve's last light." And the music of man and bird that charmed the ear in *An Evening Walk* is not lacking in the neighborhood of Como, where the sounds of "lutes and voices down th'enchanted woods Steal," while "Evening's solemn bird melodious weeps." Wordsworth does not specifically mention hearing "th'unwearied glance of woodman's echo'd stroke" in *Descriptive Sketches,* but he must have heard it, for the lines—

>   From thickly-glittering spires the matin-bell
>   Calling the woodman from his desert cell—

clearly reveal his knowledge that at least one woodman lived in the vicinity of Como.

Evidence that the pleasures and joys yielded by nature in Switzerland were, for the most part, the same as those for which Wordsworth developed an early fondness in the English Lake District, and that the impulse which caused the composition of *An Evening Walk* was also largely responsible for *Descriptive Sketches,* is scattered throughout the poem. One passage in particular deserves quotation because of its close correspondence to the details and outline of *An Evening Walk* and of the favorite sonnet which Dorothy copied for Jane Pollard:

>   On as we move, a softer prospect opes,
>   Calm huts, and lawns between, and sylvan slopes.
>   While mists, suspended on th'expiring gale,
>   Moveless o'er-hang the deep secluded vale,
>   The beams of evening, slipping soft between,
>   Light up of tranquil joy a sober scene;
>   Winding it's dark-green wood and emerald glade,
>   The still vale lengthens underneath the shade;
>   While in soft gloom the scattering bowers recede,
>   Green dewy lights adorn the freshen'd mead,
>   Where solitary forms illumin'd stray

THE EARLY POEMS

Turning with quiet touch the valley's hay,
On the low brown wood-huts delighted sleep
Along the brighten'd gloom reposing deep.
While pastoral pipes and streams the landscape lull,
And bells of passing mules that tinkle dull,
In solemn shapes before th'admiring eye
Dilated hang the misty pines on high,
Huge convent domes with pinnacles and tow'rs,
And antique castles seen thro' drizzling show'rs.

Many years later, when he was dictating the Fenwick notes, Wordsworth himself admitted that his description of this "valley filled with mist" had been inspired by the close similarity of its lakes, Lungarn and Sarnen, to those of his native country: "Nothing that I ever saw in nature left a more delightful impression on my mind than that which I have attempted, alas, how feebly! to convey to others in these lines. Those two lakes have always interested me especially, from bearing, in their size and other features, a resemblance to those of the North of England."

No swans appear in *Descriptive Sketches,* but there are verses[45] in the poem which prove beyond question that Wordsworth's interest in domestic felicity, already recorded in *An Evening Walk,* continued unabated on his Alpine tour, and that his enjoyment of the tender sentiments aroused by the contemplation of parental affection was undiminished. Wordsworth tells us that he loved to roam by "silent cottage doors," and that on one occasion near the Lake of Como he had the good fortune to come upon a lonely cabin, situated in a wood. Although the peasant-owner of the cabin was absent on the business of the day, the little home was not devoid of life. Before the door a "hoary-headed sire Touch'd with his wither'd hand an aged lyre"; at his feet lay his grandchildren, gazing upon him with admiration, and joining in the "holy sound." This, Wordsworth explains, was "A hermit—with his family round."

No great feat of the imagination is required to conceive of the pleasure which this scene and situation must have given Wordsworth. Perfect household bliss was guaranteed of

[45] Vv. 164–175.

course by the fact that the father and mother were still alive, but these children knew the further blessing of a surviving grandparent, an advantage hitherto unencountered in Wordsworth's speculations upon family happiness.[46] We observe, moreover, that the life of this fortunate group was lacking in none of the specifications which Wordsworth deemed necessary for the ideal existence, for they dwelt in the vicinity of Lake Como, a neighborhood qualified in every respect to provide the pleasures afforded by the ideal environment. Finally, the grandfather's performance on the lyre and the children's exemplary behavior as auditors and chorus show clearly that the musical culture of the region was not confined to the talented innkeeper whose harpsichord and collection of Italian music had provoked Wordsworth's admiration and comment in his letter to Dorothy in 1790.

It is evident, then, that these passages of *Descriptive Sketches* are little more than a restatement of the details of the ideal life and situation which Wordsworth celebrated in *An Evening Walk,* and which Dorothy frequently described in her letters to Jane Pollard. Thus far, if we except the emphasis placed upon the value of pedestrian traveling, we have discovered nothing of importance to distinguish *Descriptive Sketches* from the earlier poem. In a passage beginning in the two hundred and eighty-third line, however, where Wordsworth paints the picture of "Uri's lake," the influence of his experience in revolutionary France in 1791 and 1792 asserts itself, and *Descriptive Sketches* begins to acquire significance as a transitional document. A larger world is opened up to the reader of his verse when Wordsworth, for the first time in his career, manifests an interest in politics, and when the joys which he finds emanating from nature, from the contemplation of domestic bliss, and from the exercise of humanitarianism become dependent upon and subordinate to the basic requirement of political liberty.

At first glance the characteristics of the scenery and the

---

[46] One recalls that William and Dorothy Wordsworth were not always appreciative of the survival of their own maternal grandparents (see particularly Dorothy's letter to Jane Pollard of the summer of 1787 [*The Early Letters,* pp. 1–5]).

THE EARLY POEMS

human habitations in the region of Uri appear to be so undesirable as to preclude completely the possibility of true happiness, despite the fact that the situation bears a superficial resemblance to those described in *An Evening Walk* and the earlier passages of *Descriptive Sketches*. Here man has built himself a "small wood-hut"; he has a little garden which perfumes the "desert air"; an orchard blooms among the pine trees. But there is no shaded pathway down which the peasant can go to his "domestic skiff." He is forced to descend a "zig-zag path" instead, so steep and precipitous are the shores of the lake. The residents of the neighborhood are unfortunate, in Wordworth's judgment, for their cottages are so isolated and unapproachable as to make the pleasures arising from "conversation and the exercise of the social affections" quite impossible. Travelers never pass that way, and the peasant is consequently ignorant of the delight gained from gossip with a curious passer-by. Even the cottage watchdog suffers from the solitude, cut off as he is from the ecstasy, well known by dogs in more populated regions, of withholding his "angry bark" when touched by human misery and sympathy for itinerant beggars. And the "grassy seat" beneath the window of the little hut is unhallowed by the blessing of any "pilgrim's wistful eye." So wild and bleak is the scene on Uri's banks, moreover, that fear is the predominant emotion. Terror fills the breast of the "love-sick maiden," for example, as she waits at midnight high upon the treacherous cliffs for her lover to arrive safely at the end of the dangerous mountain path. Wordsworth insists, however, that in spite of these many disadvantages the people who live on the shores of Uri are truly happy. The single fact that the district affords materials with which "Freedom" can make herself a suitable "crest" compensates them abundantly for their lack of more trivial sources of satisfaction:

> Ev'n here Content has fix'd her smiling reign
> With Independance child of high Disdain.
> Exulting mid the winter of the skies,
> Shy as the jealous chamois, Freedom flies,
> And often grasps her sword, and often eyes,
> Her crest a bough of Winter's bleakest pine,

> Strange "weeds" and alpine plants her helm entwine,
> And wildly-pausing oft she hangs aghast,
> While thrills the "Spartan fife" between the blast.

The truth of the matter is that the natives of this region are doubly happy: they experience not only the inestimable advantages of present political liberty, but also the salutary influence of a long tradition of liberty and independence, a tradition ennobled by the mighty name of William Tell! Wordsworth specifically describes the powerful effect of this tradition of freedom upon a local boatman, who has been caught on the lake in his boat during a violent storm:

> 'Tis storm; and hid in mist from hour to hour
> All day the floods of deeper murmur pour,
> And mournful sounds, as of a Spirit lost,
> Pipe wild along the hollow-blustering coast,
> 'Till the Sun walking on his western field
> Shakes from behind the clouds his flashing shield.
> Triumphant on the bosom of the storm,
> Glances the fire-clad eagle's wheeling form;
> Eastward, in long perspective glittering, shine
> The wood-crown'd cliffs that o'er the lake recline;
> Wide o'er the Alps a hundred streams unfold,
> At once to pillars turn'd that flame with gold;
> Behind his sail the peasant strives to shun
> The west that burns like one dilated sun,
> Where in a mighty crucible expire
> The mountains, glowing hot, like coals of fire.
>   But lo! the boatman, over-aw'd, before
> The pictur'd fane of Tell suspends his oar;
> Confused the Marathonian tale appears,
> While burn in his full eyes the glorious tears.
> *And who but feels a power of strong controul,*
> *Felt only there, oppress his labouring soul,*
> *Who walks, where honour'd men of ancient days*
> *Have wrought with god-like arm the deeds of praise?*[47]

The patriotic inspiration that results inevitably from such a vision as this is not limited to particular individuals or to the residents of any one district of Switzerland. Further on in *Descriptive Sketches* Wordsworth suggests that Switzerland's glorious record of liberty is an irresistible influence for

---

[47] The italics here and in the verses immediately following are my own.

THE EARLY POEMS

good with every inhabitant of the country. This happy circumstance, according to Wordsworth, is one of the various traces yet remaining in republican Switzerland of a bygone Golden Age:

>   Once Man entirely free, alone and wild,
> Was bless'd as free—for he was Nature's child.
> *He, all superior but his God disdain'd,*
> Walk'd none restraining, and by none restrain'd,
> Confess'd no law but what his reason taught,
> Did all he wish'd, and wish'd but what he ought.
> As Man in his primaeval dower array'd
> The image of his glorious sire display'd,
> Ev'n so, by vestal Nature guarded, here
> The traces of primaeval Man appear.
> The native dignity no forms debase,
> The eye sublime, and surly lion-grace.
> The slave of none, of beasts alone the lord,
> He marches with his flute, his book, and sword,
> Well taught by that to feel his rights, prepar'd
> With this "the blessings he enjoys to guard."
>   And as on glorious ground he draws his breath,
> Where Freedom oft, with Victory and Death,
> Hath seen in grim array amid their Storms
> Mix'd with auxiliar Rocks, three hundred Forms;
> While twice ten thousand corselets at the view
> Dropp'd loud at once, Oppression shriek'd, and flew.
> Oft as those sainted Rocks before him spread,
> *An unknown power connects him with the dead.*
> *For images of other worlds are there,*
> *Awful the light, and holy is the air.*
> *Uncertain thro' his fierce uncultur'd soul*
> *Like lighted tempests troubled transports roll;*
> *To viewless realms his Spirit towers amain,*
> *Beyond the senses and their little reign.*
>   *And oft, when pass'd that solemn vision by,*
> *He holds with God himself communion high,*
> When the dread peal of swelling torrents fills
> The sky-roof'd temple of th'eternal hills,
> And savage Nature humbly joins the rite,
> While flash her upward eyes severe delight.[48]

These verses I have quoted at length because they have been generally neglected by Wordsworth's critics, and because

[48] Inevitably of course the noble Swiss experiences the joys which Wordsworth held most precious and leads a life whose chief characteristic is

they are the most significant passages in *Descriptive Sketches* to the student of Wordsworth's development. They are incontrovertible proof, first of all, that Wordsworth possessed as early as 1793 many of the ideas to which he later gave immortal expression in his political sonnets. They reveal, moreover, his early disposition to go "Beyond the senses and their little reign" in his quest for essential truth. They show, in fact, that, in 1792 and 1793, when Wordsworth was fresh from his experience in republican and freethinking France— when, that is, his revolutionary enthusiasm had reached its highest pitch—his political convictions were unmistakably interwoven with and dependent upon sheer pious mysticism, just as they were some ten years later when the mature Wordsworth was well along the road to conservatism in politics and orthodoxy in religion.

A glance at Wordsworth's noble and impassioned invocations of the great English tradition of liberty and independence in two of the representative sonnets of 1802 shows clearly that his later philosophy of political liberty differed from that of *Descriptive Sketches* chiefly in the beauty of its expression. First:

> Great men have been among us; hands that penned
> And tongues that uttered wisdom—better none:
> The later Sidney, Marvel, Harrington,
> Young Vane, and others who called Milton friend.
> These moralists could act and comprehend:
> They knew how genuine glory was put on;
> Taught us how rightfully a nation shone
> In splendour: what strength was, that would not bend
> But in magnanimous meekness. France, 'tis strange,
> Hath brought forth no such souls as we had then.
> Perpetual emptiness! unceasing change!

---

simplicity. Outstanding among his pleasures are those of memory and association: "No vulgar joy is his," writes Wordsworth,

> For as the pleasures of his simple day
> Beyond his native valley hardly stray,
> Nought round its darling precincts can he find
> But brings some past enjoyment to his mind....
> (Vv. 512-517)

Thus, in more ways than one, is the Swiss mountaineer a prototype of the shepherd Michael.

THE EARLY POEMS

> No single volume paramount, no code,
> No master spirit, no determined road;
> But equally a want of books and men!

And again:

> It is not to be thought of that the Flood
> Of British freedom, which, to the open sea
> Of the world's praise, from dark antiquity
> Hath flowed, "with pomp of waters, unwithstood,"
> Roused though it be full often to a mood
> Which spurns the check of salutary bands,
> That this most famous Stream in bogs and sands
> Should perish; and to evil and to good
> Be lost for ever. In our halls is hung
> Armoury of the invincible Knights of old:
> We must be free or die, who speak the tongue
> That Shakespeare spake; the faith and morals hold
> Which Milton held.—In everything we are sprung
> Of Earth's first blood, have titles manifold.

Here Wordsworth merely repeats his faith in the efficacy of famous names, and reaffirms his conviction that a record of freedom such as that of England, with its long line of illustrious heroes and sages, can belong only to a people directly descended from the moral and physical titans who distinguished the Golden Age of storied antiquity. And in the sonnet entitled "Thought of a Briton on the Subjugation of Switzerland" it is plain that Wordsworth in later years came to think of his native land and the Switzerland he had celebrated in *Descriptive Sketches* as copartners in and joint contributors to the holy and historic cause of political liberty:

> Two Voices are there; one is of the sea,
> One of the mountains; each a mighty Voice:
> In both from age to age thou didst rejoice,
> They were thy chosen music, Liberty!
> There came a Tyrant, and with holy glee
> Thou fought'st against him; but hast vainly striven:
> Thou from thy Alpine holds at length art driven,
> Where not a torrent murmurs heard by thee.
> Of one deep bliss thine ear hath been bereft:
> Then cleave, O cleave to that which still is left;
> For, high-souled Maid, what sorrow would it be
> That Mountain floods should thunder as before,

WORDSWORTH'S FORMATIVE YEARS

> And Ocean bellow from his rocky shore,
> And neither awful Voice be heard by thee!

Special emphasis must be given to the mystical nature of Wordsworth's earliest utterance upon the glorious stream of political liberty as it flows from the heroic past to modern times, for critics have declared that Wordsworth was definitely an unbeliever when he composed *Descriptive Sketches,* and have suggested that the religious overtones of the political sonnets mark a departure from his youthful philosophy and reflect the influence of increasing age, fear of Napoleon, and a general tendency toward orthodoxy. Professor Harper and H. W. Garrod in particular have insisted that Wordsworth in 1792 and 1793 was a religious skeptic.[49] They base this conclusion upon four lines descriptive of Wordsworth's feelings at the Catholic shrine of Einsiedeln, where suffering pilgrims, full of faith, come and hope to be relieved of their various woes:

> —Without one hope her written griefs to blot,
> Save in the land where all things are forgot,
> My heart, alive to transports long unknown,
> Half wishes your delusion were it's own.

Close scrutiny of these lines in their context shows, however, that they are by no means evidence of "religious unbelief." They tell us merely that Wordsworth had no faith in latter-day miracles.[50]

That Wordsworth had faith in the abiding presence and

---

[49] See Harper, *op. cit.,* p. 138, and Garrod, *op. cit.,* pp. 49-51.

[50] The passage introductory to the lines in question here makes it perfectly clear that Wordsworth was writing of miracles in particular and not of religious faith in general. It should be noted, moreover, that, although he himself cannot believe in the wonders ascribed by the superstitious to the shrine of Einsiedeln, he generously refrains from holding in contempt all those who can and do:

> Oh give not me that eye of hard disdain
> That views undimm'd Einsiedeln's wretched fane.
> Mid muttering prayers all sounds of torment meet,
> Dire clap of hands, distracted chafe of feet,
> While loud and dull ascends the weeping cry,
> Surely in other thoughts contempt may die.
> If the sad grave of human ignorance bear
> One flower of hope—Oh pass and leave it there.

THE EARLY POEMS

the intelligent benign activity of a mighty power whose source lay somewhere outside the little world of time and space is affirmed by the lines of *Descriptive Sketches* italicized above. The boatman on the Lake of Uri is overwhelmed and confused as the "Marathonian tale" of William Tell flashes before his vision in the blinding light of the western sun. "Glorious tears" burn in his dazzled eyes as the profound mystical significance of the experience bursts upon his understanding and he feels the presence of "a power of strong controul." So is it with all the men of Switzerland. When they lay eyes upon the "sainted Rocks" which commemorate the valiant deeds of their heroic forebears, they—like the boatman of Uri—enjoy the marvelous stimulus of a mystical experience. The inscrutable operations of an "unknown power" uplift their spirits; "images" other than those produced by ordinary sense perception appear to them, while the light and air of common day mysteriously take on the wonderful aspect of a "solemn vision." The "power" responsible for such visions is not "unknown," however, either to the Swiss, to nature, or to Wordsworth: once the vision has passed, Wordsworth assures us, the Swiss hold "with God himself communion high," and "savage Nature humbly joins the rite."[51]

In view of the fact that Wordsworth admitted in his letter of 1790 to Dorothy that their ignorance of German had made it impossible for him and his friend Jones to converse with others than "innkeepers, and those corrupted by perpetual intercourse with strangers," critics have been obliged to search for the source of the detailed and ostensibly close information

---

[51] The significance of *Descriptive Sketches* as a sort of repository for ideas and attitudes which were to become focal points in his mature philosophy is even more apparent when Wordsworth's early description of the mystical experience is compared with the opening lines of a famous passage from "Lines Written a Few Miles above Tintern Abbey":

>   And I have felt
> A presence that disturbs me with the joy
> Of elevated thoughts; a sense sublime
> Of something far more deeply interfused, etc.

I find it impossible to make any vital distinction between the "power of strong controul" of *Descriptive Sketches* and the disturbing "presence," the "something far more deeply interfused" of "Tintern Abbey."

concerning Swiss manners and traditions which Wordsworth displayed in *Descriptive Sketches*. This source was discovered years ago by Émile Legouis, who—following an acknowledgment made by Wordsworth himself in a note to the poem[52]—proved beyond question that Wordsworth found materials made to order for his purpose in *Lettres de M. William Coxe à M. W. Melmoth sur l'État politique, civil et naturel de la Suisse, traduites de l'anglais et augmentées des observations faites dans le même pays, par le traducteur* (Paris, 1788), by Ramond de Carbonnières.[53]

Legouis and subsequent critics have been inclined to believe that Ramond exerted upon Wordsworth an influence of considerable extent and significance. Legouis, for example, remarks that Wordsworth borrowed from Ramond "a certain number of thoughts and feelings which he first expressed in the *Sketches*, and afterwards scattered over the work of his maturity,"[54] and suggests that "It may have been through Ramond that he first became acquainted with Rousseau, the greatest of his predecessors, of whom Ramond was an enthusiastic admirer."[55] Legouis observes that Wordsworth was less favorably impressed by the Swiss than by the French and Italians in 1790. Consequently, when Wordsworth reveals himself in *Descriptive Sketches* as a zealous enthusiast for the Swiss and endorses the notion that they represent the descendants of "primaeval man," Legouis feels forced to conclude that Wordsworth was writing under the influence of Ramond, who endorsed Rousseau's idea that the Swiss were the closest approximation to primitive man that one could find in Europe.[56] This view is supported by Arthur Beatty, the most recent critic to consider the relationship of Wordsworth to Ramond. Professor Beatty also maintains that Wordsworth took from Ramond "the thesis that Switzerland is the representative of primeval man, who is free, independent, hospitable . . . ."[57] He notes that Ramond inherited the

---

[52] See Wordsworth's note to v. 372.
[53] See Legouis, *op. cit.*, pp. 113–114, 475–477.
[54] *Ibid.*, p. 114.   [55] *Ibid.*   [56] *Ibid.*
[57] *Wordsworth: Representative Poems*, p. 34 (introductory note to *Descriptive Sketches*).

THE EARLY POEMS

idea from Rousseau and Coxe, but insists that "in neither is this belief a flaming conviction, as it is with Ramond, which fires others with an unquenchable zeal for the betterment of mankind."[58] Since Wordsworth lacked this zeal in 1790 and expressed it two years later in *Descriptive Sketches,* it follows, according to Professor Beatty, that Wordsworth's enthusiasm for the Swiss was entirely the result of his acquaintance with the provocative observations of Ramond de Carbonnières.

Now it is true that Wordsworth gives evidence in *Descriptive Sketches* of an enthusiasm for the Swiss that is not apparent in his letter to Dorothy in 1790. It is also true that he may have acquired the idea that the Swiss were descended from the primeval heroes of a Golden Age from his perusal of Ramond's inspiring pages. Nevertheless, it is somewhat unrealistic to suppose that Ramond alone is responsible for the attitude toward the Swiss which Wordsworth registers in *Descriptive Sketches.* We must remember, first of all, that Wordsworth told Dorothy in 1790 that he was partial to Switzerland, that because of the pleasure he had received from her natural charms he was "induced to hope that the manners of the inhabitants would prove amiable." And we must remember, moreover, that Ramond de Carbonnières was not Wordsworth's only source of inspiration and knowledge between 1790 and 1793, when *Descriptive Sketches* was published.

Credit for Wordsworth's newly acquired political faith and fervor should be given not to Ramond de Carbonnières, but to Michel Beaupuy, to whom Wordsworth pays ample tribute in *The Prelude.*[59] All who have read *The Early Life of William Wordsworth* by Émile Legouis will recall the description of the intellectual equipment brought by Beaupuy to the instruction of Wordsworth in the basic principles and aims of the French Revolution. Michel Beaupuy, according to Legouis,

was a man rich in the knowledge of philosophers and political writers with whose teachings Wordsworth was little acquainted. "Philosophy" was the passion of his family. He and his brothers were less proud of

[58] *Ibid.*   [59] Bk. IX.

79

their titles than of their ancestor Montaigne, from whom they were descended on the female side. The house at Mussidan in which they were born contained a huge library, where not one of the great authors of the eighteenth century was missing, and the folios of the Encyclopaedia towered above the rest.[60]

Beaupuy and Wordsworth became fast friends. They walked together along the banks of the Loire, where their "chief delight," as Legouis observes—following Wordsworth's own account in *The Prelude*—was in picturing to themselves the miseries

> Of royal courts, and that voluptuous life
> Unfeeling, where the man who is of soul
> The meanest thrives the most; where dignity,
> True personal dignity, abideth not;
> A light, and cruel, and vain world cut off
> From the natural inlets of just sentiment,
> From lowly sympathy and chastening truth:
> Where good and evil interchange their names.

Following Rousseau [Legouis continues], they took especial delight also in glorifying "man and his noble nature." They shared the faith of their age in the infinite perfectibility of the human race, a subject which at that very time was occupying the thoughts of Condorcet and of Godwin. Man's blind desires would impel him to break his bondage; his higher faculties, "capable of clear truth," would enable him to build liberty on firm foundations.[61]

These, among others, writes Legouis, "were the sentiments of Beaupuy, and from the outset they were echoed by Wordsworth."[62]

It is this association with Michel Beaupuy that is the true source of Wordsworth's inspiration for that part of *Descriptive Sketches* in which he bestows lavish praise upon the Swiss as a people who perpetuate the virtues possessed by men in the Golden Age and for the concluding passages, in which his celebration of abstract freedom is loud and vehement. We know that under the tutelage of this philosophic Frenchman Wordsworth discussed Rousseau and "Man and his noble nature." We know that under Beaupuy's influence Wordsworth became imbued with revolutionary ardor for the prin-

[60] *Op. cit.*, p. 203.   [61] *Ibid.*, p. 207.   [62] *Ibid.*, p. 208.

THE EARLY POEMS

ciples of republican government and with hatred for the numerous evils emanating from the "voluptuous life" led in the courts of European monarchies. And Wordsworth is explicit in *The Prelude* when he tells us that on his rambles with Beaupuy,

> We summon'd up the honorable deeds
> Of ancient Story, thought of each bright spot
> That could be found in all recorded time
> Of truth preserv'd and error pass'd away,
> Of single Spirits that catch the flame from Heaven,
> And how the multitude of men will feed
> And fan each other .... (IX, 370-376)

In view of these facts, it is unlikely that the influence of Ramond de Carbonnières upon *Descriptive Sketches* is as significant as has been supposed.

What probably happened is this: Late in 1791 or very early in 1792 Wordsworth determined to write a poem about Switzerland that would differ only superficially from *An Evening Walk*. For the first several hundred lines of the poem, following his original purpose, he emphasized chiefly the beauties of nature to be observed in the Alps, and, as in *An Evening Walk*, made cursory comments upon the activities of the human beings who lived and worked in the region he was describing. Then suddenly in 1792, either during his companionship with Beaupuy or shortly after Beaupuy's departure for military service on July 27, 1792,[63] Wordsworth's interest in Switzerland broadened to such an extent that he wished to supply himself with information concerning the manners, politics, and traditions of the people—information which he had failed to obtain on his walking tour in 1790. This new and wider interest was the result of his residence in France and particularly of his communion with Beaupuy. Naturally, in his quest for sources of this information, Wordsworth would have been attracted to one with whose general principles he was sympathetic. It is quite probable that the highly educated and widely read Beaupuy aided him in his search and put him on the track of French writers who had

[63] According to Legouis, Wordsworth never saw Beaupuy after this date (*ibid.*, p. 214).

made observations upon the Swiss. Beaupuy of course would have been careful to recommend to his recently converted protégé writers known to have a republican bias. One of these writers, perhaps the only one, was Ramond de Carbonnières.

In Ramond Wordsworth found the information, principles, and sentiments which he had determined to find. Because Switzerland had long enjoyed the political liberty for which Beaupuy and the French masses were struggling, Wordsworth's freshly acquired republican enthusiasm merely increased that partiality for Switzerland which had begun in 1790. Switzerland combined the natural charms that Wordsworth had long worshiped in England with the republican form of government which his most recent experience taught him was good; inevitably, then, he was ready and eager to extol the people who inhabited that wonderful country, and to consider them as the noble and appreciative beneficiaries of the various joys and pleasures that he associated with nature and political independence. Ramond had already thus described them; he therefore proved to be an extremely congenial and convenient source for Wordsworth, who had no scruples about appropriating much of his predecessor's imagery and phraseology.[64] Despite the fact, how-

[64] The importance of Wordsworth's frequent and rather extensive use of Ramond's language has probably been overestimated by Professor Beatty. Legouis, who was the first to record the parallel passages in *Descriptive Sketches* and Ramond's work (*op. cit.*, pp. 114, 136, 475–477), ventured no opinion as to the permanent effect of Ramond's influence upon Wordsworth's practice of the art of writing. With less caution, Professor Beatty opines that Ramond taught Wordsworth "a lesson in style and language" (*Wordsworth, Representative Poems*, p. 34 [introductory note to *Descriptive Sketches*]), and showed him how "to render the object in its essential truth, directly and not by figure or circumlocution or comparison" (*ibid.*, p. xlii). But Professor Beatty's position here is certainly untenable. Critics have long agreed that the style of *Descriptive Sketches* is worse than the bad style of *An Evening Walk*. Wordsworth himself, as we have seen, dated his ability to observe and describe accurately "the infinite variety of natural appearances" from his eighteenth year. And the concluding twenty-four lines of *An Evening Walk*, as well as many of the passages quoted above, are incontrovertible evidence that Wordsworth had learned how "to render the object in its essential truth, directly and not by figure or circumlocution or comparison" years before he became acquainted with the prose of Ramond de Carbonnières.

THE EARLY POEMS

ever, that parallels between Ramond's book and *Descriptive Sketches* are frequent and unmistakable, and despite the fact that Ramond unquestionably perpetuates the Swiss legend of a Golden Age, there is nothing to suggest that Wordsworth was indebted to Ramond for his concept of and his abiding faith in the miraculous and mystical continuity of the tradition of liberty and independence.[65] It would seem, therefore, that Ramond's influence upon Wordsworth, like that of the early eighteenth-century poets whose style Wordsworth imitated and whose phrases he echoed in *An Evening Walk*, was primarily verbal and of permanent importance only in so far as it reinforced and contributed to Wordsworth's predisposition in favor of republican principles—a predisposition already greatly strengthened by the teachings of Michel Beaupuy.

The hundred-odd lines with which Wordsworth brings *Descriptive Sketches* to a close, although they must be numbered among the poorest that he ever wrote, are of considerable interest, for they reveal strikingly the intensity of his desire for freedom and represent his first clearly defined attempt to compose republican propaganda. In Savoy Wordsworth discovers evidence calculated to convince the greatest skeptic that life without freedom is not to be endured. Slavery prevails in Savoy and the results are catastrophic: even

---

[65] The view expressed here—that Wordsworth did not take from Ramond those ideas which were to become basic in his political sonnets—is necessarily tentative, for I have been unable to gain access to Ramond's book. None of the parallel passages listed by Legouis (see note 64), however, indicates that these ideas were available in Ramond. The one passage quoted by Legouis which touches upon the legend of the Golden Age concerns neither the heroic tradition of the Swiss, nor their mystical experiences, of which Wordsworth makes so much: "Malgré cette prodigieuse fécondité [des vaches en laitage], ces bous bergers imaginent un tems où elle a été plus considérable: le tradition leur a, disent-ils, transmis la mémoire d'un âge heureux où les glacières n'avaient pas encore envahi la plus belle partie de leurs Alpes; alors les plantes maintenant vénéneuses étaient saines: les *tithymales* augmentaient de leur lait celui des vaches, et l'on pouvait les traire trois fois par jour. Les péchés des hommes, ajoutent-ils, ont attiré la malédiction du Ciel et les glaces sur leurs paturages. Ces traditions sont précieuses, dan quelque sens qu'on les considère." It is reasonable to assume, I think, that Legouis would have chosen a more significant parallel than this from Ramond had he found any such at his disposal.

the pedestrian traveler is deprived of pleasure in such a region. Wordsworth heaves "the human sigh" as he passes through this sad district, and observes that

> not for thee, delicious vale! unfold
> Thy reddening orchards, and thy fields of gold;
> That thou, the slave of slaves, art doom'd to pine,
> While no Italian arts their charms combine
> To teach the skirt of thy dark cloud to shine;
> For thy poor babes that, hurrying from the door,
> With pale-blue hands, and eyes that fix'd implore,
> Dead muttering lips, and hair of hungry white,
> Besiege the traveller whom they half affright.

And the verses which follow prove conclusively that Wordsworth's conception of the perfect life is now inextricably involved with the idea of political independence. Wherever there is despotism, he suggests, there can be no happiness:

> In the wide range of many a weary round,
> Still have my pilgrim feet unfailing found,
> As despot courts their blaze of gems display,
> Ev'n by the secret cottage far away
> The lilly of domestic joy decay....

Far different is it, however, where "Freedom" lives. Every conceivable blessing is enjoyed in the most remote and insignificant village of a region where political liberty exists:

> The casement shade more luscious woodbine binds,
> And to the door a neater pathway winds,
> At early morn the careful housewife, led
> To cull her dinner from it's garden bed,
> Of weedless herbs a healthier prospect sees,
> While hum with busier joy her happy bees;
> In brighter rows her table wealth aspires,
> And laugh with merrier blaze her evening fires;
> Her infant's cheeks with fresher roses glow;
> And wilder graces sport around their brow;
> By clearer taper lit a cleanlier board
> Receives at supper hour her tempting hoard;
> The chamber hearth with fresher boughs is spread,
> And whiter is the hospitable bed.

It is manifest that Wordsworth had learned well the lessons of Michel Beaupuy and that political liberty was defi-

THE EARLY POEMS

nitely associated in his mind with republican government from the passage which he dedicates to the "fair favoured region" of the Loire, where he has passed many a happy day. This lovely district of republican France has lost the charms she knew in time of peace. Where once the "grey-clad peasant stray'd" among the trees, "war's discordant habits" now appear. No more do the village "maids their voices suit To the low-warbled breath of twilight lute"; instead there are the sounds of the strident fife and the rumbling drum. But in Wordsworth's view, ample compensation has been made for such losses as these:

> —Yet, hast thou found that Freedom spreads her pow'r
> Beyond the cottage hearth, the cottage door:
> All nature smiles; and owns beneath her eyes
> Her fields peculiar, and peculiar skies.
> Yes, as I roam'd where Loiret's waters glide
> Thro' rustling aspins heard from side to side,
> When from October clouds a milder light
> Fell, where the blue flood rippled into white,
> Methought from every cot the watchful bird
> Crowed with ear-piercing power 'till then unheard;
> Each clacking mill, that broke the murmuring streams,
> Rock'd the charm'd thought in more delightful dreams;
> Chasing those long long dreams the falling leaf
> Awoke a fainter pang of moral grief;[66]
> The measured echo of the distant flail
> Winded in sweeter cadence down the vale;
> A more majestic tide the water roll'd,
> And glowed the sun-gilt groves in richer gold.

The contemplation of the manifold blessings of republicanism stirs Wordsworth's spirit to such an extent that he abandons his disguise as a leisurely and observant pedestrian traveler whose interest in nature, manners, and politics is essentially passive, and prophesies in militant vein the success

---

[66] It is perhaps worth noting here that Wordsworth's observation on the "falling leaf" is an early manifestation of that preoccupation with mutability which was to direct most of his poetry after 1806, if not before, and which was to produce a philosophy of life whose most economical and best-known expression is found in the concluding verses of the "Ode on Intimations of Immortality":

> To me the meanest flower that blows can give
> Thoughts that do often lie too deep for tears.

of the Revolution. Liberty, he asserts, shall soon rise in indignation and, to the sounds of bells and cannon, sweep in triumph through the land, "tho' Pride's perverted ire Rouse Hell's own aid, and wrap thy hills in fire." Miraculously, he forecasts, from the flames of revolutionary conflict there will come a new birth of virtue. The Golden Age will live again, for "Nature, as in her prime," will govern, assisted by love, truth, and justice. When this happy time arrives, instead of wiping out whole hamlets as has been his wont, "On his pale horse shall fell Consumption go." The imminent prospect of such a victory for the forces of good leads Wordsworth, in conclusion, to call upon God for the quick and total destruction of despotism in general and, in particular, of the monarchs who band together in base conspiracy against the progress of liberty:

> Oh give, great God, to Freedom's waves to ride
> Sublime o'er Conquest, Avarice, and Pride,
> To break, the vales where Death with Famine scow'rs,
> And dark Oppression builds her thick-ribb'd tow'rs;
> Where Machination her fell soul resigns,
> Fled panting to the centre of her mines;
> Where Persecution decks with ghastly smiles
> Her bed, his mountains mad Ambition piles;
> Where Discord stalks dilating, every hour,
> And crouching fearful at the feet of Pow'r,
> Like Lightnings eager for th'almighty word,
> Look up for sign of havoc, Fire, and Sword;
> —Give them, beneath their breast while Gladness springs,
> To brood the nations o'er with Nile-like wings;
> And grant that every sceptred child of clay,
> Who cries, presumptuous, "here their tides shall stay,"
> Swept in their anger from th'affrighted shore,
> With all his creatures sink—to rise no more.

Artistically inept and hackneyed in style as these closing lines are, they nevertheless reflect a high seriousness of purpose which Wordsworth did not possess when he wrote *An Evening Walk* or when he began the composition of *Descriptive Sketches*. His experience in revolutionary France—especially his conversations with Beaupuy—convinced him that his adolescent dream of a cottage prettily set in a wooded landscape of the English Lake District was seriously incomplete. True happiness, he now knew, was dependent upon freedom, and freedom, in turn, was dependent upon republican government, like that enjoyed by the inhabitants of the "fair favoured region" of the Loire. Before his dream of the perfect life in the ideal home could be realized, therefore, it was necessary for the principles of republicanism to spread throughout the world. To the championing of these principles Wordsworth dedicated himself and his art in 1792; the later lines of *Descriptive Sketches* are the written record of this dedication.

CHAPTER III

The Letter to the Bishop of Llandaff

THE zeal for the principles of the French Revolution with which Wordsworth returned from his sojourn in France continued unabated even after his native land became embroiled in warfare with her republican neighbor across the Channel. Indeed, the height of his revolutionary fervor, so far at least as it is reflected in his work, was reached in 1793, when Wordsworth wrote his letter *To the Bishop of Llandaff on the Extraordinary Avowal of His Political Principles, Contained in the Appendix to His Late Sermon,* and composed the first draft of *Guilt and Sorrow*. And so pronounced and persistent was Wordsworth's radicalism that his free association with Englishmen of dangerous political repute caused the government to place a secret agent in the vicinity of Racedown in 1797, lest the revolutionary machinations of Wordsworth and his circle contribute to the subversion of English constitutional government.

Critics and biographers, however, have paid insufficient attention to the causes of Wordsworth's open and continued endorsement of the principles of liberty, equality, and fraternity after his return from France early in 1793, and to the permanent influence of his early allegiance to the French Revolution upon his later poetry. The general tendency has been to regard Wordsworth's youthful political eccentricity as a matter of somewhat minor interest, revealing—especially when it is associated with the Annette Vallon episode—that the respectable poet of later decades once had hot red blood in his veins, but yielding little of significance for the under-

LETTER TO THE BISHOP OF LLANDAFF

standing and appreciation of those poems to which Wordsworth owes his reputation as a major English poet.[1] Later chapters will show, among other things, that Wordsworth's mature poetry, *Lyrical Ballads* in particular, would have been quite different in purpose and substance had he in his youth remained unmoved by the broad principles which underlay the social and political cataclysm of the French Revolution. The purpose of this chapter is to examine the crisis experienced by Wordsworth immediately after his return to England, and to show that the events of the early months of 1793 combined to change his fervid but vague and abstract enthusiasm for the principles of the Revolution into flaming hatred for the society and the monarchical government of his native land.

When Wordsworth set foot on English soil in the winter of 1792/93, he had been drinking deep at the springs of French optimism. He had been long enough under the spell of Michel Beaupuy to be convinced of the perfectibility of man and the efficacy of republican government. He was full of hope for the future. In love with France, where he had experienced the thrill of history in the making and intimate association with at least one man who was making visible contributions to human progress, Wordsworth doubtless entertained the belief that England would fall in step behind enlightened France, cast off the hated fetters of monarchy, and march triumphantly forward to the millennium that was certain to follow the establishment of universal justice and equality under republican auspices. Before the catastrophes of 1793 Wordsworth conceived of England as a sanctuary for freedom, despite the fact that she was ruled by a king and

[1] See Émile Legouis, *The Early Life of William Wordsworth, 1770–1798,* tr. by J. W. Matthews (New York, 1918) (hereafter referred to as *The Early Life*), pp. 221–252; George McLean Harper, *William Wordsworth, His Life, Works, and Influence* (New York, 1929), pp. 127–159; and H. W. Garrod, *Wordsworth: Lectures and Essays* (Oxford, 1923), pp. 40–42. Professor Garrod is particularly disdainful of the importance of Wordsworth's early faith in the French Revolution to his later work. According to him, "The strength of Wordsworth's supreme period is, in fact, not the Revolutionary Idea, but his own reaction, first upon the failure of that Idea, and then upon the failure of Godwinism" (*op. cit.*, p. 42).

despite the fact that she harbored tyrannical descendants of the feudal age who successfully employed their medieval power to cheat worthy young men of their patrimony. That Wordsworth held his country in such high esteem during his residence in France we know from the contents of the letter he wrote on May 17, 1792, urging his friend Mathews away from melancholy: "Educated as you have been, you ought to be above despair. You have the happiness of being born in a free country, where every road is open, and where talents and industry are more liberally rewarded than amongst any other nation of the Universe."[2] But this faith in England, unshaken, so far as we know, before his return, was destined to complete destruction in the early months of 1793.

Wordsworth's homecoming was complicated by emotions other than those generated by zeal and hope for political principles. On December 15, 1792, he had become the father of a daughter, and the evidence suggests that he was in love. Annette Vallon and Caroline Wordsworth took their rightful places beside Dorothy in Wordsworth's dreams of domestic felicity. At least two passages in the letters written by the unfortunate Annette to Wordsworth and his sister—letters which miscarried pathetically to the hands of the French police—clearly indicate that Wordsworth planned to give an honorable position to Annette and Caroline in that fair rural cottage which he described in *An Evening Walk* as the "Sole bourn, sole wish, sole object of my way." "Ta sœur me parle [de notre] petit ménage avec un entousiasme qui me fait grand [plaisir]," Annette wrote to Wordsworth on March 20, 1793—"Que nous serons heureux, ô mon tendre ami; oui [on] sera heureux."[3] And on the same day, in a letter to Dorothy, whom she addressed as her "chère sœur," Annette looked hopefully ahead to the moment

quand nous serons réunit; mais quand viendra-t-il? Ah! que je le croit encore éloignez! Il faut que je l'achette encore par bien des soupires.

---

[2] *The Early Letters of William and Dorothy Wordsworth (1787–1805)*, ed. by Ernest de Selincourt (Oxford, 1935) (hereafter referred to as *The Early Letters*), p. 76.

[3] Émile Legouis, *William Wordsworth and Annette Vallon* (London, Toronto, and New York, 1922), p. 126.

LETTER TO THE BISHOP OF LLANDAFF

Mais quand nous y serons, ô ma sœur, que nous serons heureux! Et toi, mon ami, désire-tu ce jour aussi ardament que ton Annette? Quand tu sera environéz de ta sœur, ta femme, ta fille, qui ne respirerons que pour toi, nous naurons qu'un même sentiment, qu'un coeur, qu'une âme, et tout sera reportée à mon cher Williams. Nos jours coulerons tranquillement.[4]

Although we can only imagine what mingled hopes and fears for Annette and Caroline crowded Wordsworth's mind in the early months of 1793, we are certain that the twenty-two-year-old poet, forced to return to England by lack of funds, then faced a problem more serious than any he had ever before encountered.

Two possible solutions to this problem were available to Wordsworth after his departure from France. The first and easier of course was outright desertion of Annette and Caroline. But this facile and dishonorable means of escape, if indeed it ever occurred to him, was not contemplated for long by Wordsworth. His forced separation from Annette probably intensified, at least temporarily, his love and his loyalty; and it would have been ironic in the extreme had Wordsworth, in this difficult situation, failed to put into practice those humanitarian principles which he had endorsed with great enthusiasm in *An Evening Walk* and *Descriptive Sketches*. Whether through love or sympathy for innocence in distress which he himself had caused, Wordsworth, with the aid of his obliging sister Dorothy, communicated the truth about the whole affair to his righteous relatives.[5] It is hardly necessary to point out that this would have been a ridiculous tactical blunder had Wordsworth's intentions been false and prudential.

The alternative to desertion was a reunion, either in France or in England, marriage, and, if fate would permit, the cottage felicity of Wordsworth's dreams. Annette's letters are clear proof that this was the plan which Wordsworth

---

[4] *Ibid.*, p. 129.
[5] See Legouis, *William Wordsworth and Annette Vallon*, p. 28, and Annette's letter to Dorothy, where she writes, "Avant de finire ma lettre, ma bonne amie, je vous recomande bien de ne pas vous affligée, de chacher autems que vous le pourez à votre oncle et votre tante les raisons qui comande à vos larmes de couler" *(ibid.,* p. 132).

had determined to effect. For the realization of this desirable scheme, however, money was necessary, and it was money that Wordsworth lacked. What expectations, then, did Wordsworth have upon his return to England of fulfilling his promises to Annette?

Wordsworth knew that there were but three sources—none of them good—from which he might possibly secure the money necessary for a reunion with Annette and Caroline. The publication and sale of his poems, *An Evening Walk* and *Descriptive Sketches,* might bring in something. There was a chance, also, that he and his brothers and sister might receive justice in the courts of law, where their patrimony was tied up by Lonsdale. These failing, he could appeal to his guardians for help. It is interesting to speculate upon what Wordsworth hoped to accomplish, as a last resort, with these hitherto difficult if not absolutely unfriendly guardians. Believing without reservation in the innate goodness and perfectibility of man, did Wordsworth hope that the sentimental and pathetic history of Annette and Caroline would soften the heart of his pious Uncle William to the extent that he would be willing to contribute to their financial support? Did he expect his published poems—concrete evidence that he "could do something"—to convince his shocked and suspicious aunts and uncles that he was not a wastrel and a ne'er-do-well, as they now had ample reason to suppose, but a man of worth and promise? Some such expectations he must have entertained. How else can we explain his risking complete alienation from the elder members of his family by permitting Dorothy to reveal to them the truth about Annette?

Whatever was the extent of Wordsworth's hope, when he arrived in England early in 1793, not only for the status of political freedom in his native land, but also for a happy solution of his complex personal difficulties, he was doomed to immediate and bitter disillusion and disappointment. His first source of information was no doubt his brother Richard, in London. In answer to his urgent inquiry, Richard, it is safe to assume, informed Wordsworth not only that his funds were all but exhausted, but also that they were not at all likely to be replenished in the near future by any favorable judgment of the Lonsdale case in the courts of law.[6] In his rôle as financial agent for the family, Richard probably described in great detail the outrageous methods employed by Lonsdale in his successful effort to defeat justice, and thereby placed at his brother's disposal all the evidence necessary to shatter completely his illusory belief that England was a free and progressive country. It is reasonable to suppose, finally, that Richard, with natural interest and curiosity, soon engaged William, just returned from abroad, in conversation concerning the events and merits of the French Revolution. William of course spoke high words of praise for all things French, and was probably rebuked by the conservative Richard, who could give him prompt and unequivocal notification that his wild enthusiasm for radical French political philosophy would meet with no approval either in family ranks or in any corner of respectable British society. Shortly after his arrival in London, in other words, Wordsworth had learned that he had no chance of getting any large sum of money, and that England, far from being the enlightened and liberal country that he had described the previous spring in his letter to Mathews, was in truth a stronghold of all that was dull and reactionary, feudal and base.

Wordsworth's fears for himself, for Annette and Caroline, and for the social and political health of England were doubtless soon increased by Joseph Johnson, a sympathizer with the English Jacobins,[7] an enthusiast of the Revolution, and the publisher of *An Evening Walk* and *Descriptive Sketches*. Johnson could appreciate and praise the principles endorsed in the later lines of *Descriptive Sketches,* and he could agree to publish Wordsworth's poem; but he could hold out to Wordsworth little or no hope that the venture would be a profitable one.[8] Few men in England, moreover, were better

[6] Dorothy's letters reveal that hopes for a just settlement of the case were at a very low ebb in June, 1793. No evidence suggests that the prospects had been brighter six months before.

[7] For more information concerning Johnson's affiliations with the English Jacobins than would be appropriate here see Harper, *op. cit.*, pp. 153–154.

[8] That *An Evening Walk* and *Descriptive Sketches* contributed nothing

equipped than Johnson, the friend of Tom Paine, William Godwin, and Joseph Priestley, to provide Wordsworth with accurate information on the true condition of England. In Johnson's shop Wordsworth surely idled away many hours against the publication of his poems. There he was certain to find ears willing to listen to his tales of the Revolution and to his account of the criminality of the Earl of Lonsdale; there he could find voices eager to join with his in protest—at least in private protest—against the corruption of the British courts of law; and there he must have secured full and authentic confirmation of his new and dread suspicion—that England, so far as social and political progress was concerned, was little better than the France of the *ancien régime*.

Thus did Wordsworth discover, almost immediately after his return to England, that he was penniless and likely to continue so for an indefinite period of time; that because of the injustice prevalent in England there was little or no chance of his obtaining a home for himself and for Annette, Caroline, and Dorothy; and that he was likely to become a pariah in his native land and in the heart of his own family by virtue of political beliefs which staunch and unselfish conviction caused him to support. However bitter Wordsworth's disappointment may have been, and however dark the future may have appeared to him in January, 1793, sharper disappointments and blacker days were still to come. On February 1 Wordsworth's despair for the favorable course of the Revolution and for the political integrity of England reached its zenith, for on that day England went to war against France, the country where—so Wordsworth thought—the hopes of all mankind were centered. The state of war between the two countries made Annette and Caroline even more inaccessible and the possibility of a reunion with them even more remote than before. And early in the spring, probably in late March or April, Wordsworth's last hope for

---

to the solution of Wordsworth's financial problems is all too clearly shown in the letter to Mathews of May 23, 1794: ". . . pray let me request you to have the goodness to call on Johnson, my publisher, and ask him if he ever sells any of those poems, and what number he thinks are yet on his hands" (*The Early Letters*, p. 117).

LETTER TO THE BISHOP OF LLANDAFF

a satisfactory solution of his personal problems vanished completely—his Uncle William, instead of responding to the piteous tale of Annette and Caroline with sympathy and an offer of cash, replied with indignation, and informed his nephew that he would not be welcome at Forncett and that his association with his sister Dorothy at any time, in any place, could only provoke high family displeasure.

It is against this background of chagrin and personal despair that we must read Wordsworth's *Letter to the Bishop of Llandaff*, written early in 1793.[9] Richard Watson, the Bishop of Llandaff, had published on January 15 a sermon on "The Wisdom and Goodness of God in Having Made Both Rich and Poor" which he supplemented ten days later, after the news of the execution of Louis XVI had reached England, with an "Appendix" full of strictures on the French Revolution. It was this appendix, apparently, that inflamed Wordsworth—already predisposed to cry out angrily against abuses from which he himself was suffering—and first moved him to compose the bitter and comprehensive social criticism of England that was to be his chief preoccupation for at least two years.

In the appendix to his sermon the Bishop of Llandaff undertook to condemn the principles of the French Revolution and to praise with all the authority and unction pertaining to his holy station the divine efficacy and providential benignity of the British Constitution and of British government

---

[9] The exact date of composition of the letter is unknown. Despite the strength of the convictions he expressed therein, Wordsworth was prudent enough not to publish his letter. Indeed, there is nothing to suggest that a copy of it was ever sent to Watson. Wordsworth may have written the letter soon after Watson published the "Appendix" to his sermon, on January 25, 1793, for Wordsworth refers to the "Appendix" as having been "lately given to the world." On the other hand, internal evidence suggests that a considerable period of time elapsed between the publication of the "Appendix" and Wordsworth's reply. In his conclusion Wordsworth attacks Watson for having failed to comment upon the war. By so doing, however, Wordsworth was taking unfair advantage and was clearly in error, for the "Appendix" was published almost a week before the war between France and England was declared. Wordsworth's lapse may be explained in one of two ways: either Wordsworth read Watson's "Appendix" some time after its publication, of whose date he was ignorant, or he delayed the writing of his reply long enough for his memory to confuse the chronology.

under that constitution. His purposes he undoubtedly accomplished to his own satisfaction and to that of all Englishmen whose personal interests in maintaining the *status quo* provided them with more potent and convincing arguments than were ever created by sound reason and common sense. But Wordsworth was not satisfied with the tenor of Watson's complacent lucubrations. To Wordsworth—and, we may suppose, to any informed and impartial Englishman of the day—the Bishop, previously known as a liberal in politics, was an apostate and a sham, a smug sophister whose arguments—like those of his abler and better-known contemporary, Edmund Burke—were the vicious spawn of corrupt monarchical tradition and of ignorance of the truth or refusal to admit it.

The philosophy underlying Watson's criticism of French Republicanism and his defense of British monarchical government was calculated to outrage Wordsworth and any other man interested in the application of reason to the administration of human affairs. When Watson concluded that God was both wise and good in creating "both Rich and Poor," he betrayed his allegiance to the doctrine of the Chain of Being, and his faith in its divine origin and in the desirability of its perpetuation. This doctrine, complicated and ingenious in its details, and long employed by ecclesiastics to calm the people whenever they groaned beneath the weight of social and political injustice and gave evidence of wishing to improve their lot,[10] had for its primary and essential mes-

---

[10] For a detailed study of the social and political implications of the Chain of Being, see Arthur O. Lovejoy, *The Great Chain of Being* (Cambridge [Mass.], 1936), pp. 200–207. Writing of two of the basic principles of this doctrine, those of "plenitude and gradation," Professor Lovejoy asserts that they might "be made to serve the purposes of a species of pessimistic and backhanded apologetic both for the political *status quo* and for the accepted religion. They provided a damper for the zeal of the reformer. Since men are not and were not meant to be angels, let us cease to expect them to behave as if they were; and let us avoid the error of imagining that by an alteration of the form or mechanism of government we shall put an end to those limitations of human nature which are essentially unalterable, because they are inherent in the scheme of the universe which required just such a creature, as well as all other kinds, to make it 'complete' " (p. 204).

sage the cheerful affirmation that "Whatever is, is right." As it applied to organized society, the idea of the Chain of Being was well expressed in the following lines:

> Wise Providence
> Does various parts for various minds dispense;
> The meanest slaves or they who hedge and ditch,
> Are useful, by their sweat, to feed the rich;
> The rich, in due return, impart their store,
> Which comfortably feeds the lab'ring poor.
> Nor let the rich the lowest slave disdain,
> He's equally a link of nature's chain;
> Labours to the same end, joins in one view,
> And both alike the will divine pursue.[11]

That the Bishop of Llandaff endorsed this philosophy and based his social and political thinking upon it there can be no reasonable doubt. His strongest argument against republican government shows plainly that he conceived of society, whether French or British, with its economic and social stratification, in terms of the Chain of Being, whose origin was divine:

That the constitution of this country is so perfect as neither to require or admit of any improvement, is a proposition to which I never did or ever can assent; but I think it far too excellent to be amended by peasants and mechanics. I do not mean to speak of peasants and mechanics with any degree of disrespect; *I am not so ignorant of the importance, either of the natural or social chain by which all the individuals of the human race are connected together, as to think disrespectfully of any link of it.* Peasants and mechanics are as useful to the State as any other order of men; but their utility consists in their discharging well the duties of their respective stations; it ceases when they affect to become legislators; when they intrude themselves into concerns for which their education has not fitted them.[12]

From this utterance alone the reader can by simple deduction reconstruct the remainder of Watson's argument against republicanism in general and against the execution of

[11] Cited by Lovejoy, *op. cit.*, p. 207. Professor Lovejoy has been unable to discover the source of these lines.

[12] "Appendix to Bishop Watson's Sermon," reprinted in *The Prose Works of William Wordsworth*, ed. by Alexander B. Grosart (London, 1876) (hereafter referred to as *The Prose Works*), I, 28. The italics are my own.

Louis XVI in particular. Peasants and mechanics were sent into this world by the Almighty to fill the places of peasants and mechanics and to behave as peasants and mechanics. The Almighty, following His inscrutable but infinitely wise and beneficent plan, created legislators and placed them upon the earth that they might legislate, not only for themselves, but also for peasants and mechanics. Since this was clearly the intention of the Almighty, it is sinful for peasants and mechanics to legislate, or for legislators to perform the functions of peasants and mechanics. The usurpation by either group of the position of the other would tend to weaken the Great Chain and would result inevitably in chaos and disorder.[13] Since the British Constitution provides for legislation by legislators rather than by peasants and mechanics, since it recognizes a vertical "social chain" with the legislating aristocracy at the top and the laboring poor at the bottom, the British Constitution is manifestly in accordance with His plan, and must not suffer change except at the hands of those authorized by the Almighty to effect such change. Englishmen must profit from the example of the sinful French. In France peasants and mechanics have desecrated the excellent plan of the Almighty by presuming to legislate. The result is that chaos and disorder of which the execution of Louis XVI is the incontrovertible proof. It is therefore earnestly to be hoped that Englishmen will not sin so atrociously as have the French. Bishop Watson hopes indeed that Englishmen will not sin at all, and the irregular alteration of the British Constitution would be sin. To save them from so heinous an offense, Bishop Watson urges peasants, mechanics, and all other Englishmen whose suffering might incline them to violence to "look round the globe, and see if you can discover a single nation on all its surface so powerful, so rich, so beneficent, so free and happy as our own. May Heaven

---

[13] As Professor Lovejoy remarks, "The doctrine of the Chain of Being . . . gave a metaphysical sanction to the injunction of the Anglican catechism: each should labor truly 'to do his duty in that state of life'—whether in the cosmical or the social scale—'to which it hath pleased God to call him.' To seek to leave one's place in society is also 'to invert the laws of Order'. . . . Any demand for equality, in short, is 'contrary to nature'" (*op. cit.*, p. 206).

avert from the minds of my countrymen the slightest wish to abolish their constitution!"[14]

The weakness of this argument for the preservation of the *status quo,* as Watson well knew, lay in the possibility that the peasants and mechanics of England might perform their rôles in the "natural or social chain" faithfully and well, while the legislators, moved by cupidity and selfishness, were derelict in the discharge of their sacred and appointed duties. The latter might forget the ethical injunction implicit in the doctrine of the Chain of Being:

> Nor let the rich the lowest slave disdain,
> He's equally a link of nature's chain;
> Labours to the same end, joins in one view,
> And both alike the will divine pursue.

Self-interest might influence legislation, and injury might be done to those in the lower ranks of the social hierarchy.

The Bishop, however, was not disturbed by this weakness in his argument; for such an unfortunate situation he had a course of action to recommend. If the peasants and mechanics become the victims of unjust laws which work to the advantage of their aristocratic authors, they should not resist or rise against their oppressors; they should rather submit and patiently await elevation to a happier and more just world, where, according to orthodox theology, handsome rewards fall to the virtuous, dire punishments to the vicious. Such a course of passive acquiescence Watson suggests in opposition to his wicked adversaries who insist that the execution of Louis XVI was justifiable on the ground of his failure to deal honestly and fairly with the people over whom the Almighty had set him to rule:

> The monarch, you will tell me, was guilty of perfidy and perjury. I know not that he was guilty of either; but admitting that he has been guilty of both, who, alas, of the sons of men is so confident in the strength of his own virtue, so assured of his own integrity and intrepidity of character, as to be certain that, under similar temptations, he would not have been guilty of similar offences? Surely it would have been no diminution of the sternness of new republican virtue, no disgrace to

[14] *Op. cit.,* in *The Prose Works,* I, 29.

the magnanimity of a great nation, if it had pardoned the perfidy which its own oppression had occasioned, if it had remitted the punishment of the perjury of the king to the tribunal of Him by whom *kings reign and princes decree justice*.[15]

This was the position defended by the Bishop of Llandaff in his published message to the people of England. Had he confined his remarks to animadversions upon the French and to mere generalizations concerning the blessings of life under the British Constitution, it is likely that Wordsworth, fresh from France, in a dangerous frame of mind, and with the revolutionary dialectic on the tip of his tongue, would have considered it his duty as a lover of truth and a friend of France to expose the fallacies lurking beneath the Bishop's pompous rhetoric. But the Bishop was not content to make only general remarks about the virtues of English government; he went on to particulars, and listed as an outstanding advantage of Englishmen their unparalleled equality in the eyes of the law:

> The courts of British justice are impartial and incorrupt; they respect not the persons of men; the poor man's lamb is, in their estimation, as sacred as the monarch's crown; with inflexible integrity they adjudge to every man his own. Your property under their protection is secure. If your personal liberty be unjustly restrained, though but for an hour, and that by the highest servants of the crown, the crown cannot screen them; the throne cannot hide them; the law, with an undaunted arm, seizes them, and drags them with irresistible might to the judgment of whom?—of your equals—of twelve of your neighbours. In such a constitution as this, what is there to complain of on the score of liberty?[16]

Once Wordsworth had scanned this passage, his reply to Watson was inevitable. Knowing as we do of Wordsworth's distressing personal experience with the British courts, we have no difficulty in understanding why he found himself impelled to give the Bishop full satisfaction. In his reply Wordsworth took pains to provide the complacent Bishop with some inkling of what there was in England "to complain of on the score of liberty."

The general outline of the *Letter to the Bishop of Llandaff*

[15] *Op. cit.,* in *The Prose Works,* I, 25.   [16] *Ibid.,* p. 26.

has been presented by earlier biographers,[17] and it is unnecessary here to review all the details of Wordsworth's spirited defense of republicanism, of his arguments against monarchy, and of his attack upon contemporary English society. These biographers, however, have been content to discover in the reply to Watson no more than evidence showing that Wordsworth was a republican in 1793. They regard the letter, in other words, merely as more abundant proof of what was already obvious in the concluding lines of *Descriptive Sketches*. Legouis remarks, for example, that "The letter to Watson . . . contains the most complete statement of Wordsworth's political and social ideas in his twenty-third year,"[18] and proceeds to a disquisition upon the general state of the patriotic sentiment in eighteenth-century Europe. And Professor Harper, after briefly summarizing and praising the letter, advances impatiently to his study of *Guilt and Sorrow*.[19] Neither, however, makes a concise distinction between the stage of development represented in the reply to Watson and that reflected in *Descriptive Sketches,* and both fail to recognize in the letter Wordsworth's first clear and specific statement not only of his republican faith in 1793, but also of those political, social, and educational principles which were to provide the materials for *Guilt and Sorrow* as well as the very basis and foundation of *Lyrical Ballads*.

It is true that the *Letter to the Bishop of Llandaff* and the later lines of *Descriptive Sketches* are alike in that both are dedicated to the support of Wordsworth's new republican ideal. A comparison of the two documents reveals, however, considerable differences between Wordsworth's first and second efforts to champion republican principles. In *Descriptive Sketches* Wordsworth was clearly hopeful of seeing the early realization of his ideal. Apparently convinced that the French Revolution was divine in origin and purpose and that

[17] Legouis, *The Early Life,* pp. 226–232; Harper, *op. cit.,* pp. 154–159.
[18] *The Early Life,* p. 231.
[19] Harper's account of the letter differs from that of Legouis only in intensity of appreciation. "Wordsworth's noble pamphlet," writes Professor Harper, "in its buoyant eloquence, its fearless logic, its trust in the supremacy of goodness, is splendidly youthful. One would rather live in his ideal world than in the ideal world of his antagonist" (*op. cit.,* p. 158).

it would therefore be guaranteed a prosperous course and a successful conclusion, Wordsworth was satisfied in *Descriptive Sketches* to utter vague generalities about the blessings of liberty, as he found them in Switzerland and France, and about the curse of slavery, as he found it in Savoy. Full of the rosy optimism of inexperience and youth, he seems to have been certain that, because republican government was, in his estimation, superior to monarchical government, all nations would very soon, if not immediately, discard their antiquated forms of political administration in favor of a more just and efficient republican model. Kings and emperors of course might be expected to object and to offer some resistance, but their contrary efforts must prove vain before the irresistible might of republican crusaders. In short, nothing in *Descriptive Sketches* suggests that Wordsworth understood that freedom, even with the help of God and France, was not likely to spread throughout the civilized world in the twinkling of an eye.

But in the interval between his return to England and his composition of the reply to Watson, Wordsworth experienced his baptism of fire. The tempestuous emotions which he felt in the early weeks of 1793, his disappointment at learning of the wretched state of his finances, his anxiety over the desperate situation of Annette and Caroline, his despair at the prevalence of injustice in his native land and at the declaration of war between England and France, his resentment of the treatment meted out to him by his Uncle William—all these things somehow combined to produce in Wordsworth some degree of intellectual, if not emotional, maturity. At last he was face to face with harsh reality; unpleasant and insoluble problems surrounded him, and this time events and circumstances made complete escape impossible. At last Wordsworth understood that the world was no dream, that ideals did not realize themselves. The world instead was a stage in time and space on which was acted an eternal struggle between the forces of good and evil. In England, all about him, the forces of evil, already powerful, were gaining strength; his republican ideal was threatened by a

LETTER TO THE BISHOP OF LLANDAFF

public opinion whetted to sharp hostility by such arguments from vested authority as those of Richard Watson. Unless evil were to triumph in England, the opposition must have able and doughty champions; such a champion Wordsworth chose to be. Ready and eager for the fray, he brought to the contest a clearly focused political and social point of view, an abundance of concrete information on the condition of England, and a program for the future. In this emergency he would provide not merely an affirmation but also a demonstration of the excellence of republican principles, and he would base his indictment of despotism and monarchical society not upon broad, general allusions to the unhappiness regnant in Savoy, a land of which he knew almost nothing, but upon specific facts derived from his personal knowledge of English government and society. It is this direct and detailed criticism of the evils of English society and Wordsworth's recommendations for their elimination or alleviation that constitute the chief strength of the *Letter to the Bishop of Llandaff* and give it considerable significance for any study of Wordsworth's development.

In the introductory paragraphs of his reply to Watson Wordsworth calls attention to the fact that the Bishop, after gaining some reputation as a "levelling prelate,"[20] has at last revealed himself in his true colors and moved so far to the political right as to endorse the servile arguments and opinions traditionally associated with "the ministers of the Church of England,"[21] who "have appeared as writers upon public measures only to be the advocates of slavery civil and religious...."[22] The Bishop has asked his countrymen never to forget and never to permit their children to forget "that we are in possession of both (liberty and equality), of as much of both as can be consistent with the end for which civil society was introduced among mankind."[23] By so doing he has shown himself to be an ally of Mr. Edmund Burke, who,

by a refinement in cruelty superior to that which in the East yokes the living to the dead ... strove to persuade us that we and our posterity

---

[20] *Prose Works*, I, 4.
[21] *Ibid.*, p. 3.
[22] *Ibid.*, pp. 3–4.
[23] *Ibid.*, p. 21.

to the end of time were riveted to a constitution by the indissoluble compact of—a dead parchment, and were bound to cherish a corse at the bosom when reason might call aloud that it should be entombed.[24]

Bishop Watson, in fact, has gone even further than Edmund Burke: "Your Lordship," Wordsworth avers,

aims at the same detestable object by means more criminal, because more dangerous and insidious. Attempting to lull the people of England into a belief that any inquiries directed towards the nature of liberty and equality can in no other way lead to their happiness than by convincing them that they have already arrived at perfection in the science of government, what is your object but to exclude them for ever from the most fruitful field of human knowledge?[25]

Because of the vicious purpose of Watson's arguments, and because Englishmen might be swayed by the magic of his name and the authority of his position rather than by the merit of his doctrines, Wordsworth proposes to do all in his power to destroy Watson's influence by exposing his errors and his ignorance.

To begin with, Wordsworth attacks his opponent's stand in regard to the execution of Louis XVI, the necessity of violence in a time of revolution, and the confiscation of Church property in France. Wordsworth supports all three of these features of the French Revolution on the broad humanitarian ground that, whereas a few people suffered therefrom, the great masses of the French people benefited immensely. He then proceeds to make Watson's allegation that "the liberty of man in a state of society consists in his being subject to no law but the law enacted by the general will of the society to which he belongs," the basis for his defense of republican government and for his indictment of monarchy.

Not wishing the attention of the English people to be diverted from the evils of their government and governors by Watson's blandishments, Wordsworth points out that the Bishop, in endorsing the static conception of society afforded by a conservative interpretation of the Chain-of-Being doctrine, has confused the distinction between human suffering

[24] *Prose Works*, I, 21.   [25] *Ibid*.

caused by the inscrutable ways of God and that caused by the selfish and unjust acts of mortal men in political office. Unfortunately, according to Wordsworth, Englishmen have been so long deluded and misled by such arguments as the Bishop's that they have become almost incapable of perceiving this vital distinction. In consequence, they live in a sordid and wretched condition which they must change if they are to regain the dignity of true men. "Slavery is a bitter and a poisonous draught," Wordsworth reminds the Bishop:

> We have but one consolation under it, that a Nation may dash the cup to the ground when she pleases. . . . We submit without repining to the chastisements of Providence, aware that we are creatures, that opposition is vain and remonstrance impossible. But when redress is in our own power and resistance is rational, we suffer with the same humility from beings like ourselves, because we are taught from infancy that we were born in a state of inferiority to our oppressors, that they were sent into the world to scourge, and we to be scourged. Accordingly we see the bulk of mankind, actuated by these fatal prejudices, even more ready to lay themselves under the feet of *the great* than the great are to trample upon them.[26]

These "fatal prejudices," which have poisoned men's souls from the cradle, and which such writers as Watson and Burke strive to perpetuate, must be destroyed if humanity is to realize to the full its potentialities for development. That mankind is possessed of such potentialities Wordsworth is certain, for he has seen incontrovertible evidence of man's perfectibility in both Switzerland and France. Contrary to the Bishop's allegation that peasants and mechanics should not legislate, Wordsworth's experience in these two enlightened nations has revealed that peasants and mechanics, despite the humble circumstances of their birth, make excellent legislators:

> If your Lordship has travelled in the democratic cantons of Switzerland, you must have seen the herdsman with the staff in one hand and the book in the other. In the constituent Assembly of France was found a peasant whose sagacity was as distinguished as his integrity, whose blunt honesty overawed and baffled the refinements of hypocritical patriots.

[26] *Ibid.*, p. 8.

The people of Paris followed him with acclamations, and the name of Père Gerard will long be mentioned with admiration and respect through the eighty-three departments.[27]

In the light of these facts it becomes clear that the very foundations of Watson's argument, derived as they are from the doctrine of the Chain of Being, are false. Since this is the case, Watson's pious recommendation that the lower classes of society submit meekly to injustice during their brief sojourn on this earth, confident that wrongs will be righted in the hereafter, can have only the most disastrous consequences for society as a whole, unless the masses of men can be roused from their lethargy and persuaded to set up a republican form of government.

Ample evidence exists in English society that the aristocratic legislators, to whom the Bishop of Llandaff would continue to entrust the general welfare, are corrupt and swayed by avarice and ambition from the just and proper execution of their responsibilities to the peasants and mechanics. Wordsworth notes, for example, the protection of wealth and property afforded by English law. The prosperous, it is true, are assured of "the possession of lands and movables against the depradation of the necessitous," but what protection have the legislators provided for the property of the poor?—"They have unjustly left unprotected that most important part of property, not less real because it has no material existence, that which ought to enable the labourer to provide food for himself and his family."[28] Wordsworth admits that the "distinction of wealth ... always will attend superior talents and industry,"[29] but he calls attention to the fact that the aristocrats have greatly exaggerated the gap between wealth and poverty in England by passing "innumerable statutes, whose constant and professed object it is to lower the price of labour, to compel the workman to be *content* with arbitrary wages, evidently too small from the necessity of legal enforcement of the acceptance of them."[30] Such artificially produced "extremes of

[27] *Prose Works*, I, 11–12.
[28] *Ibid.*, pp. 15, 16.
[29] *Ibid.*, p. 15.
[30] *Ibid.*, p. 16.

LETTER TO THE BISHOP OF LLANDAFF

poverty and riches," Wordsworth insists, "have a necessary tendency to corrupt the human heart...."[31]

The dreadful social consequences of such monopolistic legislation, the legislation characteristic of a monarchical form of government, are everywhere visible in England. They are seen in the "depopulation of the country,"[32] in the necessary reliance of the poor upon "the ostentatious bounty of their oppressors,"[33] in the "class of wretches called mendicants ... [who] shock the feelings of humanity,"[34] and in that "promiscuous intercourse" to which the poor are "impelled by the instincts of nature and the dreadful satisfaction of escaping the prospect of infants, sad fruit of such intercourse, whom they are unable to support."[35] The fearful results of monarchy are apparent, finally, not only in the "tendency to dishonour labor,"[36] in the "prostitution which miserably deluges our streets,"[37] in the "hypocrisy and sycophancy of our intercourse in private life,"[38] and in a general disintegration of human dignity,[39] but also—and most reprehensibly—in that "infatuation which is now giving up to the sword so large a portion of the poor, and consigning the rest to the more slow and more painful consumption of want."[40] All this Wordsworth, haunted as he is by his dreams of republican happiness, finds insupportable.

But if the policy of meek and patient submission urged by the Bishop of Llandaff and by scores of ecclesiastics before him is ineffective and ill-advised, what are English peasants and mechanics to do to escape from the burdens and suffering imposed upon them by legislators who consciously strive to perpetuate their ignorance and wretchedness? Wordsworth provides no direct and explicit answer to this question in his *Letter to the Bishop of Llandaff*. The implications of his remarks upon the necessity for violence in France, however, make it perfectly clear that Wordsworth favors recourse to open revolt, if need be, for "the safety of the people."[41]

[31] *Ibid.*, p. 15.
[32] *Ibid.*
[33] *Ibid.*, pp. 15–16.
[34] *Ibid.*, p. 16.
[35] *Ibid.*
[36] *Ibid.*, p. 18.
[37] *Ibid.*
[38] *Ibid.*
[39] *Ibid.*, pp. 18, 19.
[40] *Ibid.*, p. 22.
[41] *Ibid.*, p. 6.

But violence is to be employed only as a last resort and, even then, for as short a time as possible. Wordsworth admits that violence and revolution are productive of results not wholly desirable. In a period of revolution, he perceives, "Political virtues are developed at the expense of moral ones; and the sweet emotions of compassion, evidently dangerous when traitors are to be punished, are too often altogether smothered."[42] This disadvantage, however, must be welcomed and endured when it is certain that "a fairer order of things" will eventually result.[43] Besides, the moral virtues and the "sweet emotions of compassion," always held in high regard by Wordsworth, will not be long neglected. Once the salutary change to republicanism has been effected, and once the oppressive principle of monarchy has been forcibly thrust into the past, education will play its part and men will live at peace with one another. "It is the province of education," Wordsworth declares,

to rectify the erroneous notions which a habit of oppression, and even of resistance, may have created, and to soften this ferocity of character, proceeding from a necessary suspension of the mild and social virtues; it belongs to her to create a race of men who, truly free, will look upon their fathers as only enfranchised.[44]

It is important to note that Wordsworth already understands that education is the only means by which true liberty can be achieved. The mere destruction or forcible removal from office of the oppressors will not guarantee the disappearance of injustice or the establishment of genuine freedom. Satisfactory social and political progress must be slow and difficult of attainment, but come it will once the canker of monarchical prejudice has been extirpated and the seeds of republican truth planted in its place. "I am well aware," Wordsworth admits to Richard Watson,

from the abuse of the executive power in States, that there is not a single European nation but what affords a melancholy proof that if, at this moment, the original authority of the people should be restored, all that could be expected from such restoration would in the beginning be but a change of tyranny. Considering the nature of a Republic in

[42] *Prose Works*, I, 6.   [43] *Ibid.*   [44] *Ibid.*

LETTER TO THE BISHOP OF LLANDAFF

reference to the present condition of Europe, your Lordship stops here; but a philosopher will extend his views much farther: having dried up the source from which flows the corruption of the public opinion, he will be sensible that the stream will go on gradually refining itself.[45]

Thus Wordsworth gave expression in the *Letter to the Bishop of Llandaff* not only to a deep enthusiasm for the French Revolution and the republican form of government, but also to a specific criticism of English life and society, confidence in the efficacy of education, and firm faith in the perfectibility of the common man. His criticism of England Wordsworth was soon to make the matter of *Guilt and Sorrow*, his most bitter and provocative poem. His articles of faith, his confidence in education and the inexhaustible virtues of the common people—first openly declared in the spring of 1793, when he had more reasons to give up hope for the future and turn pessimist than he was ever to have again—were to become, as later chapters will disclose, the basic principles of Wordsworth's mature philosophy of poetry.

[45] *Ibid.*, pp. 10-11.

CHAPTER IV

Guilt and Sorrow

I

NO SINGLE poem of any length written by Wordsworth, save possibly *The Borderers*, has received less attention from his critics and biographers than *Guilt and Sorrow*. The cause of this neglect is not far to seek. *Guilt and Sorrow* is a poor and quite unpleasant poem. Nothing else that Wordsworth wrote seems at first glance less characteristic of the poet usually revered for his interpretation of nature and for his repeated affirmation that the world and humanity are full of love, benevolence, and joy. There is no interpretation of nature in *Guilt and Sorrow;* there is little love and less joy. The world of *Guilt and Sorrow* is a hard and evil world, devoid of beauty and of comfort. Moreover, a single reading of the poem is not likely to yield much of importance to the student of Wordsworth's intellectual or artistic development. The reader may conclude hastily that *Guilt and Sorrow* was merely one of Wordsworth's youthful mistakes, a kind of poetic wild oats, and may, with Professor Garrod, turn from its stanzas in righteous indignation and high moral disgust to recharge his faith in Wordsworth by way of the only too obvious cheerfulness of "To My Sister," or the unmistakable excellence of "Tintern Abbey" or the "Ode on Intimations of Immortality."[1]

No one, so far as I know, has made a sustained attempt to relate *Guilt and Sorrow* to the work which preceded it. It is

[1] H. W. Garrod, *Wordsworth: Lectures and Essays* (Oxford, 1923), Chap. V, and particularly pp. 85–86.

110

GUILT AND SORROW

true that biographers have been wont to associate the poem with the *Letter to the Bishop of Llandaff*, but they have ventured no further than to suggest that both were works of Wordsworth's so-called "Republican" period. Usually *Guilt and Sorrow* is hailed as the work in which Wordsworth's indebtedness to William Godwin's *Political Justice* first appears; and since it is generally assumed that Godwin's influence on Wordsworth ceased in *The Borderers*, it is generally believed that *Guilt and Sorrow* and *The Borderers* are comparatively insignificant so far as the main current of Wordsworth's development is concerned. The Godwin influence, it is supposed, brought Wordsworth to a dead end. He repudiated this influence at Racedown and, under the guidance of his sister Dorothy and Samuel Taylor Coleridge, continued his interrupted progress with such astonishing rapidity that he was capable of writing his cheerful contributions to the successful *Lyrical Ballads* as early as 1798. I believe that no more than two of the studies thus far devoted to *Guilt and Sorrow*, and *The Borderers*—its companion piece in Godwinism—have been written with the purpose of showing the connection between these early poems and the later work. I refer to the essays of Oscar James Campbell and Paul Mueschke.[2] These critics, however, while demonstrating the unmistakable significance of these poems to *Lyrical Ballads* in the evolution of Wordsworth's aesthetic, pay slight attention to the view of the world here entertained by Wordsworth, or to the vital ideational connections between this early work and that which preceded and followed it. Professors Campbell and Mueschke, in short, have established beyond question the value of *Guilt and Sorrow* and *The Borderers* as experiments in aesthetic, but they have done little to destroy the conventional and mistaken belief that these poems throw no light on the general philosophical development that culminated in *Lyrical Ballads*.[3]

[2] *"Guilt and Sorrow:* A Study in the Genesis of Wordsworth's Aesthetic," *Modern Philology*, XXIII (1926), 293–306; and *"The Borderers* as a Document in the History of Wordsworth's Aesthetic Development," *ibid.*, XXIII (1926), 465–482.

[3] The most succinct expression of this traditional attitude is that of

WORDSWORTH'S FORMATIVE YEARS

The recent publication by Ernest de Selincourt of the original manuscript version of *Guilt and Sorrow*[4] makes it possible now to demonstrate the close relationship both in content and purpose between this neglected poem and Wordsworth's letter to Richard Watson. The first draft of the poem was equipped with introductory and concluding stanzas —deleted from all subsequent versions—which prove beyond question that Wordsworth's desire for militant republican reform in England was not exhausted by his vehement denunciation of the arguments of the learned Bishop. Moreover, a study of the text already familiar to students of Wordsworth reveals that the narratives of the sailor and the female vagrant, the two chief characters of *Guilt and Sorrow*, are permeated with Wordsworth's bitter criticism of the English society of 1793, and that much more of the matter of *Guilt and Sorrow* than has previously been supposed has autobiographical significance. It shows, in fact, that in *Guilt and Sorrow* Wordsworth was once again exploiting for poetic purposes those parts of his early experience which he had already used extensively in *An Evening Walk, Descriptive Sketches,* and the *Letter to the Bishop of Llandaff*. Finally, a reconsideration of the artistic character and worth of *Guilt and Sorrow* and an examination of Wordsworth's first revision of the poem correct some of the views of Professors Campbell and Mueschke, and enable us to reach a better understanding of the technical problems that troubled Wordsworth in his first attempt to write primarily narrative verse.

II

On November 20, 1795, Wordsworth wrote Francis Wrangham that the object of *Guilt and Sorrow* was "partly

---

H. W. Garrod. He remarks that *Lyrical Ballads* presents to us a "radiant and settled health of genius. Indeed, whatever is new and wonderful in the *Lyrical Ballads,* nothing is more wonderful than that they should have come from the Wordsworth whom we have hitherto known. They usher in, without any forewarning, a swift springtime of clear song. Without preparation we pass at once from a condition drearily morbid to a puissant and settled serenity" (*op. cit.,* p. 102).

[4] *The Poetical Works of William Wordsworth: Poems Written in Youth, Poems Referring to the Period of Childhood,* ed. by Ernest de Selincourt

GUILT AND SORROW

to expose the vices of the penal law and the calamities of war as they affect individuals."[5] But this description, Wordsworth's own, of the purpose of the poem has been misleading. Actually there is not a single reference to the penal code, its vices or its virtues, in the only version of the poem Wordsworth published.[6] And that part of Wordsworth's statement which mentions the "calamities of war as they affect individuals" has caused students of the poem to regard it chiefly as a pacifist harangue in verse, noteworthy perhaps for betraying Wordsworth's membership in the fraternity of antiwar writers popular in the 1790's,[7] but of no genuine importance in any other connection. This has resulted in the general neglect of those aspects of *Guilt and Sorrow* most revealing to the student of Wordsworth's youth and development.

A more accurate and comprehensive account of *Guilt and Sorrow* than Wordsworth sent to Wrangham is the "Advertisement: Prefixed to the First Edition of This Poem, Published in 1842." The second and third paragraphs of the "Advertisement" describe in some detail the circumstances and reflections that inspired the composition of the poem:

> During the latter part of the summer of 1793, having passed a month in the Isle of Wight, in view of the fleet which was then preparing for sea off Portsmouth at the commencement of the war, I left the place with melancholy forebodings. The American war was still fresh in memory.

(Oxford, 1940) (hereafter referred to as *The Poetical Works*), pp. 94-127, 334-341.

[5] *The Early Letters of William and Dorothy Wordsworth (1787-1805)*, ed. by Ernest de Selincourt (Oxford, 1935) (hereafter referred to as *The Early Letters*), p. 145.

[6] For the lengthy and somewhat involved history of the text of *Guilt and Sorrow* see de Selincourt in *The Poetical Works*, Notes, pp. 330-333. Here it need only be remarked that when he wrote to Wrangham Wordsworth had just completed his first and most radical revision of the poem. But in neither the first nor the second manuscript version of *Guilt and Sorrow* are there more than the most oblique and inconsequential references to the penal code. One may therefore be permitted to wonder if Wordsworth, in his letter to Wrangham, did not confuse his intention in *Guilt and Sorrow* with his achievement in "The Convict," a minor poem of the same period.

[7] See, for example, Arthur Beatty, "Joseph Fawcett: *The Art of War*, Its Relation to the Early Development of William Wordsworth," *Studies by Members of the Department of English*, University of Wisconsin Studies in Language and Literature, No. 2 (Madison, 1918), 224-269.

The struggle which was beginning, and which many thought would be brought to a speedy close by the irresistible arms of Great Britain being added to those of the allies, I was assured in my own mind would be of long continuance, and productive of distress and misery beyond all possible calculation. This conviction was pressed upon me by having been a witness, during a long residence in revolutionary France, of the spirit which prevailed in that country. After leaving the Isle of Wight, I spent two days in wandering on foot over Salisbury Plain....

The monuments and traces of antiquity, scattered in abundance over that region, led me unavoidably to compare what we know or guess of those remote times with certain aspects of modern society, and with calamities, principally those consequent upon war, to which, more than other classes of men, the poor are subject. In those reflections, joined with particular facts that had come to my knowledge, the following stanzas originated.

Here, as in the letter to Wrangham, Wordsworth emphasizes the "calamities of war," but in this more complete account of the poem he also recalls having attempted a comparison of "what we know or guess of . . . remote times with certain aspects of modern society." Except war, just what those "aspects of modern society" were which provoked the first draft of *Guilt and Sorrow* in 1793 the Wordsworth of 1842 does not explain. By 1842 Wordsworth, like Richard Watson before him, had become an eminent conservative, a veritable pillar of society. This Wordsworth had no qualms about acknowledging a poem that exposed the evils of war, but he could and did in his preface to that poem conveniently fail to specify or to invite too close attention to the details of his youthful attack upon a society which he defended in his riper years. The later Wordsworth published *Guilt and Sorrow* only after he had blunted the edge of its social criticism and removed its more violent and inflammatory passages. But the original version preserves those details which Wordsworth was reluctant to emphasize or enumerate in 1842 and enables us to determine the nature of the comparison Wordsworth once felt obliged to draw between the savage age of the Druids and the England of 1793.

To Wordsworth the huge gray monoliths of Stonehenge were grim reminders of a culture that was brutal, barbarous, and inhuman. The ancient priesthood, whose gigantic

GUILT AND SORROW

monuments loomed before him and summoned dreadful thoughts to mind, was composed of ignorant, misguided, and bloodthirsty men whose cursed spirits return at night to the scene of their ancient crimes. This much Wordsworth suggests in two stanzas descriptive of a supernatural experience suffered by one of the harassed characters of *Guilt and Sorrow*, whose wanderings have brought him at night to the unholy precincts of Stonehenge:—"A voice as from a tomb in hollow accents cried":

> "Oh from that mountain-pile avert thy face
> Whate'er betide at this tremendous hour.
> To hell's most cursed sprites the baleful place
> Belongs, upreared by their magic power.
> Though mixed with flame rush down the crazing shower
> And o'er thy naked bed the thunders roll
> Fly ere at once the fiends their prey devour
> Or grinning, on thy endless tortures scowl
> Till very madness seem a mercy to thy soul.
>
> "For oft, at dead of night, when dreadful fire
> Unfolds that powerful circle's reddening stones
> Mid priests and spectres grim and idols dire
> Far heard the great flame utters human moans
> Then all is hushed: again the desert groans
> A dismal light its farthest bounds illumes,
> While warrior spectres of gigantic bones
> Forth issuing from a thousand rifted tombs
> Wheel on their fiery steeds amid the infernal glooms."[8]

The horror which Wordsworth feels as he recreates in imagination those remote and superstitious days when human flesh was used to feed the sacrificial fires does not yield to a milder emotion when he contemplates the society in which he lives. Eighteenth-century Englishmen, it is true, did not burn one another alive in the worship of false gods, but the England of 1793 had evils of her own—refined and subtle sources of human pain and suffering beside which the crass physical tortures of the Druids seemed impressive by their

---

[8] *The Poetical Works*, p. 100. Here it is interesting to note the resemblance between the "warrior spectres" wheeling "on their fiery steeds amid the infernal glooms" in the second stanza, and the "horsemen-shadows" of *An Evening Walk*, vv. 183-190.

innocence. In the introductory stanzas of the original *Guilt and Sorrow* Wordsworth suggests that the savage of antiquity, inured to hunger, cold, and incessant war, was "strong to suffer" because of his ignorance of anything better. The lot of the modern poverty-racked Englishman, haunted as he is by memories of vanished pleasures and former prosperity, is immeasurably more difficult and unhappy, for he is

> Beset with foes more fierce than e'er assail
> The savage without home in winter's keenest gale.[9]

After telling the tale of the female vagrant, which he presents as a concrete illustration of the desperate plight of thousands of his countrymen, Wordsworth repeats with emphasis his gloomy conviction that a comparison of the barbarous past with the presumably civilized present serves only to illuminate "the terrors of our day." So far as Wordsworth can tell, little or no progress in the amelioration of human suffering has been made through all the ages: "For proof," he writes,[10]

> I
>
> if man thou lovest, turn thine eye
> On realms which least the cup of Misery taste;
> For want how many men and Children die;
> How many, at Oppression's portal placed,
> Receive the scanty dole she cannot waste;   5
> And bless, as she has taught, the hand benign.
> How many, by inhuman toil debased,
> Abject, obscure and brute, to earth incline
> Unrespited, forlorn of every spark divine!
>
> II
>
> Nor only is the walk of private life   10
> Unblessed by Justice and the kindly train
> Of Peace and truth, while Injury and strife
> Outrage and deadly Hate usurp their reign.
> From the pale line to either frozen main
> The nations, forced at home in bonds to drink   15
> The dregs of Wretchedness, for empire strain;

---

[9] *The Poetical Works*, pp. 334–335.

[10] The following four stanzas and their lines are numbered to facilitate reference to them below.

GUILT AND SORROW

> And when by their own fetters crushed they sink
> Move their galled limbs in fear, and eye each
>   silent link.[11]

The features of modern society here described—starvation, extreme economic inequality, domestic injustice, lust for empire, and international hate—were, in Wordsworth's judgment, more dreadful than the ancient tortures of the Druids.

But Wordsworth was aware that there were men—Richard Watson was one, Edmund Burke, another—whose esteem for English monarchical society was higher and more flattering than his own. The views of such champions of the *status quo* he acknowledged in the original *Guilt and Sorrow* in stanzas that probably have been lost forever. But the lines immediately following the gap in the manuscript left by these lost stanzas show that Wordsworth in the autumn of 1793, as in the spring when he wrote to the Bishop of Llandaff, found the dulcet apologies and bland explanations of the Watsons and the Burkes worthy only of ridicule and contempt in a world and country where the virtuous and the poor were repeatedly given up to the sword, where rulers ignored the lucubrations of the rational and wise, and where the penal code instead of discouraging succeeded only in generating crime:

III

> How weak the solace such fond thoughts afford
> When with untimely stroke the virtuous bleed.   20
> Say, rulers of the nations, from the sword
> Can aught but murder, pain, and tears proceed?
> Oh, what can war but endless war still breed?
> Or whence but from the labours of the sage
> Can poor benighted mortals gain the meed   25
> Of happiness and virtue, how assuage
> But by his gentle words their self-consuming rage?

IV

> Insensate they who think, at wisdom's porch,
> That Exile, Terror, Bonds and Force may stand;
> That Truth with human blood can feed his torch,   30
> And Justice balance with her gory hand
> Scales whose dire weight of human heads demand

---
[11] *The Poetical Works*, p. 339.

> A Nero's arm. Must Law with its own scourge
> Still torture crimes that grew a monstrous band
> Formed by his care, and still his victims urge 35
> With voice that breathes despair to death's tremendous
>   verge?[12]

The answers to such questions, Wordsworth was sure, could only be sharply negative. He reasoned accordingly that progress would come only after the extermination of monarchy, that a society so evil and irrational as England's in 1793 should be immediately and utterly destroyed. With this grim and violent end in mind Wordsworth wrote the concluding stanza of the original *Guilt and Sorrow:*

> Heroes of Truth, pursue your march, uptear
> The oppressors' dungeon from its deepest base;
> High o'er the towers of Pride undaunted rear
> Resistless in your might th'Herculean mace
> Of Reason, let foul Error's monstrous race
> Dragged from their dens start at the light with pain
> And die! pursue your toils till not a trace
> Be left on earth of Superstition's reign
> Save that eternal pile which frowns on Sarum's plain.[13]

The points of similarity between this version of *Guilt and Sorrow* and Wordsworth's earlier work are unmistakable. The stanzas quoted above represent little more than a verse paraphrase of Wordsworth's arguments in his *Letter to the Bishop of Llandaff*,[14] while the last stanza in particular merely

---

[12] *The Poetical Works*, p. 340.   [13] *Ibid.*, pp. 340-341.

[14] For a detailed understanding of Wordsworth's use in the early *Guilt and Sorrow* of material from his reply to Watson, compare vv. 3-9 of the numbered lines above with the passage in the letter beginning, "Aware of this, and that the extremes of poverty and riches . . . ," and ending, ". . . owe their very existence to the ostentatious bounty of their oppressors" (*The Prose Works of William Wordsworth*, ed. by Alexander B. Grosart [London, 1876], I, 15-16), with that beginning, "Your Lordship tells us that the science of civil government . . . ," and ending, ". . . whom they are unable to support" (*ibid.*, p. 16), and with that beginning, "Reflecting on the corruption of the public manners . . . ," and ending, ". . . snatching the bread from their mouths to eke out the *'necessary* splendour' of nobility" (*ibid.*, pp. 18-19). Read also against vv. 10-11 the passage beginning, "I congratulate your Lordship . . . ," and ending, ". . . the perpetual contrariety in our judicial decisions" (*ibid.*, p. 20); against vv. 24-27 the passage beginning, "Alas, the obstinacy and perversion of man . . . ," and ending, ". . . will look upon their fathers as only

GUILT AND SORROW

reiterates sentiments he had already expressed in the closing lines of *Descriptive Sketches*. In its original form *Guilt and Sorrow*, like the reply to Watson, was a bitter attack on English society and its conservative defenders. It was a document of revolutionary propaganda provided with a narrative illustrating the dire effects of monarchy upon the well-being of the individual—a narrative specially designed to inflame all thinking readers and to incite them to action against a government which Wordsworth insisted was vicious and indecent. And just as Wordsworth had ended *Descriptive Sketches* with a militant prayer to God for the obliteration of sceptered tyranny, so did he conclude the first draft of *Guilt and Sorrow* with a spirited apostrophe to the "Heroes of Truth" that was intended to rouse apostles of republicanism to fever pitch and to more strenuous exertions in the interests of liberty, equality, and fraternity. To these "Heroes" Wordsworth offered the high task of ridding the world of those evils and terrors which rendered embarrassing and abhorrent a comparison of English society in 1793 with the superstitious age of which Stonehenge was the monument and symbol.

III

The version of *Guilt and Sorrow* that Wordsworth published in 1842 bears little external resemblance to the poem that he wrote in 1793. According to his own account, when he revised *Guilt and Sorrow* in 1795 he made "alterations and additions so material as that it may be looked on almost as

---

enfranchised" (*ibid.*, p. 6); against vv. 33-36 the passage beginning, "I have spoken of laws partial and oppressive . . . ," and ending, ". . . incurring the contempt of his fellow-citizens" (*ibid.*, pp. 12-13); against vv. 3, 21-23 the passage beginning, "From your omitting to speak upon the war . . . ," and ending, ". . . consigning the rest to the more slow and more painful consumption of want" (*ibid.*, p. 22), and that beginning, "that, deprived almost of the necessaries of existence . . . ," and ending, ". . . about to smart under the scourge of labour, of cold, and of hunger" (*ibid.*, p. 10).

The idea expressed in vv. 14-18, concerning the domestic wretchedness of nations engaged in the struggle for empire, is not found in the letter to Watson. Tom Paine in particular makes much of it in his *The Rights of Man*. Wordsworth had no doubt been long familiar with the thesis, which was a commonplace among radical thinkers of the day.

another work."[15] The only part of the first draft that Wordsworth thought worth keeping was the narrative of the female vagrant, and this he decided to expand. The most radical change, of course, was the deletion of the original argumentative and hortatory introduction and conclusion—those parts of the poem in which he had given strident voice to his youthful indignation and, without any pretense of subtlety or indirection, denounced in his own person the time-honored institutions of his native land. For the disparaging comparison of modern society with the savagery of times remote he now substituted the newly created personal history of the sailor and the incident of the maltreated child. The revised *Guilt and Sorrow* is thus composed of three narratives which Wordsworth permitted to stand without the support of authorial exegesis. Analysis of these tales reveals, however, that despite this more objective, if less forceful and insistent, mode of presentation finally adopted by Wordsworth, the revised and published *Guilt and Sorrow*,[16] no less than the original, is a reworking of old material and a stern criticism, not only of the evils of war, but of those other aspects of English monarchical society which Wordsworth, for reasons at least partly personal, found most offensive in 1793.

Guilt and Sorrow begins with a description of the sailor as he wanders alone at night over the desolate waste of Salisbury Plain. Several years before, after completing a lengthy voyage, he had started for his home when he was impressed

---

[15] Letter to Francis Wrangham, November 20, 1795 (*The Early Letters*, p. 145).

[16] Except for that part of the poem entitled "The Female Vagrant" and published independently in 1798 in *Lyrical Ballads*, the following discussion of *Guilt and Sorrow*, unless otherwise indicated, is based upon the published text of 1842. References to the narrative of the female vagrant are to the text of 1798. This procedure, admittedly somewhat awkward, is less difficult and confusing than the available alternatives. The 1842 text, except for the tale of the female vagrant, differs in no important respect from the manuscript version of 1795. It is, moreover, the text most readily accessible to all readers. The 1798 text of "The Female Vagrant" combines the version of 1793 with the additions Wordsworth made in 1795. This text differs markedly from that of 1842, Wordsworth having taken pains in his later years to erase or alter those lines and stanzas which were most explicit in their criticism of English society.

GUILT AND SORROW

and forced to go to sea again, this time on a British man-o'-war. Against his will he experienced the horrors of battle and became an agent of death. When at last he earned release his heart was cheered by the joyful expectation of a quick reunion with his wife and children. His hopes now prove vain, however, for evil men defraud him of his money. This catastrophe, the loss of the wherewithal to buy food for his dependents, breaks his weakened spirit. Within sight of his doorstep he suffers a kind of psychological disintegration, loses control of mind and body, and in a fit of maniacal desperation robs and murders a traveler on the road. To escape detection and ultimate capture he avoids his home and wanders aimlessly about the countryside, tortured by the memory of his crime. On the night described in the early stanzas of *Guilt and Sorrow* the sailor takes shelter from a storm in a "lonely Spital" on Salisbury Plain. Here he meets the female vagrant who, after assurance of his friendliness, tells him her tale.

The vagrant's history is even more pathetic than the sailor's. Hers had been a good life with her aged and pious father until a wealthy tyrant forced them from their "old hereditary nook." In their distress they sought and found a new home with a youth whom the vagrant had loved from childhood. Their marriage was a happy one, eventually blessed—as Wordsworth puts it—by "Three lovely infants." For several years all went well, and they might have lived happily ever after had not the threat of war "reduced the children's meal." Desperate for money, the vagrant's husband went to America to fight for the king. The hapless woman and her children, lacking any means of support, followed him to the theater of war. There tragedy overtook them: one year of war with its dread attendants—"Disease and famine, agony and fear"—destroyed all but the vagrant, who was left by a merciless fate to face the world and her sorrow alone.

On her return to England the vagrant's troubles began anew. Too proud to beg, she soon collapsed from hunger. In a hospital to which she had been carried by strangers, she received treatment—most inhumanely administered but sufficient to restore her strength. Then she fell in with a band of cheerful gypsies who pitied her and gave her food. They stole, however, and her conscience forced her to desert them and face the world alone again.[17]

The sailor hears the vagrant's tale with sympathy, and at daybreak they pursue their way together. On the road they meet a peasant who, despite the protests of his wife, and for no good reason, has struck his small son a series of brutal blows on the head. The sailor intervenes in this family quarrel and by means of a few pious reflections succeeds in reconciling father and son.

Continuing on their way, the sailor and the vagrant pass proud mansions, where they are certain to receive no hospitality, and eventually reach a "cottage in the dale," where a breakfast of bread and milk is gladly given them. Here the vagrant takes leave of the sailor. She returns in a moment, however, with the information that not far from the cottage door is "A pale-faced Woman, in disease far gone." This unfortunate, though almost dead, has enough strength in her wasted body to tell her story before she dies. She is the wife of a sailor who several years before had been forced to serve in the navy. One of her two sons had recently been murdered, and her safety was made precarious by the rumor that her husband, who had been reported lurking near their home, had committed the crime. Finally, unable longer to secure food for herself and her surviving son, she was seeking the shelter of her father's house when illness overcame her. At this point the sailor recognizes his wife, embraces her, and receives her blessing just prior to her death. Then, serene in his trust in God, he surrenders himself to British justice.[18]

This brief summary makes it plain that these simple tales accomplish their ostensible first purpose—the exposure of the "calamities of war as they affect individuals." The narratives

[17] The vagrant's experiences in the hospital and with the philanthropic gypsies are the parts of her narrative that Wordsworth added in 1795.

[18] The only noteworthy alteration Wordsworth made after 1795 in the sailor's narrative was in the conclusion of the poem. In the version of 1795 the sailor does not give himself up, but is exposed to the law by the peasants

GUILT AND SORROW

of the sailor, the female vagrant, and the sailor's dying wife indicate only too clearly how war broke up the families of the poor. War was preceded, accompanied, and followed by economic depression. Men were either driven by material want to enlist in the armed forces of the realm, or they were seized by press gangs and compelled to fight against their will. Wives and children either became camp followers, fated to suffer the manifold afflictions of life in the wake of an army, or drifted inevitably into beggary, prostitution, and thievery. If they endeavored to exist by honest means they experienced the unkindness of their fellow men; if in desperation they turned from lawful paths to find the necessities of life they risked the dreadful punishments and hideous death rigorously meted out under an antiquated and barbaric penal code. The soldiers themselves—if they survived the "mine's dire earthquake," "the bomb's incessant thunder-stroke," and the pestilence and famine that oppress all armies—returned to their ruined homes to face the hardships of peace already encountered by their families. Not infrequently, we may suppose, good men like the sailor became murderers.

But the narratives of the sailor and the female vagrant reveal more than the evil effects of war upon individuals. In the original *Guilt and Sorrow,* as we have seen, Wordsworth wished to make his readers the implacable opponents of imperialist war. But this desire was only a part of the broader purpose which inspired him to write the poem. His main objective was the destruction of monarchy. War was but one of the "aspects of society" that earned his animosity in 1793. Under the cover of his barrage upon war Wordsworth launched against English monarchical society a general attack equal in bitterness and extent to that contained in the *Letter to the Bishop of Llandaff.* Vestiges of this attack, first

---

who have just given him breakfast. In the early version, moreover, the authorities hang him in an "iron case," where his dead body excites the curiosity of dissolute and idle men. In the published version, when his attitude toward the law had mellowed, Wordsworth wrote:
> His fate was pitied. Him in iron case
> (Reader, forgive the intolerable thought)
> They hung not . . . .

sketched in detail in the concluding stanzas of the original *Guilt and Sorrow,* remain in the final version of the poem. These must here be stressed, for hitherto they have been generally neglected.

In the published *Guilt and Sorrow,* as in the reply to Richard Watson, Wordsworth criticized no single feature of English society, but the entire social structure of the nation. Wordsworth found England an evil place, not only because she forced her "peasants and mechanics" to risk or give up their lives in futile and murderous imperialist contest, but also because of the manner in which she dealt with the dependents of these men—the wives and children who had been left behind and entrusted to the protection of the infinitely good and efficacious British Constitution of which Watson and Burke were so inordinately fond. England was wicked, too, because of the reception she afforded the men themselves when they returned to the land and government whose honor they had defended and whose wealth they had increased or protected at the peril of their lives. In *Guilt and Sorrow,* finally, Wordsworth revealed that England was an evil land and nation because of the rank injustice suffered by the poor, not merely in occasional seasons of war, but in times of peace as well.

War alone was not responsible for the tragedy that overtook the sailor. At least three circumstances contributed to his undoing. His experience as a killer in time of war had, to be sure, conditioned him psychologically to become a murderer in time of peace, but he would not have murdered had he not been cheated of his money. This misfortune resulted not merely from the corruption to be expected in a monarchy at war, but at least partly from human greed—from a vice, that is, which thus far has made itself manifest in all societies. Wordsworth might have called it bad luck, a "chastisement of Providence." But still more was necessary to make a criminal of the innately good sailor. His war experience and the loss of his money could not effect such a transformation in his character. The final and crucial factor in his moral collapse was his knowledge of the certain difficulty—if not the certain impossibility—of earning more money for the family made destitute by his enforced absence.

The sailor's experience subsequent to his crime shows clearly that his estimate of the essential injustice of English society—the estimate which drove him to murder—was a sound one. Penniless and forlorn in the land for which he has fought,[19] he feels only too keenly the inhumanity of his countrymen. As he wanders weary and hopeless in foul weather across Salisbury Plain, he is full of melancholy thoughts, for he knows that he is welcome nowhere. Kipling's Tommy Atkins could teach Wordsworth's sailor nothing of cynicism or disillusionment. The hearts of rich Englishmen, he knew, were as hard as the silver and gold they treasured; they had no pity, no kindliness for him:

> While thus he journeyed, step by step led on,
> He saw and passed a stately inn, full sure
> That welcome in such house for him was none.
> No board inscribed the needy to allure
> Hung there, no bush proclaimed to old and poor
> And desolate, "Here you will find a friend!"
> The pendent grapes glittered above the door;—
> On he must pace, perchance 'till night descend,
> Where'er the dreary roads their bare white lines extend.

His only hope for shelter from an unfriendly nature lay in the discovery of "Some labourer" or "some shepherd's spreading thorn Or hovel." Only from these members of England's oppressed classes was there the faintest hope of hospitality. No wonder is it that Wordsworth enters the poem for a stanza, as the sailor passes Stonehenge, and inquires of the great gray stones if ever they have seen a human being more wretched:

> Pile of Stone-henge! so proud to hint yet keep
> Thy secrets, thou that lov'st to stand and hear
> The Plain resounding to the whirlwind's sweep,
> Inmate of lonesome Nature's endless year;
> Even if thou saw'st the giant wicker rear

---

[19] Evidently the sailor gained nothing from murdering and robbing his son, for Wordsworth describes him as "needy," with worn-out clothes and feet half bare.

> For sacrifice its throngs of living men,
> Before thy face did ever wretch appear,
> Who in his heart had groaned with deadlier pain
> Than he who, tempest-driven, thy shelter now would gain?

The history of the sailor's wife and his two children throws still more light on aspects of English society other than war. Their case was an unusual one to be related with the other chronicles in *Guilt and Sorrow*, for, in ways which Wordsworth does not trouble to explain, they apparently had been able to make ends meet during the long years of the sailor's absence. At least they managed to keep body and soul and the remnant of the family together until the fatal night when the sailor, in his momentary fit of madness, killed his son. This of course aroused the neighborhood. The rumor that the dead man's father had been seen thereabouts and that he had done the deed cast suspicion upon the poor woman and her remaining son. To escape the possibility of arrest and brutal punishment for a crime they had not committed,[20] they abandoned their humble cottage "Near Portland lighthouse" and threw themselves separately into the struggle for existence. We are told nothing of the fate of the son, but we know that the poor woman's efforts were destined to fail in an England where help for the poor was forthcoming only from those who could least afford to give it. With her last breath the sailor's wife discloses that no employment was available; disease claimed her, and her aged father was her sole remaining hope:

> Barred every comfort labour could procure,
> Suffering what no endurance could assuage,
> I was compelled to seek my father's door,
> Though loth to be a burthen on his age.

---

[20] Wordsworth offers scant information as to why the sailor's wife and son were forced to flee from their home after the murder. It is clear, however, that they were ostracized by their neighbors: "In vain," she says, "to find a friendly face we try." We may infer from what evidence there is that the neighbors suspected the sailor and his wife and son of having been in communication with one another and of committing the murder for some motive which has never come to light. To live under such suspicion was extremely dangerous, as Eldred the Peasant in *The Borderers* (Act IV, sc. iii) knew full well.

GUILT AND SORROW

> But sickness stopped me in an early stage
> Of my sad journey ....

We cannot, however, understand or appreciate the full extent of the atrocities perpetrated and permitted by British society merely from our knowledge of the fate of the sailor and his family. The sailor's wife most assuredly was unfortunate, but hers was by no means the unkindest destiny of all in the England described by Wordsworth in *Guilt and Sorrow*. She had lost her own home, but there was shelter awaiting her beneath her father's roof when she was cut down by disease. By just so much was her lot happier than the female vagrant's.

Only in the narrative of the vagrant are we introduced to the more subtle types of terror and injustice characteristic of the society which Wordsworth in 1793 hated with singular intensity. The vagrant had no place to go. Her father was dead, of course, but had he been alive he would have had no door for her to seek in her distress: he, too, before his death, had felt the full weight of British oppression and social inequality.

In better days the old man and his daughter lived idyllically upon the banks of the Derwent. For twenty years they knew no hardship but that of honest toil. Their life might have continued happy and unoppressed in any land where society was humane and government just. But England was no such land. In the woods near their cottage, a "mansion proud" arose, whose owner immediately endeavored to bend his poorer neighbors to his tyrannical will and to acquire their meager properties:

> And cottage after cottage owned its [the proud
> mansion's] sway,
> No joy to see a neighbouring house, or stray
> Through pastures not his own, the master took ....

The vagrant's father, however, possessed the stubborn virtues ascribed by Wordsworth in *Descriptive Sketches* to the patriots of Switzerland. Proud of his hereditary land, conscious of his rights as a man and determined to assert and defend them, the old Englishman defied his offensive superior and refused to sell his small estate. In a nation where justice was available only to the rich—in England—such defiance was an invitation to disaster. The powerful landlord used his economic might to frustrate his poor neighbor's efforts to buy or sell with profit. That part of Derwent's water which belonged to him by right was denied him, apparently by the British courts:[21] no longer could he fish, use his boat, or water his sheep there. Finally, according to the vagrant,

> All but the bed where his old body lay,
> All, all was seized, and weeping, side by side,
> We sought a home where we uninjured might abide.

Such distress as this, it is obvious, did not result from imperialistic war, the favorite sport of monarchy. The vagrant and her father were forced from their home in time of peace by the savage machinations of a representative of the upper class of the British socioeconomic hierarchy, the landed gentry, the class cast by the Almighty, according to the Bishop of Llandaff, in the rôle of legislator, the class, finally, which along with the king was responsible under the British Constitution for the execution of justice in the English courts of law, where, according to Richard Watson, "peasants and mechanics" were the peers of dukes and earls. The old man, innocently believing that justice was available in the courts of his land, was presumptuous enough to insist upon his rights, with the result that he lost everything but his life.

But death soon released the father from the suffering that lurked around the corner of the future for his daughter. No sooner had she begun life anew as a wife and mother than other varieties of the evil that inevitably attends monarchical government combined to destroy her happiness, this time forever. The approach of war plunged the nation into economic depression. Her husband lost his work, and the children were undernourished; the cottage loom was empty, the wheel silent, and the hearth cold: there were "tears that flowed for ills which patience could not heal." Suffering such

---

[21] The vagrant is not clear on this point. "His little range of water was denied," is all she says. It must be concluded, therefore, that the landgrabber somehow gained a legal title to the water.

GUILT AND SORROW

as this was general throughout the country. The masses were in utter despair, and there was danger of riot and public disorder. According to the vagrant, however, the government knew how to insure against embarrassing demonstrations:

> an evil time was come;
> We had no hope, and no relief could gain.
> But soon, with proud parade, the noisy drum
> Beat round, to sweep the streets of want and pain.

England, it is true, could not be held entirely responsible for the horrible conditions which the vagrant found in America:

> groans, that rage of racking famine spoke,
> Where looks inhuman dwelt on festering heaps!
> The breathing pestilence that rose like smoke!
> The shriek that from the distant battle broke!
> The mine's dire earthquake, and the pallid host
> Driven by the bomb's incessant thunder-stroke
> To loathsome vaults, where heart-sick anguish toss'd,
> Hope died, and fear itself in agony was lost!

But Wordsworth held England to account for her treatment of the woman, an English soldier's widow, after her return to her native land.

The vagrant's experiences after her homecoming are similar to those of the sailor. She has no money. She is hungry and cold, and there is no one willing to extend a helping hand, no offer of food or shelter, no place to go. She is forced to sleep with chickens in an outhouse and, finally, to beg. Public aid she receives when she faints from hunger, but it is the kind of aid that makes her wish that she had died instead. The inhumanity of the hospital attendants in the performance of their routine duties is scarcely known to her, however, for the calamities that have befallen her have rendered her insensible. "I heard," she says,

> my neighbors, in their beds, complain
> Of many things which never troubled me;
> Of feet still bustling round with busy glee,
> Of looks where common kindness had no part,
> Of service done with careless cruelty,

> Fretting the fever round the languid heart,
> And groans, which, as they said, would make a dead
>   man start.

When her strength revives the female vagrant finds herself adrift once more in a merciless and inhospitable society. In her distress she meets the gypsies, who pity her and give her food. These wild and unconventional creatures, living a life outside of British law and organized society, are unique among those whom the vagrant has hitherto encountered, for they alone possess the virtues of kindliness and generosity. The vagrant's

> heart is touched to think that men like these,
> The rude earth's tenants, were my first relief:
> How kindly did they paint their vagrant ease!
> And their long holiday that feared not grief,
> For all belonged to all, and each was chief.

The communistic, humane, and hospitable gypsies, however, are thieves, and the unhappy woman finds it impossible to reconcile their antisocial mode of life with her moral nature. Mindful of the training she has received in childhood from her pious and law-abiding father, and harassed by the memory of domestic tragedy, she is both unwilling and unable to live by criminal means. Accordingly, she deserts her uncouth benefactors and decides to face the world alone.

The adventures which befell her, the means by which she lived during the three-year interval that separated her voluntary parting from the philanthropic gypsies and her encounter with the sailor on Salisbury Plain, are only hinted at in the following cryptic lines:

> I lived upon the mercy of the fields,
> And oft of cruelty the sky accused;
> On hazard, or what general bounty yields,
> Now coldly given, now utterly refused.
> The fields I for my bed have often used:
> But, what afflicts my peace with keenest ruth
> Is, that I have my inner self abused,
> Foregone the home delight of constant truth,
> And clear and open soul, so prized in fearless youth.

GUILT AND SORROW

In these and the foregoing lines it is clear that the instinct for self-preservation has driven the female vagrant into thievery and into beggary. But what of the last four lines of the stanza just quoted? The unfortunate creature reveals that she has "Foregone the home delight of constant truth, And clear and open soul"; she has abused her "inner self." What does she mean by this? Does she refer to her brief experience with the gypsies—to the petty larcenies in which she apparently took part before her early training caused her to revolt and go her way alone? Probably not, for although she is concluding her tale in the stanza under consideration and is, consequently, summarizing, she seems to refer to another, more recent and more disturbing, aberration, which she is reluctant to describe with perfect clarity.

Professors Campbell and Mueschke make much of these curious lines. They argue that Wordsworth, when he wrote the story of the female vagrant, felt remorse for his desertion of Annette Vallon, that the effect of this remorse was a "disorganized personality,"[22] and that Wordsworth was entertaining unruly emotions which clamored for and received furtive expression in *Guilt and Sorrow* despite his most strenuous efforts to repress them. In this instance they conclude that the vagrant is suffering from "spiritual disharmony brought about by . . . moral delinquency,"[23] that there is nothing in the poem to indicate that she was a moral delinquent, and that it is therefore Wordsworth's remorse for his own sins of the body that here receives surreptitious expression.[24] The suspicion that these lines refer, however indefinitely, to sexual sin seems justified, but the contention that Wordsworth here releases an irrepressible feeling of moral dissatisfaction with his own illicit adventure rests rather too precariously on the dubious assumptions of Freudian psychology to be entirely satisfactory. We have seen, moreover, that Wordsworth's intentions toward Annette Vallon were wholly honorable when he returned to England. In 1793 his purpose

---

[22] "*Guilt and Sorrow* . . . ," p. 306.
[23] *Ibid.*, p. 303.
[24] *Ibid.*, pp. 303–306.

was to make her his wife. So far as we know, events—not Wordsworth's change of heart—made this impossible. In any case, Wordsworth had very little reason to feel remorse for his treatment of her at the late date of 1795, the year in which the lines in question were composed.[25]

A more convincing explanation for these lines is to be found in the *Letter to the Bishop of Llandaff*. There, as we have remarked, Wordsworth informs Richard Watson that the extreme economic inequality prevalent under British monarchy inevitably produces crime, beggary, and prostitution. We have seen, moreover, that Wordsworth's purpose in *Guilt and Sorrow* was to reveal to his readers the appalling evils of British society, and that he used his *Letter to the Bishop of Llandaff* as a source for the poem. Wordsworth presents the history of the female vagrant as evidence in support of his thesis that the fruits of monarchy among the poor are crime, beggary, and prostitution. She has been a thief and she has been a beggar; to fulfill the formula of the reply to Watson and exploit to the full the potentialities for revolutionary propaganda inherent in her case, it remains for this unfortunate—once a happy country girl, of pious parents born and bred—to sully her immortal soul with prostitution.[26]

After the conclusion of the vagrant's narrative, one might reasonably suppose that Wordsworth had exposed enough distress and misery to convince the most skeptical reader of the truth of his contention that oppression reigned in England and that the poorer classes suffered in times of peace as well as in war. But, desirous of driving home his argument with yet greater force, Wordsworth could not resist the temptation to present one more incident—that of the maltreated child—before bringing his poem to a close. This child is the victim of one of the most startling examples of

---

[25] See note 34 below.

[26] If it be objected that Wordsworth would have made this clear had he intended such an interpretation of these lines, let allowance be made for the vagrant's diffidence in conversation with a strange man, and let it be remembered that Wordsworth, though a realist in many senses of the word, was yet no Hemingway or Dreiser.

gratuitous brutality to be encountered in literature outside of Dostoevsky. In a "simple freak of thoughtless play," the ill-starred infant had "provoked his father." Seized by a towering passion which overrode reason and the paternal instinct, the adult rained heavy blows upon his son until his head was battered and bloody. Such behavior was singular, to say the least, and the reader is naturally curious concerning the peasant's motives, his background, and present circumstances. Such information, however, Wordsworth does not vouchsafe, and the reader, left to his own devices and the knowledge he has of British society from his perusal of the earlier tales, must conclude that the peasant also had suffered the sad vicissitudes of English life that had wrought a similar moral and psychological collapse in the sailor and driven him to the commission of a brutal crime.[27] It is significant, however, that there is nothing in the incident to suggest that war was in any way responsible for the savagery displayed by the father in his effort to correct his son.

IV

Critics hitherto have agreed that *Guilt and Sorrow* represents the first stage of Wordsworth's allegiance to the philosophy of William Godwin, and that his intention to expose here "the vices of the penal law and the calamities of war as they affect individuals" reveals clearly his debt to Godwin,

[27] The similarities between the two actions are too striking to be mere coincidence. Like the sailor, the peasant father possesses kind and humane instincts. This is evident from the fact that he bestows a paternal kiss upon his suffering son once his senses have been restored to him by the benevolent intervention of the sailor. The wounds inflicted upon the child's head, moreover, remind the sailor of the fatal hurt received at his hands by the unfortunate traveler:

> as the boy turned round
> His battered head, a groan the Sailor fetched
> As if he saw—there and upon that ground—
> Strange repetition of the deadly wound
> He had himself inflicted.

These lines show that the two actions were related in Wordsworth's mind, and provide ample warrant, it seems to me, for the conclusion that the peasant's brutality, like the sailor's crime, was regarded by Wordsworth as an example of the violent behavior to be expected of individuals who had suffered long and unjustly in a bad society.

who had much to say against war and the British penal code in *Political Justice,* published in 1793. But this view, given authority by frequent repetition, rests on little more than sheer assumption on the part of the critics.

When Wordsworth wrote *An Evening Walk,* several years before the publication of Godwin's *Political Justice,* he was already exposing the "calamities of war as they affect individuals": the soldier's widow in *An Evening Walk* is definitely a prototype of the female vagrant. In the absence of any sustained reflections by Wordsworth on the penal code in any of the several versions of *Guilt and Sorrow,* it is difficult to determine whether his early ideas on this subject were Godwinian or not.[28] We have seen, furthermore, that *Guilt and Sorrow* is little more than Wordsworth's *Letter to the Bishop of Llandaff* put into verse and fitted out with appropriate narrative illustrations; and thus far no effort to connect *Political Justice* with the reply to Watson has been crowned with success.[29]

The ideas in the *Letter to the Bishop of Llandaff* and *Guilt and Sorrow* were well established in the climate of opinion with which Wordsworth was familiar. They were available, before Godwin published *Political Justice,* in the works of Tom Paine, in the *Vindiciae Gallicae* of Mackintosh, in the sermons of Dr. Price, and in the essays, tracts, and pamphlets of innumerable French writers. It should be evident that Wordsworth, with a year in revolutionary and re-

---

[28] Some critics detect Godwin's doctrine of "Necessity" in Wordsworth's account of the sailor's crime (see, for example, C. H. Herford, *Wordsworth* [New York: E. P. Dutton and Company, 1930], p. 57). Godwin, in his novel *Caleb Williams* (1794), they explain, showed how environment might force a good man to commit a crime. But there is no proof that Wordsworth had read *Caleb Williams* when he invented the sailor's crime for the 1795 version of *Guilt and Sorrow.*

[29] It has never been established that Wordsworth had read *Political Justice* before starting work on either the first or the second draft of *Guilt and Sorrow.* He may have seen it, it is true, early in 1793 in Johnson's bookshop, either in manuscript or in its published form. But our only definite knowledge is that he had read it before March 21, 1796, for on that date he wrote to Mathews: "I have received . . . Godwyn's second edition. I expect to find the work much improved" (*The Early Letters,* p. 156). This is Wordsworth's earliest reference to Godwin.

GUILT AND SORROW

publican France behind him—part of which was spent in close communion with the informed and philosophic Beaupuy—did not have to go to William Godwin's *Political Justice* to discover that war was evil, that the poor suffered in times of war as well as in peace, or that the British penal code needed reform. It is certain, moreover, that Wordsworth had no need of *Political Justice* to inform him on the condition of England. The bitterness of his indictment of English society suggests a personal animus rather than an attitude inspired and cultivated simply by a book. A study of *Guilt and Sorrow* in the light of what we know of Wordsworth's personal circumstances in 1793 discloses that most of the materials for the poem were mere extensions of his personal experience, that *Guilt and Sorrow*, like nearly everything else that Wordsworth wrote, was basically autobiographical.

The sufferings of the sailor, almost without exception, are exaggerations of those experienced by Wordsworth in 1793. The sailor was separated from his wife and children by war; so, too, was Wordsworth separated from Annette Vallon and his daughter by war. Even if Wordsworth had possessed the money necessary for a return to France, he could not have crossed the English Channel without exposing his life to grave danger. As matters stood, the war made even a successful correspondence between him and Annette impossible, their letters—most of them, at least—being seized by secret agents. Had it not been for the state of war existing between France and England, some sort of reunion between the two lovers would surely have been effected.

The circumstances in which the sailor found himself on Salisbury Plain and the events which befell him there are remarkably like those faced by Wordsworth. The sailor, for example, has a terrifying encounter with a dead criminal hanging on a gibbet: in the ninth stanza,

> as he plodded on, with sullen clang
> A sound of chains along the desert rang;
> He looked, and saw upon a gibbet high
> A human body that in irons swang,
> Uplifted by the tempest whirling by;
> And, hovering, round it often did a raven fly.

It is well known that this was a moment of melodrama which Wordsworth salvaged from his memories of childhood, and which he describes again in *The Prelude*, XI, 279–294. The sailor, moreover, was alone on Salisbury Plain, penniless, friendless, hungry, and—after he had committed murder—with no place to go. Wordsworth was in a similar situation after a capering horse had landed him and his traveling companion, William Calvert, in a ditch near Salisbury in the summer of 1793. Calvert rode off on the horse, leaving Wordsworth to shift for himself. Wordsworth can have had but very little money; he could expect nothing from his family; and his nearest friend, geographically speaking, was Robert Jones, miles away in the north of Wales. Wordsworth wandered about Salisbury Plain for two days and saw Stonehenge in that frame of mind which the bitterness of *Guilt and Sorrow* reflects. Where and how he spent his nights, how and where and what he ate during these and succeeding days which saw him into Wales on foot, we may never know, but it is very likely that the sailor's sufferings had a basis in Wordsworth's personal experience, and that the picture presented by the female vagrant—

> And homeless near a thousand homes I stood,
> And near a thousand tables pined, and wanted food—

was not entirely a figment of his imagination.[30]

Still more striking evidence of Wordsworth's use in *Guilt and Sorrow* of material from his own experience abounds in the narrative of the female vagrant. Let us read stanzas XXIII–XXV, where Wordsworth describes the early life and environment of the vagrant:

---

[30] There is of course an important difference between the experience of the sailor and that of Wordsworth. The misfortunes which befall the sailor result in his complete loss of self-control, and he commits murder. Wordsworth suffered similar catastrophes, but no such moral disintegration. I doubt, however, that the murder committed by the kind and gentle sailor was any more than the vicarious expression of Wordsworth's own desire. In the fits and seizures of self-pity which he must have experienced in 1793 Wordsworth probably slew his guardians, his brother Richard, and the Earl of Lonsdale many times. This is a point, however, which I have no wish to labor.

GUILT AND SORROW

My father was a good and pious man,
An honest man by honest parents bred,
And I believe that, soon as I began
To lisp, he made me kneel beside my bed,
And in his hearing there my prayers I said:
And afterwards, by my good father taught,
I read, and loved the books in which I read;
For books in every neighbouring house I sought,
And nothing to my mind a sweeter pleasure brought.

Can I forget what charms did once adorn
My garden, stored with pease, and mint, and thyme,
And rose and lilly for the sabbath morn?
The sabbath bells, and their delightful chime;
The gambols and wild freaks at shearing time;
My hen's rich nest through long grass scarce espied;
The cowslip-gathering at May's dewy prime;
The swans, that, when I sought the water-side,
From far to meet me came, spreading their snowy pride.

The staff I yet remember which upbore
The bending body of my active sire;
His seat beneath the honied sycamore
When the bees hummed, and chair by winter fire;
When market-morning came, the neat attire
With which, though bent on haste, myself I deck'd;
My watchful dog, whose starts of furious ire,
When stranger passed, so often I have check'd;
The red-breast known for years, which at my casement
      peck'd.

In 1842 Wordsworth changed the first lines of the first stanza to

> By Derwent's side my father dwelt—a man
> Of virtuous life, by pious parents bred,

and the first line of the second stanza to

> A little croft we owned—a plot of corn.

By so doing he rendered even more easily recognizable a description of the life and situation praised by him in *An Evening Walk* and *Descriptive Sketches* and actually enjoyed by Dorothy when she went to live with her Uncle William and his bride in 1788.

Teaching the children to pray was no doubt the common practice in English families of all classes. But the presence of books in the vagrant's cottage, the ability to read them, and the enthusiasm which caused her to seek out other volumes in neighboring houses, presuppose a degree of literacy surely extraordinary in an English peasant of the eighteenth century. Wordsworth almost certainly was describing here, not the intellectual opportunities and ambition of the average English maiden, but those of his precocious sister Dorothy.[31] The second and third stanzas, moreover, simply repeat details already stressed in Dorothy's letters to Jane Pollard and in *An Evening Walk* and *Descriptive Sketches,* and include a few floral and vegetable decorations which Wordsworth thought would render the picture more idyllic and attractive. The "croft" is taken from Dorothy's experience—there was a croft in Halifax where Dorothy and Jane Pollard had memorable adventures.[32] The swans, symbolic of domestic perfection, we remember from *An Evening Walk,* while we recognize the redbreast as one of the two or more redbreasts fortunate enough to partake of Dorothy's largesse and to have the run of her Uncle William's house in 1788. The vagrant's father, staying his aged steps upon a staff, sitting beneath a "honied sycamore" as the "bees hummed" about him, and occupying a "chair by winter fire," merely presents again that picture of mellow old age which Wordsworth cherished throughout his life and celebrated first in *Descriptive Sketches.* Even the antics of the vagrant's dog recall that conception of domestic bliss, denied to the young Wordsworths except in correspondence, dreams, and poetry, which William bodied forth in the earlier work. This gentle beast, like the active but benevolent dogs of Switzerland, barks but never bites. It is perhaps worth noticing that Wordsworth was at some pains in the delineation of the character of the vagrant's dog. In the harsher 1798 version of the stanza the

---

[31] I think there can be no other explanation than this one for the presence of these details in the vagrant's narrative, for it is unlikely that the sailor was keenly interested in the cultural background of his chance companion, or that the vagrant could have supposed that he would be so interested.

[32] See Dorothy's letter to Jane, May 23, 1791 (*The Early Letters,* p. 45).

GUILT AND SORROW

young girl had to check his "starts of furious ire." In 1842, however, the reader's natural concern for the ankles of the besieged wayfarer is relieved, for Wordsworth then specifies that the threats of the animal were mere sound and fury, signifying nothing:

> Our watchful house-dog, that would tease and tire
> The stranger till its barking-fit I checked.

But such domestic felicity as that temporarily enjoyed by the vagrant and her father could not be of long duration in corrupt, monarchical England. Their happiness and hope for the future were blasted by the avarice and tyranny of the man of property, who so controlled the courts of the land that he could perpetrate injustice according to his whim without danger of penalty or retaliation from any source. Even the most casual reader will here recognize a reflection of the injustice worked upon Wordsworth, his sister, and his brothers, by the tyrannical practices of the Earl of Lonsdale. And the lament in stanza XLVIII, "Poor Father! gone was every friend of thine," is almost identical with that voiced by Dorothy Wordsworth in 1787, when she and her brothers had learned that friends too often were of the fair-weather variety: ". . . amongst all those who visited at my father's house he had not one real friend."[33] Finally, the vagrant's experience, paralleling Wordsworth's once more, includes two separations from her lover and husband: the first one is temporary and brought about by financial necessity—her young man "to a distant town . . . repair[ed], to ply the artist's trade"; the second, which divorces her not only from her husband but from her children as well, is permanent and caused by the "calamities of war."[34]

---

[33] *Ibid.*, p. 7.

[34] It is probable, though of course not certain, that stanzas XXVIII and XXIX, in which Wordsworth describes the emotions of the separated lovers, reflect still further the influence of the affair with Annette Vallon:

> There was a youth whom I had loved so long,
> That when I loved him not I cannot say.
> 'Mid the green mountains many and many a song
> We two had sung, like little birds in May.
> When we began to tire of childish play

WORDSWORTH'S FORMATIVE YEARS
V

Guilt and Sorrow is not great art, although it compares favorably with many poems which the eighteenth century praised. Had Wordsworth in his old age chosen not to publish this creation of his revolutionary youth, his reputation would not therefore have suffered. Nevertheless it is a mistake to suppose that the only facts about *Guilt and Sorrow* of interest to the student of Wordsworth's technical progress are that he here used the Spenserian stanza—a medium better suited to his narrative purpose than the stiff heroic measure he had employed in *An Evening Walk* and *Descriptive Sketches*—and that the poem contains a few lines which might have been written by the Wordsworth of 1798. A study of the construction of *Guilt and Sorrow* contributes much to an understanding of the growth of Wordsworth's artistic power; and a search for the causes of the failure of the poem reveals the elementary problems of composition which Wordsworth had to solve before he could take his place among the great poets of the English tradition.

Professors Campbell and Mueschke are the only critics who have examined *Guilt and Sorrow* with the specific purpose of illuminating the development of Wordsworth's art. In their study of the poem as a document significant in the evolution of his aesthetic practice, they seek primarily to explain his inability to achieve complete success with *Guilt and Sorrow*. According to them, Wordsworth's efforts to create a

---

> We seemed still more and more to prize each other:
> We talked of marriage and our marriage day;
> And I in truth did love him like a brother,
> For never could I hope to meet with such another.
>
> His father said, that to a distant town
> He must repair, to ply the artist's trade.
> What tears of bitter grief till then unknown!
> What tender vows our last sad kiss delayed!
> To him we [the vagrant and her father] turned:—
>   we had no other aid.
> Like one revived, upon his neck I wept,
> And her whom he had loved in joy, he said
> He well could love in grief: his faith he kept;
> And in a quiet home once more my father slept.

GUILT AND SORROW

thoroughly effective poem were thwarted by his attempt to combine the aesthetic modes of sentimental morality and Gothic horror. The poem as a whole, in their opinion, was intended to arouse "that pity which is evoked by the contemplation of undeserved suffering. ... the reader is supposed to close the book, suffused with pity."[35] Wordsworth, however, attracted to the Gothic as well as to the sentimental mode, could not exclude the paraphernalia of horror popularized in England by poets of the "graveyard school" and by the writers of Gothic fiction; hence, the first twenty-one stanzas of the poem are full of those properties "habitually employed by the authors of Gothic Romance."[36] *Guilt and Sorrow*, consequently, is "weak because it is a piece of aesthetic patchwork, the product of two distinct and inharmonious artistic modes. ... a work utterly devoid of aesthetic unity."[37]

The critics are mistaken, it seems to me, in their belief that *Guilt and Sorrow* fails because it is "the product of two distinct and inharmonious artistic modes." It is true that sentimental morality and Gothic horror are both employed, and that the poem is a failure, but the connection between these two facts is not that of cause and effect. Indeed, we must question the assertion that these two aesthetic modes are intrinsically antipathetic, incapable of being harmoniously employed in a single work. They have been effectively combined in numerous poems, plays, and novels—Schiller's *The Robbers*, perhaps too much admired by Coleridge, is one example—and are related to one another in the melodramatic literature of the late eighteenth century much as pity and terror are related in Shakespeare's *The Tragedy of King Lear*. In particular is it true, I believe, that there was nothing incongruous or inept in Wordsworth's plan to fuse the two aesthetics in *Guilt and Sorrow*, although it must be granted that he left much to be desired in his execution of the plan.

Wordsworth's original intention in *Guilt and Sorrow* was to present arguments, and a narrative illustration of those

---
[35] "*Guilt and Sorrow* ... ," p. 298.
[36] *Ibid.*, p. 300.
[37] *Ibid.*, pp. 302-303.

arguments, with such effect that his appeal in the concluding stanza to the "Heroes of Truth" might be enthusiastically received and result in reformatory action. To achieve this end he sought to engage both the sympathy and the instinct for self-preservation of his reader; the best literary practice of the day assured him that the sentimental and Gothic modes were best calculated to bring success.

The manner in which Wordsworth endeavored to enlist the sympathies of his readers for the masses of oppressed Englishmen whom the various characters of the published *Guilt and Sorrow* represent, how he described the innumerable woes of the sailor and the female vagrant, the astonishing plight of the maltreated child, and the wretched death of the sailor's wife especially to evoke the emotion of pity, are effectively described by Professors Campbell and Mueschke.[38] But, owing to their lack of concern for the relationship of the poem to the *Letter to the Bishop of Llandaff*, these critics overlook one interesting and important source of effect in Wordsworth's use of the aesthetic of sentimental morality in *Guilt and Sorrow*.

Had Wordsworth published his poem in 1793, when the arguments of Richard Watson were still fresh in the minds of his readers, the effect of the poem must have been much greater than it was in 1842, or than it is today, when the "Great Chain of Being" is no more than an academic term. The sailor, the female vagrant, and the sailor's wife belong to the class of Watson's "peasants and mechanics." Before the inhumanity of British society and the ravages of war left their mark upon them they had been happy with their lot. And even in their sore distress, with their manifold woes, they do not clamor for the overthrow of the monarchy which has caused their pain. They remain ever true to the *status quo*. They do not question the ways of God with men, nor do they express any desire to usurp the places and the powers of the born legislators of the realm, although they know full well that on this earth little else than heartbreak and injustice can be expected from God and the aristocracy. They suffer

[38] *"Guilt and Sorrow . . . ," passim.*

GUILT AND SORROW

meekly the hardships and vicissitudes of the lowly, and patiently await the merciful death which is the first sign of the blissful life to come in the hereafter. The beatific integrity of the social and political hierarchy presupposed in the arguments of the Bishop of Llandaff—the strength of the Great Chain itself—is never endangered by any rebellious impulse in the sailor or the vagrant. The unfortunate woman has had occasion to question the efficacy of the method of meeting evil recommended by Watson and by scores of ecclesiastics before and after him—she has shed tears "for ills which patience could not heal"—but she plots no revolution. So steadfast is she, in fact, that she associates only briefly with the sympathetic gypsies who prey on a society which she has every reason to hate. And the sailor, despite the tragedies that have overtaken him, remains loyal to the teachings of the church and consoles the vagrant in her distress with "Proverbial words of comfort." After his single crime the wisdom of Watson's recommendation of uncomplaining submission to social injustice comes home to him with extra force; this we know from the humble words he addresses to the maltreated child in the fifty-sixth stanza of the poem:

> Yet happy thou, poor boy! compared with me,
> Suffering not doing ill—fate far more mild.[39]

It is this docility, this patience, this loyalty to the principles of the society which has so abused them—especially when these qualities are contrasted, as they are in *Guilt and Sorrow*, with the degeneracy and predatory inhumanity of the rich and noble, whose prerogative in the Great Chain these sufferers do not question—that render the characters of the sailor and the vagrant unusually pathetic, the picture of England doubly

---

[39] This is a curious anticipation of the philosophy expressed by Wordsworth in *The Borderers*, most notably in the well-known lines:

> Action is transitory—a step, a blow,
> The motion of a muscle—this way or that—
> 'Tis done, and in the after-vacancy
> We wonder at ourselves like men betrayed:
> Suffering is permanent, obscure and dark,
> And shares the nature of infinity.
>   (Act III, vv. 405–410)

incriminating, and the mode of sentimental morality unusually effective in *Guilt and Sorrow*.[40]

Wordsworth was not to be satisfied, however, with the mere evocation of pity in *Guilt and Sorrow,* and it must not be supposed that his artistic purpose in this poem was similar to that in *Peter Bell,* "The Thorn," or "The Complaint of a Forsaken Indian Woman," poems written later in accordance with a philosophy of composition not formulated in 1793. In *Guilt and Sorrow* Wordsworth was crying out for republican action of the French variety against the monarchical society of his native land. It was not enough, therefore, for him to soften his reader's heart with liberal applications of sentimental morality; this would have sufficed only if he had intended to promote merely the mild social virtues and domestic affections. But his chief desire was to arouse the champions of liberty, perhaps to create new ones, to fight for the rights of man. With this muscular purpose in mind, Wordsworth provided his poem with atmosphere and episodes characteristic of the Gothic school of terror; these were sup-

[40] Wordsworth's anticipation in *Guilt and Sorrow* of the formula exploited by twentieth-century writers of "proletarian literature" is remarkable. The latter, like Wordsworth before them, employ literature for purposes of revolutionary propaganda. They present good, kind, and deserving lower-class characters who are tormented by the economic and social dislocations peculiar to the society in which they are trapped. The circumstances and suffering of these maltreated people are portrayed with meticulous care for the edification of the reader whom the writer is attempting to sway. Invariably, the virtues of the submerged third are contrasted pointedly and invidiously with the vices of the degenerate upper class. The chief difference between the formula followed by Wordsworth in *Guilt and Sorrow* and that used by modern revolutionary writers concerns the attitude of the characters toward the correction of abuse. Wordsworth's creatures submit meekly to injustice, and wait for God to punish tyrants and reward the suffering in the life after death. This behavior in the 1790's was best calculated to win the sympathies of the reader for oppressed characters of the lower class. In the twentieth century, however, when the influence of the Church is on the wane, when the Great Chain of Being clanks only in graduate seminars and the dusty corners of college libraries, when men respect only those who shed blood in defense of their inalienable rights, Wordsworth's sailor and female vagrant would excite little admiration and less respect. "Proletarian" writers, as familiar with the climate of opinion and the springs of social action in their day as Wordsworth was in his, endow their characters with the revolutionary spark, cause them to spring exuberantly to platform or stage with a banner of ruddy hue and cry out with heroism and a curse their determination to cast off their chains.

posed to shock the reader's nervous system, stimulate the activity of the suprarenal glands of the "hero," and induce him to give free expression to his instinct for self-preservation.

That there was nothing inept in Wordsworth's plan to exploit both the sentimental and the Gothic modes in *Guilt and Sorrow* is established, I believe, by the comparative effectiveness of the first eighteen stanzas of the poem. The Gothic elements in these stanzas contribute much to the intensity of the sailor's situation. The description of the night, for example, which follows the account of the murder and the sailor's encounter with the gibbet and the hanged criminal in his clanking chains, provides an excellent and harmonious backdrop for the conflict of emotions raging within the sailor's tortured consciousness:

> Hurtle the clouds in deeper darkness piled,
> Gone is the raven timely rest to seek;
> He seemed the only creature in the wild
> On whom the elements their rage might wreak;
> Save that the bustard, of those regions bleak
> Shy tenant, seeing by the uncertain light
> A man there wandering, gave a mournful shriek,
> And half upon the ground, with strange affright,
> Forced hard against the wind a thick unwieldy flight.

Just here the unhappy sailor discovers Stonehenge and thinks it an "antique castle" where he can find shelter from the storm. But Stonehenge affords no rest or refuge:

> Within that fabric of mysterious form,
> Winds met in conflict, each by turns supreme;
> And, from the perilous ground dislodged, through storm
> And rain he wildered on, no moon to stream
> From gulf of parting clouds one friendly beam,
> Nor any friendly sound his footsteps led;
> Once did the lightning's faint disastrous gleam
> Disclose a naked guide-post's double head,
> Sight which tho' lost at once a gleam of pleasure shed.

Wordsworth's plan to use the paraphernalia of Gothic terror to render his account of the sailor more poignant breaks down in the eighteenth and nineteenth stanzas, not because of any weakness inherent in the aesthetic itself, but because Wordsworth momentarily forgot that terror, for his purpose, was the means to an end, and not the end itself. When the sailor and the vagrant have been brought together beneath the roof of a chapel "named the 'Dead House' of the plain," Wordsworth loses sight of his narrative purpose, reverts to the descriptive technique of his early poems—in which he leisurely recounted local legends associated with natural and man-made objects—and devotes a stanza to a preposterous tale of terror. The vagrant, it seems,

> Had heard of one who, forced from storms to shroud,
> Felt the loose walls of this decayed Retreat
> Rock to incessant neighings shrill and loud,
> While his horse pawed the floor with furious heat;
> Till on a stone, that sparkled to his feet,
> Struck, and still struck again, the troubled horse:
> The man half raised the stone with pain and sweat,
> Half raised, for well his arm might lose its force
> Disclosing the grim head of a late murdered corse.

Ostensibly, Wordsworth spins this ridiculous yarn to account for the vagrant's fear at the appearance of the sailor. Since, however, it is reasonable for any defenseless woman housed in a "lonely Spital" in the middle of a waste to feel uneasiness when she is awakened from an already troubled sleep by the sudden approach of a strange man in the middle of the night, Wordsworth was under no obligation to provide such an elaborate explanation for the vagrant's fright. The reader's concern for the sufferings of the sailor is temporarily relaxed; he is distracted by the gruesome detail, and—what is more important for the effectiveness of the poem as a whole—he has occasion to doubt the poet's sincerity, to suspect even that he is trifling with human emotions. This "grim head of a late murdered corse," in other words, is a gratuitous and unfortunate interruption of the poem's main line of narrative interest.

Later stanzas of the poem seem to confirm the suspicion that the chief cause of the failure of *Guilt and Sorrow* was Wordsworth's lack of narrative skill. There is a bad break in interest and in mood in the middle of the tale of the female vagrant. Just after she has informed us that her husband

and children were carried off by sword and plague "in one remorseless year," she is seized with a fit of weeping that delays the business of the poem for three stanzas. The sailor takes advantage of her momentary indisposition and moves to the portal of the ruin, where he discovers that there has been a marked change in the weather:

> the dawn opening the silvery east
> With rays of promise, north and southward sent;
> And soon with crimson fire kindled the firmament.

These lines alone suffice to destroy the mood and atmosphere of unrelieved gloom and despair which the earlier stanzas of the poem have effectively established, and when Wordsworth dedicates the next two stanzas to a delineation of the beauties of the morning and their cheerful effect upon the vagrant, there is little if anything left of the reader's conviction that all is for the worst in the worst of all possible worlds:

> "O come," he [the sailor] cried, "come, after weary night
> Of such rough storm, this happy change to view."
> So forth she came, and eastward looked; the sight
> Over her brow like dawn of gladness threw;
> Upon her cheek, to which its youthful hue
> Seemed to return, dried the last lingering tear,
> And from her grateful heart a fresh one drew:
> The whilst her comrade to her pensive cheer
> Tempered fit words of hope; and the lark warbled near.
>
> They looked and saw a lengthening road, and wain
> That rang down a bare slope not far remote:
> The barrows glistered bright with drops of rain,
> Whistled the waggoner with merry note,
> The cock far off sounded his clarion throat;
> But town, or farm, or hamlet, none they viewed,
> Only were told there stood a lonely cot
> A long mile thence . . . .

Fifteen stanzas further on, when the original tone of the poem has been somewhat restored by the completion of the vagrant's tale of woe, and when she has been once more reduced to tears, Wordsworth again destroys the effectiveness of his narrative by diverting the reader's attention to the charms of the countryside through which his characters are walking:

> Ere long, from heaps of turf, before their sight,
> Together smoking in the sun's slant beam,
> Rise various wreaths that into one unite
> Which high and higher mounts with silver gleam:
> Fair spectacle . . . .

The incident of the maltreated child serves to recall to mind Wordsworth's initial purpose of exposing the inhumanity manifest in English society, but the point of this episode is blunted in turn by Wordsworth's third lapse into the lazy descriptive vein of his early poems:

> Forthwith the pair passed on; and down they look
> Into a narrow valley's pleasant scene
> Where wreaths of vapour tracked a winding brook,
> That babbled on through groves and meadows green;
> A low-roofed house peeped out the trees between;
> The dripping groves resound with cheerful lays,
> And melancholy lowings intervene
> Of scattered herds, that in the meadow graze,
> Some amid lingering shade, some touched by the sun's rays.

These passages, pleasant enough in their own right, but offensive in *Guilt and Sorrow,* meet in all important respects the requirements of the eighteenth-century landscape school of poetry, to which Wordsworth paid homage in *An Evening Walk* and *Descriptive Sketches.* The wain and whistling wagoner, the cock with "clarion throat," the "lonely cot," Wordsworth's favorite "wreaths of vapour," the "winding brook" and "dripping groves," the meadow with its grazing herds—"some amid lingering shade, some touched by the sun's rays"—affording an opportunity for remarks upon light and shadow, all recall the early poems. Wordsworth's reversion in these passages to the cataloguing of agreeable rural sights and sounds shows clearly that one of the causes of his failure in *Guilt and Sorrow* was his lack of artistic control, his inability to keep materials of which he was fond out of a poem in which they were only incongruities. When he interrupts the vagrant's tale to comment upon the beauty of the rising sun, when he proceeds from the account of the maltreated child to a description of dripping groves and lowing herds, he forgets that he is writing political propaganda. Instead of plucking relentlessly and without interruption at the heartstrings of the reader, Wordsworth seems to lose interest in his characters; instead of continuing to bend the Gothic elements in nature to his purpose and to sustain the intensity of the early stanzas of the poem thereby, he suddenly takes an objective view of nature and slips inadvertently into the leisurely manner of the conventional landscape poet to give us another brief glimpse of that bucolic perfection which he adores, and which we are supposed to believe cannot exist in England so long as monarchy prospers.[41]

The unmistakable confusion in the ideational implications of the stanzas following upon the female vagrant's tale contributes perhaps as much to the weakness of *Guilt and Sorrow* as does Wordsworth's ineptitude as a writer of narrative. Little justification, for example, can be found for the episode of the maltreated child. Wordsworth was exposing in *Guilt and Sorrow* the "calamities of war" and the other evils incident to British monarchical society, but only the reader's imagination can provide the connection between this episode and British monarchy. No satisfactory motivation is provided for the brutality of the father. We are not told that he has gone to war; we are not aware that he has suffered at the hands of an acquisitive earl. For all we know, the unfortunate infant's head might as well have been bloodied by the lightnings of heaven as by his father's hand. We can draw certain inferences from the analogy with the sailor's crime, but a reader unsympathetic with the purpose of the poem might very well refuse to draw such inferences; he

---

[41] These obtrusive descriptive passages—as might be suspected from their close resemblance in substance and style to *An Evening Walk* and *Descriptive Sketches*—date from 1793 (see *The Poetical Works*, pp. 111-112, 118). Wordsworth apparently was aware a few years later that they detracted from the effectiveness of the poem, for he deleted them from the *Lyrical Ballads* version of "The Female Vagrant." In 1798 there was no sun to pierce the darkness of the vagrant's despair or to violate the aesthetic unity of her tale. But in 1842, when he decided at last to publish the entire *Guilt and Sorrow*, Wordsworth restored this evidence of his youthful ineptitude without significant alteration.

might conclude instead that Wordsworth, not monarchy, caused the father's arm to be raised against his son in wrath. The episode of the maltreated child, in short, suggests the possibility that some confusion existed in Wordsworth's mind between evils caused by society and those caused by the immutable nature of things as they are.

This possibility becomes a disturbing probability, if not indeed a certainty, when Wordsworth introduces the family of peasants whose hospitality the sailor and the vagrant enjoy on the beautiful sunlit morning after the storm. They own their own house, and the title to it is apparently clear: "I have a house that I can call my own," says the good wife, in the sixty-third stanza. What is more, they have abundant bread; the master carves it "lustily," and thereby reveals that he relishes his food and enjoys good health. They are prosperous enough to afford domestic help and thriving cattle, for a milkmaid appears "with her brimming pail." They are blessed with children who are intelligent, curious, and well brought up—after breakfast they gather properly round the knees of the sailor and play innocently with his oaken staff, behaving in the manner most approved by Wordsworth in poems both early and late. All these things suggest a degree of well-being difficult to understand in the light of our knowledge of the experiences of the sailor and the vagrant. The latter has told us that she encountered no one like these peasants, excepting of course the band of gypsies, in three years of wandering about the English countryside. If her story and that of the sailor accurately describe the lower classes in England, if the sorrows and suffering which they have endured are the rule and not the exception—and Wordsworth surely intended that we accept them as such—how is it that these particular peasants have escaped the "calamities of war" and the hard necessity which has driven others of their class to the numerous vices that result from monarchical government? How have they managed to do so well? Why have the evils of British society which Wordsworth attacks failed to ruin or disrupt their lives? Wordsworth answers none of these questions in *Guilt and Sorrow*, and the result is confusion. The

GUILT AND SORROW

reader's credulity is strained to the breaking point. The suspension of disbelief, become reluctant long before, is now unwilling, and the reader wonders if the misfortunes of the sailor and the female vagrant were not, after all, the "chastisements of Providence," rather than the inevitable fruits of monarchy. There is but one other choice left to the reader—he may suppose that the prosperous peasants of the house and bread and brimming pail were immigrants recently arrived in England from some canton of democratic Switzerland, or from the "fair favoured region" of the Loire!

Guilt and Sorrow, despite such glaring faults as these, is nevertheless a remarkable anticipation of the poetry Wordsworth was to write after the experience of a few more years. The revolutionary purpose and argument of the poem throw but scant light on his development, for, as we have seen, they represent little or no advance from the ground defended by the young radical in the later lines of *Descriptive Sketches* and in the *Letter to the Bishop of Llandaff*. But in *Guilt and Sorrow* Wordsworth for the first time created real characters drawn from the world he knew and permitted them to describe in their own words the experiences they had known and the emotions they had felt. These characters, anemic and faltering though they be, are a marked improvement upon the pathetic creatures of *An Evening Walk* and *Descriptive Sketches*. The soldier's widow and her two children of *An Evening Walk* and the Grison gypsy of *Descriptive Sketches*—Wordsworth's first portraits of fellow beings in distress—were conceived in the older style, as mute and static parts or adjuncts of the scenery he was describing. They do not speak for themselves, and their sufferings never seriously engage our sympathies. In *Guilt and Sorrow*, on the other hand, Wordsworth added point and effectiveness to his social criticism by creating real and recognizable victims of society to tell us of their misery in words ostensibly of their own choosing.[42] Particularly is this true of the second or 1795

---

[42] This is not to say that *Guilt and Sorrow* is completely free of that false diction against which Wordsworth was later to inveigh. For a study of the language of *Guilt and Sorrow* see Émile Legouis, "Some Remarks on the Com-

version of the poem, wherein Wordsworth—attempting to increase its dramatic power—stripped *Guilt and Sorrow* of the original expository introduction and conclusion and gave increased emphasis and attention to the personal history and psychology of the sailor. By so doing he revealed his rising interest in the subtleties of the individual personality, rid his poetry of much of the quiet monotony and flatness that had spoiled most eighteenth-century verse, and took a long step in the direction of *Lyrical Ballads*. We must not forget, after all, that Wordsworth, with the approval of Coleridge, considered the female vagrant and her narrative distinguished enough to be included in the epoch-making publication of 1798.

---

position of the *Lyrical Ballads* of 1798," *Wordsworth and Coleridge, Studies in Honor of George McLean Harper* (Princeton [New Jersey]: Princeton University Press, 1939), pp. 6-7.

CHAPTER V

The Borderers

I

A STUDY of *The Borderers*, the all but unintelligible blank-verse tragedy which Wordsworth wrote in 1796–97, must be prefaced by a repetition of the traditional account of Wordsworth's life at Racedown—where he is thought to have experienced a "moral crisis"—and by a review of two or three passages of verse that he wrote in the two-year interval which separated his work on the original *Guilt and Sorrow,* late in 1793, and his arrival at Racedown, in September, 1795. Until quite recently almost nothing was known of Wordsworth's literary activity in this important period of his early life, and biographers were compelled to search *The Prelude* for information that might help them to solve the difficult problems of interpretation presented by *The Borderers*. Since such information as they found was, as we shall see below, vague, contradictory, and misleading, the accounts of that period of Wordsworth's life and the interpretations of *The Borderers* based upon it were unavoidably confused. Fortunately, the indefatigable labors of Ernest de Selincourt have brought forth new evidence of Wordsworth's poetic efforts in the spring of 1794. This evidence enables us to correct the conventional and mistaken descriptions of his intellectual progress in the two years preceding his settlement at Racedown, and to establish a sounder basis than has been hitherto possible for an understanding of *The Borderers*, a work almost devoid of artistic merit but of the highest significance to the student of Wordsworth's philosophical development.

WORDSWORTH'S FORMATIVE YEARS

For decades critics have agreed that Wordsworth labored through this chapter of his life under the harmful influence of William Godwin's radical rationalism. This, together with his disappointment in the course of the French Revolution and the tormenting remorse which he is assumed to have suffered without interruption as a result of his desertion of Annette Vallon and their baby daughter, supposedly drove him almost mad, and plunged him into a hellish pit of despair from which he was extricated slowly and with some pain by the joint efforts of his sister Dorothy and his friend Samuel Taylor Coleridge. The various stages of this complicated rescue of a dedicated and potentially great poet from emotional, intellectual, and spiritual purgatory are three. Dorothy, when William was tossing in a fit of profound depression in the autumn of 1795, contributed her cheerful companionship and a keen sensitiveness to natural objects more delicate than those which William had been wont to contemplate.[1] Then Wordsworth, in 1795 and 1796, assisted his own recovery by composing *The Borderers,* a morbid tragedy that gave expression and timely relief not only to the vicious rationalism of Godwin, but also to remorse for Annette Vallon—that cruel and devastating emotion which, try as he might, Wordsworth could not keep from spoiling his art.

[1] Some critics have even suggested that Dorothy at this time introduced her brother to the beauties of nature and the subtle joys derived therefrom. But *An Evening Walk,* William's letter to Dorothy from Switzerland, and *Descriptive Sketches* afford abundant evidence to the effect that if either Dorothy or William had to be formally introduced to nature, it was William, the older brother, who performed the honors. George McLean Harper believes that Dorothy became conscious of natural objects only after the beginning of her life at Racedown: "When, for instance, did Dorothy Wordsworth acquire her habit of exactly noting what she saw out of doors? Surely, if she had been so interested in natural objects three years before, she would have expressed herself to Jane Pollard on this as on so many other subjects" (*William Wordsworth, His Life, Works, and Influence* [New York, 1929], p. 259). Dorothy of course did so express herself in numerous passages—many of them have been cited above—of her extensive correspondence with Jane Pollard. But Professor Harper is certainly correct when he asserts that William "opened to her a new world, the world of natural objects. 'An Evening Walk' and 'Descriptive Sketches' prove that he had obtained access to this realm without her assistance . . ." (*ibid.,* p. 260). But this world had been opened to Dorothy at Penrith, where *An Evening Walk* was inspired, many years before she went to Racedown.

THE BORDERERS

This act of composition, it is alleged, purged Wordsworth of the Godwinism which had been as a canker in the heart of his creative vitality. But in ridding himself of Godwinism, Wordsworth did harm as well as good. He was free of the evil influence, but he was now a poet without a philosophy, a writer with nothing to say. Finally, however, like a knight of old relieving virtue in distress, came Coleridge with a philosophy, aesthetic principles, and poetic aims, all of which he gladly placed, to their mutual benefit, at his new-found friend's disposal. Wordsworth's restoration was thus complete, and his gratitude was soon made manifest in an outburst of clear, full-throated song that was to work a revolution in English poetry.

George McLean Harper has thus far been the only critic to suggest that this engaging tradition of the "second moral crisis" has no basis in fact. His reading of the correspondence of William and Dorothy relevant to the period in question prompts him to express the unorthodox opinion that Wordsworth in 1795 and 1796—when his depression is usually supposed to have reached its greatest intensity—was in reality cheerful, industrious, and spiritually undisturbed. Of William's letters, Professor Harper writes:

> There is here no trace whatever of that mental depression, that clouding of his spiritual faculties, that moroseness, which we have been so often told worked a crisis in his life and particularly characterized the early months of his residence in Dorsetshire.... We see him more cheerful than he was a year before, in the north, and intellectually more active; we feel in what he writes to Wrangham and Mathews an abounding energy, and, above all, a tone of self-confidence.... The causes of his retirement, he gives it to be understood, are poverty and a wish to study.[2]

Nor is there anything in Dorothy's letters, Professor Harper continues, to contradict the impression given by William that all was well at Racedown; her effusions, on the contrary, paint "a charming and harmonious picture of domestic happiness."[3]

Anyone who reads the Wordsworth correspondence for the years 1795 and 1796 must agree with Professor Harper that it contains no evidence to support, and much to oppose,

---

[2] *Op. cit.*, pp. 215–216.   [3] *Ibid.*, p. 216.

the traditional belief that Wordsworth was despondent at Racedown. But the legend of the moral crisis and miraculous restoration is founded not upon the correspondence but upon Wordsworth's own rather plain-spoken allegations and confessions in *The Prelude*. To the detriment of his argument, Professor Harper makes no effort to account for these utterances. Consequently, his contention that the moral crisis is a myth studiously cultivated by sentimental biographers has become a lost cause, Ernest de Selincourt citing *The Prelude*, XI, 24–25, where Wordsworth refers presumably to the spring of 1796 and admits,

> I saw the Spring return, when I was dead
> To deeper hope, yet had I joy for her,

as " a complete answer to Harper's scepticism as to his mental depression at this time."[4] Professor de Selincourt, however, virtually ignores the implications of the Racedown letters when he asserts that they prove only that Wordsworth was capable of punctuating the long season of his discontent with sporadic moments of good cheer.[5] Clearly there is some confusion here concerning the validity and significance of evidence; and a reëxamination of the facts is necessary if we are to come nearer the truth about the Racedown "crisis."

On the face of it the evidence from which Professor Harper writes seems to carry more weight than that presented by Professor de Selincourt in his effort to support the traditional view at Professor Harper's expense. Some seventeen letters written by William and Dorothy at Racedown have been preserved; they cover the period extending from September 2, 1795, when Wordsworth's Godwinian narcosis is assumed to have been at its height, to June, 1797, when his recovery is thought to have been complete; they fill more than thirty pages of Professor de Selincourt's edition of the Wordsworth letters.[6] Professor de Selincourt grants that they prove that

---

[4] *The Prelude*, ed. by Ernest de Selincourt (Oxford, 1926), Notes, p. 591.
[5] *Ibid.*
[6] *The Early Letters of William and Dorothy Wordsworth (1787–1805)* (Oxford, 1935) (hereafter referred to as *The Early Letters*), pp. 136–169. See also de Selincourt's edition of *The Letters of William and Dorothy Wordsworth: The Later Years* (Oxford: At the Clarendon Press, 1939), III, 1332–1338.

THE BORDERERS

Wordsworth "could yet at times be cheerful,"[7] but insists upon the superiority of the *Prelude* verses as a source of authentic biographic truth. Surely, however, these letters in their bulk are a more reliable source of information concerning Wordsworth's state of mind in 1795–97 than two lines of blank verse written by Wordsworth in 1805, nine years after the experience they purport to describe. So far as we know, moreover, the letters have never been tampered with, whereas an investigation of the various texts of *The Prelude* reveals that the passages upon which Professor de Selincourt and other critics have based the tradition of Wordsworth's depression and recovery have been so extensively altered, qualified, and manipulated as to render them practically worthless as evidence.

The lines, for example, which Professor de Selincourt quotes in contradiction of Professor Harper's theory were deleted from the final version of *The Prelude*. In the text of 1850 Wordsworth no longer claimed that he had been "dead to deeper hope" in 1796, although he did repeat that the times had been "distracted" and that he had found a "counterpoise" in nature, "when the spirit of evil reached its height."[8] It is true that Wordsworth never made important changes in the following passage—indispensable to the traditional argument—where he attributes to himself a period of extreme pessimism concerning the wisdom of pondering social and moral problems:

> I too͜ ͜nife in hand
> And stopping not at parts ͜ sensitive,
> Endeavoured with my best of skill to probe
> The living body of society
> Even to the heart; I push'd without remorse
> My speculations forward; yea, set foot
> On Nature's holiest places. Time may come
> When some dramatic Story may afford
> Shapes livelier to convey to thee, my Friend,
> What then I learn'd, or think I learn'd, of truth,
> And the errors into which I was betray'd

---

[7] *The Prelude*, Notes, p. 591.
[8] See *The Prelude*, pp. 424, 425.

> By present objects, and by reasonings false
> From the beginning, inasmuch as drawn
> Out of a heart which had been turn'd aside
> From Nature by external accidents.
> And which was thus confounded more and more,
> Misguiding and misguided. Thus I fared,
> Dragging all passions, notions, shapes of faith,
> Like culprits to the bar, suspiciously
> Calling the mind to establish in plain day
> Her titles and her honours, now believing,
> Now disbelieving, endlessly perplex'd
> With impulse, motive, right and wrong, the ground
> Of moral obligation, what the rule
> And what the sanction, till, demanding *proof*,
> And seeking it in everything, I lost
> All feeling of conviction, and, in fine,
> Sick, wearied out with contrarieties,
> Yielded up moral questions in despair. (X, 873–901)

But the sensational lines that immediately follow in the final version, lines which his biographers, in their effort to prove that Racedown was an infirmary where Wordsworth was a none too promising patient, are especially fond of quoting—

> This was the crisis of that strong disease,
> This the soul's last and lowest ebb—

were an afterthought recorded only in later versions apparently for spectacular effect. Moreover, anyone familiar with Wordsworth's poetry will immediately question the accuracy of his assertion, made in 1805, that he "yielded up moral questions in despair." Never did Wordsworth give up moral questions. One of his major preoccupations throughout his life was the consideration of moral questions and the expression in poetry and prose of his moral speculations. And never, so far as I have been able to discover, was his interest in moral questions greater than at the very time when he claims to have dispelled them from his consciousness "in despair."

Finally, there is an extraordinary discrepancy between the 1805 passage of *The Prelude* in which Wordsworth describes the progress of his recovery from his crisis, and the version to which he gave his final approval. In 1805 Wordsworth at-

THE BORDERERS

tributed his restoration to Coleridge, Dorothy, and nature, in that order:

>   Ah! then it was
> That Thou, most precious Friend! about this time
> First known to me, didst lend a living help
> To regulate my Soul, and then it was
> That the belovèd Woman in whose sight
> Those days were pass'd, now speaking in a voice
> Of sudden admonition, like a brook
> That did but cross a lonely road, and now
> Seen, heard and felt, and caught at every turn,
> Companion never lost through many a league,
> Maintained for me a saving intercourse
> With my true self; for, though impair'd and chang'd
> Much, as it seemed, I was no further chang'd
> Than as a clouded, not a waning moon:
> She, in the midst of all, preserv'd me still
> A Poet, made me seek beneath that name
> My office upon earth, and nowhere else,
> And lastly, Nature's Self, by human love
> Assisted, through the weary labyrinth
> Conducted me again to open day,
> Revived the feelings of my earlier life,
> Gave me that strength and knowledge full of peace,
> Enlarged, and never more to be disturb'd,
> Which through the steps of our degeneracy,
> All degradation of this age, hath still
> Upheld me, and upholds me at this day
> In the catastrophe . . . .
> . . . . when finally, to close
> And rivet up the gains of France, a Pope
> Is summon'd in to crown an Emperor.   (X, 905–934)

In the later version of *The Prelude,* however, Wordsworth evidently had forgotten that his soul once stood in need of regulation by Coleridge's "living help," for there we find no indication that Wordsworth remembered his services. In the published text of the poem Wordsworth divides the credit for his regeneration between Dorothy and nature. Professor de Selincourt, in his notes to *The Prelude,* endeavors to account for this discrepancy by suggesting that the lines expressing gratitude to Coleridge were "omitted doubtless, from later texts because the influence of Coleridge succeeded and did not precede that of Dorothy."[9] This explanation, however, is somewhat less than adequate. If it occurred to Wordsworth only after 1805 that Coleridge's influence "succeeded and did not precede that of Dorothy," why did he not simply transpose the lines and give Coleridge his due after proper acknowledgments had been made to Dorothy and to nature?

It may be that Wordsworth in the fullness of his sympathy for Coleridge's suffering in 1804 and 1805, when most of *The Prelude*—a poem dedicated to Coleridge—was written, attributed to his friend a service which he had not performed, and that after further reflection he quietly corrected the mistake. It may have been, on the other hand, the break in the friendship between the two poets in later years that caused this curious deletion, despite the fact that many passages of high praise for Coleridge remain in the final version of *The Prelude*. But no matter what the cause may be, it is clear that Wordsworth was vague, contradictory, and, we may suppose, arbitrary in his later-day accounts of what happened at Racedown in 1795-97, and that the evidence of a crisis contained in the passages just examined has been tampered with and made subject to significant alteration. Such evidence, needless to say, is of highly dubious value.

The mere casting of doubt and suspicion upon the integrity of these passages from *The Prelude* does not, of course, prove conclusively that Wordsworth did not suffer from a "strong disease" at Racedown. Nor does it show that his description of this period of his life, of his recovery from the "crisis" and the regeneration of his creative ability, was false. But there is further evidence—some of it new, some of it old but neglected—that throws a clear light upon Wordsworth's state of mind in September, 1795, as well as upon the impressive intellectual progress he had made prior to his voluntary rustication. This evidence makes it reasonably certain that Wordsworth was not "sick" when he came to Racedown, that Coleridge did not provide him with a philosophy, aesthetic principles, or poetic aims, and that *The Prelude*, in its description of this period of Wordsworth's life, is, in important

[9] *The Prelude,* Notes, p. 588.

THE BORDERERS

places, a distorted and quite unreliable history, consisting more of romantic fiction than of autobiographic truth.[10]

In the opening passage of *The Prelude* Wordsworth vividly describes his impressions of the memorable day when, after long years of vexation and disappointment, he came to Racedown to live at last with Dorothy in that cottage which he had described in *An Evening Walk* as the "Sole bourn, sole wish, sole object of my way." H. W. Garrod has "proved beyond question," to use the words of Professor de Selincourt,[11] that these fifty-four lines of blank verse were written by Wordsworth in September, 1795, at the very time, that is, when his depression is supposed to have reached its most critical stage. Let us examine these lines and see what they reveal of disease and despair:

> Oh there is blessing in this gentle breeze
> That blows from the green fields and from the clouds
> And from the sky: it beats against my cheek,
> And seems half-conscious of the joy it gives.
> O welcome Messenger! O welcome Friend!
> A captive greets thee, coming from a house
> Of bondage, from yon City's walls set free,
> A prison where he hath been long immured.
> Now I am free, enfranchis'd and at large,
> May fix my habitation where I will.
> What dwelling shall receive me? In what Vale
> Shall be my harbour? Underneath what grove
> Shall I take up my home, and what sweet stream
> Shall with its murmur lull me to my rest?
> The earth is all before me: with a heart
> Joyous, nor scar'd at its own liberty,
> I look about, and should the guide I chuse
> Be nothing better than a wandering cloud,

---

[10] A detailed demonstration of the fallibility of *The Prelude* as a source for Wordsworth's biography—especially for the years following the return from France in 1793—is the subject of a further study now in progress. Suffice it to say here that in 1805, after living for seven or eight years with his mature social and political philosophy (described in the next chapter), Wordsworth found it impossible to regard with either accuracy or equanimity the three years immediately preceding his establishment at Racedown.

[11] *The Prelude*, p. xxxi. Professor de Selincourt remarks that there is evidence suggesting that the present form of all but vv. 1–19 of this passage, particularly of vv. 20, 40–48, was probably not decided upon until 1799 (*ibid.* [Library ed., 1928], p. 608 E). This evidence, however, is inconclusive.

> I cannot miss my way. I breathe again;
> Trances of thought and mountings of the mind
> Come fast upon me: it is shaken off,
> As by miraculous gift 'tis shaken off,
> That burthen of my own unnatural self,
> The heavy weight of many a weary day
> Not mine, and such as were not made for me.
> Long months of peace (if such bold word accord
> With any promises of human life),
> Long months of ease and undisturb'd delight
> Are mine in prospect; whither shall I turn
> By road or pathway or through open field,
> Or shall a twig or any floating thing
> Upon the river, point me out my course?
>   Enough that I am free; for months to come
> May dedicate myself to chosen tasks;
> May quit the tiresome sea and dwell on shore,
> If not a Settler on the soil, at least
> To drink wild water, and to pluck green herbs,
> And gather fruits fresh from their native bough.
> Nay more, if I may trust myself, this hour
> Hath brought a gift that consecrates my joy;
> For I, methought, while the sweet breath of Heaven
> Was blowing on my body, felt within
> A corresponding mild creative breeze,
> A vital breeze which travell'd gently on
> O'er things which it had made, and is become
> A tempest, a redundant energy
> Vexing its own creation. 'Tis a power
> That does not come unrecogniz'd, a storm,
> Which, breaking up a long-continued frost
> Brings with it vernal promises, the hope
> Of active days, of dignity and thought,
> Of prowess in an honorable field,
> Pure passions, virtue, knowledge, and delight,
> The holy life of music and of verse.   (I, 1–54)

There is not a line here to suggest that Wordsworth's spirit was bowed down beneath the crushing weight of Godwin's influence, remorse for Annette, or the knowledge that the French had forsaken the pure ideals of liberty, equality, and fraternity in favor of a policy of military aggression. On the contrary, Wordsworth—usually celebrated as the poet of joy—never again gave expression to more cheerful sentiments than

THE BORDERERS

those found in this passage of magnificent blank verse.[12] He is exultant over his escape from the dreary city and over the fortunate circumstances which have set him at liberty to pursue whatever course his fancy may choose. No longer must he answer to guardian uncles or worry about earning the necessities of existence. He is joyous and unafraid; the world is all before him. He looks forward with unreserved enthusiasm to the future, when those creative powers of which he knows himself to be possessed, and which he feels intuitively will soon mature, will elevate him to a position of eminence in the field of poetry and enable him to serve his fellow men as a purveyor of "Pure passions, virtue, knowledge, and delight." These lines, in short, make it difficult for us still to believe that Wordsworth was sick with despair when he arrived at Racedown.

Just as this passage subverts the tradition of the Racedown "crisis," so does it—along with eight pentameter lines composed the year before at Windy Brow—invalidate the belief that Coleridge provided Wordsworth with a philosophy and poetic aims, and that it was Dorothy's responsibility at Racedown to stimulate or restore in her brother a love for nature. The last lines of the passage are a clear though general statement of the goal toward which Wordsworth labored for the remainder of his life:

> Pure passions, virtue, knowledge, and delight,
> The holy life of music and of verse.

And surely his devotion to nature was never more eager, nor his response to her more acute, than here where, after his apostrophe to the gentle breeze that beats against his cheek, he announces with superabundant joy that he is free of the weary days of city life—free now

> To drink wild water, and to pluck green herbs,
> And gather fruits fresh from their native bough.

---

[12] This excellent passage was not the successful issue of Wordsworth's first attempt to write blank verse. For earlier and less felicitous examples of his work in this medium see *The Poetical Works of William Wordsworth: Poems Written in Youth, Poems Referring to the Period of Childhood*, ed. by Ernest de Selincourt (Oxford, 1940) (hereafter referred to as *The Poetical Works*), pp. 285, 286-287, 292-293.

WORDSWORTH'S FORMATIVE YEARS

As a promise of the poetry to flow from Wordsworth's pen in later years these introductory lines have profound significance. Here are manifest many of the salient features of his mature verse. Here, for the first time, we discover that deep personal intimacy, that close spiritual *rapprochement,* between poet and nature from which springs not only the most beautiful and philosophically potent of Wordsworth's lyrical poetry, but also much of the best verse written by his famous successors in the so-called "Romantic school." The objects of nature noted here by Wordsworth—the green fields, the sweet stream, and the wandering cloud—have little or no significance in themselves. They continue to have some decorative value, to be sure, but their primary importance lies in their reflection of the thought or emotion—or combination of the two—that momentarily inhabits the consciousness of the poet. Similarly, the poet's mood, feeling, or idea is not all-important in the sense that the self-centered idea or *pensée* of a Pope or a Johnson was important. Part of its value at least derives from its susceptibility of description in terms of nature—in terms, that is, which suggest to the reader the marvelously complicated, mutually interactive, and dynamic relationship existing between external nature and the mind of man. The emphasis of course is on the poet's individuality. Nature provides materials with which he may fashion lovely descriptions of his innermost feelings, perceptions, and aspirations, but it is the shaping power of the poet's mind alone that bestows high metaphysical significance upon the phenomena of nature thus employed. This idea, implicit in the lines under discussion, Wordsworth later expressed most explicitly and memorably in the following passages, the first from *The Recluse:*

>How exquisitely the individual Mind
>. . . . .
>. . . . . . to the external World
>Is fitted:—and how exquisitely, too—
>Theme this but little heard of among men—
>The external World is fitted to the Mind;

the second from "Tintern Abbey":

THE BORDERERS

> And I have felt
> A presence that disturbs me with the joy
> Of elevated thoughts; a sense sublime
> Of something far more deeply interfused,
> Whose dwelling is the light of setting suns,
> And the round ocean, and the living air,
> And the blue sky, and in the mind of man,
> A motion and a spirit, that impels
> All thinking things, all objects of all thought,
> And rolls through all things.

Moreover, when Wordsworth tells us that the "sweet breath of Heaven" stirs within his breast

> A corresponding mild creative breeze,
> A vital breeze which travell'd gently on
> O'er things which it had made, and is become
> A tempest, a redundant energy
> Vexing its own creation,

he reveals that he is already practicing that keen, critical introspection which enabled him a few years later, in the Prefaces to *Lyrical Ballads,* to make what is sometimes thought to be the most remarkable of his several important contributions to critical theory, namely, the detailed description of the process of poetic creation.[18] These lines, indeed, give us Wordsworth's first preliminary sketch of the dynamic interrelationship between the poet's mind and external nature in the progressive generation of the creative act. Wordsworth is fully aware of the central position occupied by this reciprocal interaction of mental and external forces in the creative process. He knows also that he himself possesses in abundance the vital power produced by the harmonious interplay of these potent forces. At this early date, however, he is perplexed by the irrepressible surge of his own creative energy. Already certain of the power, Wordsworth is confident that time will bring the artistic check which he lacks;

---

[18] For a more complete account of Wordsworth's description of the creative process and of its significance in the history of criticism than would be appropriate here see O. J. Campbell and Paul Mueschke, "Wordsworth's Aesthetic Development, 1795–1802," *Essays and Studies in English and Comparative Literature,* University of Michigan Publications in Language and Literature, Vol. X (Ann Arbor, 1933), 40–57.

his success, three years later, in *Lyrical Ballads* proved that his confidence was not misplaced.

Since these introductory lines of *The Prelude* were written by Wordsworth before he had lived with Dorothy long enough for her to minister to his mind diseased and before Coleridge could have been more to him than an attractive name,[14] it seems obvious that the conventional account of Wordsworth's state of mind and of his intellectual and artistic equipment when he arrived at Racedown in 1795 is mistaken. If my reading of these lines is sound, it is clear that Wordsworth's spirits were high; that he had already formulated the general artistic objectives for which he strove throughout the rest of his life; that he was already conscious of that mystical and metaphysical interrelationship of his mind and external nature which was at once a consolation to him in moments of stress, the basis of his mature philosophy, and the strength and glory of his finest work; that he was about to articulate that theory of the creative process which yielded him a prominent position in the history of criticism; and that he was capable in 1795 of composing blank verse that compares favorably with any poetry he ever wrote.

But these verses, remarkable as they are, do not enable us to appreciate the full extent of the philosophical progress Wordsworth had made in the two years immediately following his work on the first version of *Guilt and Sorrow*. The Racedown soliloquy, after all, was an impassioned lyrical outburst inspired by Wordsworth's exhilaration over the opportunity to settle in the country, rent-free, with Dorothy. His joy at seeing his fondest dream about to come true quite naturally drove from his mind various impersonal metaphysical considerations to which he had recently given close attention. Consequently, the soliloquy cannot be regarded as a complete index to Wordsworth's ideas in 1795, and supplementary evidence must be reviewed before an accurate estimate of his intellectual position in this crucial year is possible.

[14] Wordsworth and Coleridge met for the first time "in the autumn of 1795" (see de Selincourt, *The Early Letters*, p. 149 n.).

THE BORDERERS

Such supplementary evidence, unfortunately denied to earlier critics, is now available in the form of eight highly revealing lines which Wordsworth wrote at Windy Brow in 1794. Ernest de Selincourt, who discovered this valuable passage and published it for the first time in 1936, informs us that Wordsworth intended it as an addition to *An Evening Walk.* "To the description of Rydal Falls," Professor de Selincourt continues,

he now added the reference to Horace's *Fons Bandusia*, which he had just translated, and after the passage, printed in 1842, which deprecates the sacrifice of an innocent kid,—such lovely scenes, he avers, should be approached with

> a mind that in a calm angelic mood
> of happy wisdom meditating love,—

the manuscript goes on:

> A heart that vibrates, evermore awake
> To feeling for all forms that life can take,
> That wider still its sympathy extends
> And sees not any line where being ends,
> Sees sense through Nature's rudest forms betrayed,
> Tremble obscure in fountain, rock, and shade,
> And while a secret power those forms endears
> Their social accents never vainly hears.[15]

Professor de Selincourt would seem to underestimate the significance of this passage when he remarks, "Here is a germ of the faith that was to inspire the *Lines written in early Spring* and *Hartleap Well*,"[16] for these verses contain as much of Wordsworth's mature philosophy of nature as could be intelligibly compressed within the narrow limits of eight lines. In this passage, written long before his alleged "repudiation" of William Godwin's radical rationalism, before the Racedown influence of Dorothy and Coleridge, and before the period in which he is thought to have discovered the associationistic psychology of David Hartley,[17] Wordsworth re-

---

[15] *The Early Wordsworth*, Presidential Address to the English Association (Oxford, 1936), pp. 20–21. See also *The Poetical Works*, p. 10.

[16] *The Early Wordsworth*, p. 21.

[17] The "heart that vibrates, evermore awake . . ." clearly anticipates the well-known stanzas of "Expostulation and Reply" which are of great importance to Professor Beatty's argument that Wordsworth, probably under the

167

veals himself in full possession and control of the ideas which are basic to *Lyrical Ballads* and the remainder of his best work. As early as 1794, in other words, Wordsworth was aware of the transcendent value of feeling, of the *beneficent* intricacies of the Chain of Being, of the presence of an essential spirit pervading all reality and making it dynamic, and of the necessity for respecting all the multifarious shapes and forms of nature, however trivial they might seem to be, because of their power to stimulate the social virtues.[18]

Wordsworth accomplished in these verses, moreover, what

influence of Coleridge, was a faithful exponent of Hartley's physiological sensationalistic psychology (Arthur Beatty, *William Wordsworth: His Doctrine and Art in Their Historical Relations*, University of Wisconsin Studies in Language and Literature, No. 24 [Madison, 1927], pp. 125, 136, 211-213):

> The eye it cannot chuse but see,
> We cannot bid the ear be still;
> Our bodies feel, where'er they be,
> Against, or with our will.
>
> Nor less I deem that there are powers,
> Which of themselves our minds impress,
> That we can feed this mind of ours,
> In a wise passiveness.

It seems apparent, therefore, that Coleridge, to whom Professor Beatty has given the credit for stimulating Wordsworth's interest in Hartley sometime between 1795 and 1798 (*op. cit.*, pp. 98-99), was much less influential than has been supposed.

[18] Joseph Warren Beach in his essay "Wordsworth and Nature's Teaching" (in *The Concept of Nature in Nineteenth-Century English Poetry* [New York, 1936], pp. 158-201), suggests that Wordsworth's mature nature philosophy was composed of some eight basic concepts. These include optimistic "Necessarianism"; the idea that virtue and benevolence are natural to man; the notion that there is in nature evidence of a design of such incomparable merit that its origin in divine wisdom cannot be questioned; the closely related ideas that nature is made up of "a graduated scale of beings descending from the highest of celestial creatures down through man and the lower animal and vegetable worlds" (p. 172), that nature is pervaded by "an active principle," that nature is universally harmonious and consequently teaches a lesson of love, that nature develops the character of man through pleasure and joy, and that the natural order of things may and should be regarded by man as a norm of conduct. Professor Beach, following the well-worn path of the biographers, is inclined to date the beginning of Wordsworth's acquaintance with these ideas at least as late as 1795, when his friendship with Samuel Taylor Coleridge began. There is scarcely one of these concepts, however, which is not present, by implication at least, in the lines written by Wordsworth at Windy Brow in 1794.

THE BORDERERS

he had tried but failed to achieve in *Descriptive Sketches* and *Guilt and Sorrow*—the fusion of his love for nature with his concept of social harmony and order. This success was easy, however, for Wordsworth was here content with a purely abstract and impersonal enunciation of general philosophic truth, whereas in the earlier poems he had attempted the more difficult task of translating his as yet imperfectly formed philosophy of nature and society into the concrete terms of human emotion. His achievement of the following year in the Racedown soliloquy was the more remarkable because he therein gave magnificent utterance to his most personal perceptions and emotions. The Racedown lines, on the other hand, are lacking in social significance; we search them in vain for any suggestion of Wordsworth's characteristic concern for the state of society. Thus, both the Windy Brow and the Racedown passages, if taken singly, represent only limited expressions of the creative personality which Wordsworth had developed before the autumn of 1795. Only when Wordsworth learned to consolidate in a single artistic unit the salient features of these two precocious performances, only when he could combine harmoniously his philosophy of nature with his deep social sympathy—only then did he rise to his full stature as a poet. Needless to say, he did not learn to effect such a comprehensive synthesis overnight. Before he could write such a poem as "Tintern Abbey" it was necessary for him to focus his attention on the psychology of the individual and the problem of the individual in society. We have already seen him turning in this direction in the 1795 version of *Guilt and Sorrow*, particularly in his consideration of the character and crime of the unfortunate sailor.[19] But

---

[19] Another of the proposed additions to *An Evening Walk* which Wordsworth wrote at Windy Brow reveals that his interest in psychology—an interest that became increasingly significant in his poetry after 1795—was firmly established in 1794. This passage, first published in 1940 by de Selincourt (*The Poetical Works*, pp. 12-13), follows lines in which Wordsworth announces his amazement that there are "souls whose languid powers unite No interest to each rural sound or sight":

> How different with those favoured souls who, taught
> By active Fancy or by patient Thought,
> See common forms prolong the endless chain

the most revealing record of Wordsworth's early explorations in this broad field of speculation is set down in *The Borderers,* which we may now study with the reassuring knowledge that it was written by a Wordsworth whose mind had not been noticeably wasted by disease.

II

The Borderers is usually regarded as the unhappy excrescence of Wordsworth's legendary Racedown despair, the anguished crying out in the night of a young poet made morbid by the discovery that he had arrived at an intellectual and spiritual dead end. Some critics, indeed, have ventured so far as to suggest that *The Borderers,* because of the perverse sentiments therein expressed, is a dangerous and subversive work. Swinburne, for example, remarked in 1886 that the tragedy was "unparalleled by any serious production of the human intellect for morbid and monstrous extravagance of horrible impossibility"; and then, remembering a great general truth uttered by a French critic, exclaimed ungraciously and, for Swinburne, somewhat inappropriately: "Il n'y a que les poëtes vertueux pour avoir de ces idées-là."[20] And more

---

>   Of joy and grief, of pleasure and of pain;
>   But chiefly those to whom the harmonious doors
>   Of Science have unbarred celestial stores,
>   To whom a burning energy has given
>   That other eye which darts thro' earth and heaven,
>   Roams through all space and [ ] unconfined,
>   Explores the illimitable tracts of mind,
>   And piercing the profound of time can see
>   Whatever man has been and man can be,
>   From him the local tenant of the shade
>   To man by all the elements obeyed.
>   With them the sense no trivial object knows,
>   Oft at its meanest touch their spirit glows,
>   And proud beyond all limits to aspire
>   Mounts through the fields of thought on wings of fire.

This passage is of unusual significance, not only because it shows that Wordsworth had found in "Science" an additional prop for his optimism, but also because it provides further evidence for the conjecture, suggested above (note 17), that Wordsworth had made the acquaintance of David Hartley's psychology long before he met Coleridge. The first four and the last four lines of this passage are particularly good Hartley.

[20] *Miscellanies* (London: Chatto and Windus, 1886), p. 119.

THE BORDERERS

recently so acute a critic as H. W. Garrod has been disturbed by the immorality of the conception, which he supposes Wordsworth set forth in *The Borderers*, that " 'sin and crime are apt to spring from their very opposite qualities,' and that, a crime once committed, 'there are no limits to the hardening of the heart.' "[21] Ernest de Selincourt has shown that Professor Garrod completely misunderstands Wordsworth's intentions;[22] this study shows that Swinburne's criticism was similarly based on an inaccurate reading of the play and that *The Borderers* is in reality a composition whose ethical import is unimpeachable.

Here is a brief account of what happens in *The Borderers*. In the first scene we are introduced to Marmaduke, the hero of the play and the leader of a band of philanthropic outlaws who protect the innocent along the lawless Scottish border in the reign of Henry III. Marmaduke loves Idonea, the daughter of Herbert, a blind baron whose lands and titles have been usurped during his absence in Palestine. Oswald, a new member of Marmaduke's gang and the villain of the play, persuades Marmaduke that Herbert is an impostor who plans to sell the beauteous Idonea to the Baron Clifford, a neighborhood lecher, in exchange for landed wealth. To accomplish his purpose of leading Marmaduke into crime, Oswald bribes a beggar woman to confess that Idonea is her daughter, purchased from her by the pretending Herbert. Marmaduke, whose appetite for justice is constantly whetted by Oswald's subtle innuendoes, determines to destroy Idonea's would-be betrayer. He and Oswald take Herbert into custody and lead him to the dungeon of a ruined castle where they plan to execute him. At the crucial moment, however, Marmaduke is unable to deliver the murderous blow. Instead, he abandons the old man in the middle of a bleak and barren moor, believing that Providence will deliver him if he is guiltless.

Oswald, thinking Herbert dead, admits the old man's inno-

---

[21] *Wordsworth: Lectures and Essays* (Oxford, 1923), p. 92.

[22] "Wordsworth's Preface to *The Borderers*," *Oxford Lectures on Poetry* (Oxford, 1934), pp. 172-173.

cence and explains why he has conspired to make Marmaduke a murderer. Years ago, it appears, Oswald himself had been the dupe of villainous circumstance and had caused the death of the innocent father of his betrothed. Though stricken temporarily by remorse, Oswald soon perceived that his crime had wrought his intellectual liberation and had elevated him to Olympian heights of rationalism whence he could see that independent reasoning, rather than conventional morality—based as it is upon weakness and emotion—constituted the only valid foundation for distinctions between right and wrong. This unusual experience has provided Oswald with a double motive for inducing Marmaduke to commit a similar crime. First of all, he has seen in Marmaduke the image of his former self and has foolishly hoped that by making Marmaduke his equal in crime he, Oswald, might somehow regain qualities which he formerly possessed. But his more compelling motive—the opposite of the first—was his desire to achieve equality with Marmaduke, who, at a time prior to the action of the play, had saved Oswald's life and thus placed him in the repulsive position of a debtor. Oswald now believes that he has more than squared the account by enabling Marmaduke to strike the fetters of custom and emotion from his powers of pure reason. Henceforth he and Marmaduke will be "coupled by a chain of adamant" and will become "fellow-labourers . . . to enlarge Man's intellectual empire."[23]

[23] Professor de Selincourt, in his analysis of Oswald's motives, seems to overlook the passage (Act IV, vv. 210–221) in which Wordsworth describes them most clearly. According to de Selincourt, Oswald is cast in the image of Shakespeare's Iago: "Oswald's real motives, like Iago's, are hatred of the good, lust for power, a loathing engendered by envy that one whom he feels to be his intellectual inferior holds a higher place in the world's esteem than he; like Iago, he bolsters himself up with a philosophy of his own, of which the main features are a cynical contempt for all human feeling and for the claims of conventional morality; like Iago, he uses as his tool a woman who is ignorant of the terrible part she is playing in the tragedy; and as in *Othello*, the woman so employed is the main agent in his final discomfiture. . . . Wordsworth is really more interested in Oswald's philosophy than in Oswald; at one time intent on his philosophy, at another on his character, he has not the dramatic skill to fuse the two, and as a consequence we are left uncertain how far Oswald really accepts his philosophy himself, and how far he is actuated by motives diametrically opposed to it" ("Wordsworth's Preface to *The Borderers*," p. 174).

There can be no doubt that Wordsworth had his eye firmly fixed on

THE BORDERERS

Thus informed of Oswald's treachery, Marmaduke rushes out upon the moor in a futile attempt to rescue Herbert, whose lifeless body has already been recovered by Idonea and taken to the cottage of Eldred, a peasant. Here *The Borderers* ends in a frenzy of confession and catharsis: Marmaduke informs Idonea of his part in the tragedy; the female beggar pleads for forgiveness and clears up one or two points of the plot that have remained obscure; Idonea swoons and is carried off the stage; Oswald invites Marmaduke to accompany him to Palestine—which he calls a fertile field for "enterprise"—and is rebuked by Marmaduke and stabbed to death by Wallace, Marmaduke's trusted lieutenant, for his pains. Marmaduke, after instructing his men to erect a monument that will record his tragic history, takes the following penitential vows:

> a wanderer *must I* go,
> The Spectre of that innocent Man, my guide.
> No human ear shall ever hear me speak;
> No human dwelling ever give me food,
> Or sleep, or rest: but, over waste and wild,
> In search of nothing, that this earth can give,
> But expiation, will I wander on—
> A Man by pain and thought compelled to live,
> Yet loathing life—till anger is appeased
> In Heaven, and Mercy gives me leave to die.[24]

Othello when he wrote *The Borderers*, or that there is an unusual resemblance between Oswald and Iago, but this resemblance is probably more apparent than real. Iago is consistently villainous. He strives to destroy Othello from purely personal motives. There is nothing constructive in Iago. Like Richard III, his Machiavellian prototype, he is merely "determined to prove a villain." Oswald, too, is driven by personal, selfish desire to achieve a kind of perverse moral superiority over Marmaduke. His pride drives him to this. But Oswald has a nobler motive. He has a sincere interest in what he calls "Man's intellectual empire." These two motives are admittedly irreconcilable; it does not follow, however, that Wordsworth's presentation of Oswald's character is confused. I suggest that Wordsworth deliberately split Oswald's personality, cursed him with ambivalence, and kept him in constant struggle with himself the better to portray the evil consequences of following the dictates of that secondary power called "reason."

[24] Act V, vv. 2312–2321. Unless otherwise indicated, this study of *The Borderers*, like that of *Guilt and Sorrow* in the previous chapter, and for the same reasons, is based upon the text which Wordsworth approved for publication in 1842. This text differs in minor details from the earlier versions of the play, but it represents, as Wordsworth stated in 1842, "not the slightest alteration . . . in the conduct of the story, or the composition of the charac-

WORDSWORTH'S FORMATIVE YEARS

The chief interest of *The Borderers* is undoubtedly philosophical, but the precise meaning and philosophical significance of the play unfortunately have not thus far been satisfactorily described by any of Wordsworth's critics and biographers. All of them save Professor Harper, who does not comment upon the importance of the play in the evolution of Wordsworth's poetic and philosophical powers, admit that *The Borderers* somehow throws much light upon its author's development, but there is virtually no agreement concerning the nature and the extent of this illumination. There are, in fact, almost as many divergent interpretations of the tragedy as there are interpreters. All the critics join, it is true, in the suspicion that somewhere within the play's five acts lurks evidence that is important to an understanding of Wordsworth's relationship to the radical philosophy of William Godwin, but they part company in their endeavors to discover and interpret the significance of this evidence. Legouis, Campbell, Mueschke, and de Selincourt, for example, are certain that *The Borderers* expresses Wordsworth's repudiation of Godwin's philosophy, but Garrod insists that Wordsworth's Godwinism is here at its height. Legouis and de Selincourt, moreover, contend that although Wordsworth was at last convinced of the worthlessness of Godwinism as a practical philosophy when he composed *The Borderers,* he possessed at that time no program or set of beliefs, no convictions or formulated view of life, to substitute in its place. Garrod, while differing with these two writers in regard to Wordsworth's allegiance to Godwin at this stage of his development, goes along with them in the belief that Wordsworth had not yet worked out, or even begun to form, that philosophy which he would express in *Lyrical Ballads.* As we have seen already, Godwinism, in Garrod's judgment, was an immoral and indecent influence of which Wordsworth had to purge himself before he could sing his healthy song of joy in "Tintern Abbey." Campbell and Mueschke, on the other

ters . . . ." For the history of the text of *The Borderers* see de Selincourt in *The Poetical Works,* Notes, pp. 343–344.

hand, concede that Wordsworth renounces Godwinism in *The Borderers,* but suggest that the tragedy is important for growth as well as decay. Theirs is a complicated and ingenious theory that Wordsworth had adopted Godwin's rationalism deliberately in a frantic effort to stifle his feeling of remorse for the abandonment of Annette Vallon. Then, while composing *The Borderers,* Wordsworth was pulled one way by reason, another way by emotion. To the great good fortune of English poetry, emotion triumphed and was immediately elevated, by way of reward for victory earned, to a position of prominence among the materials with which Wordsworth made his later poetry. To Campbell and Mueschke, in other words, the tragedy is a record of that important moment when Wordsworth turned his back upon the bleak rationalism of the later eighteenth century to expose himself and his poetry to the meridian rays of romantic emotion. According to this view, the tragedy is significant not only for what it rejects, but also for what it reveals and affirms.[25]

This study of *The Borderers* shows that these interpretations are inexact. Rather than constituting a repudiation of William Godwin's philosophy, *The Borderers* represents an unmistakable affirmation of some of Godwin's most prominent ideas. Rather than being an expression of the pessimism which Wordsworth supposedly cultivated at Racedown and later rejected, *The Borderers* is actually a presentation of ideas optimistic in their implications. Instead of forming the inauspicious conclusion to an abortive chapter of Wordsworth's youth, *The Borderers* is a document of extraordinary positive significance in the progressive development of Wordsworth's thought. The play reveals that Wordsworth's faith in the natural goodness of man is stronger than ever and that

---

[25] For the various discussions of *The Borderers* referred to here see O. J. Campbell and P. Mueschke, "*The Borderers* as a Document in the History of Wordsworth's Aesthetic Development," *Modern Philology,* XXIII (1926), 465–482; de Selincourt, "Wordsworth's Preface to *The Borderers,*" pp. 157–179; H. W. Garrod, *op. cit.,* pp. 90–93; and Émile Legouis, *The Early Life of William Wordsworth, 1770–1798,* tr. by J. W. Matthews (New York, 1918), pp. 269–278.

his hope for the future now rests, not upon a vague and perhaps ill-founded confidence in the political panaceas of French republicanism, but—as we might expect from our knowledge of the Windy Brow verses—upon a new philosophy of nature and a new theory of human psychology, both of which Wordsworth later employed successfully in *Lyrical Ballads* and subsequent poems.

The generally accepted belief that Wordsworth formally rejected the influence of Godwin's philosophy of radical rationalism in *The Borderers* is based upon miscellaneous evidence. First of all, there is the theory, discussed above, that Wordsworth suffered from a "strong disease" contracted from his reading of Godwin's *Political Justice*. This disease could not be cured without the removal of its cause; and since Wordsworth recovered from the disease, it is urged that he must first have rejected Godwinism. Then there is a letter Wordsworth wrote to William Mathews on March 21, 1796, in which he made the following remarks about *Political Justice:*

I have received from Montagu, Godwyn's second edition. I expect to find the work much improved. I cannot say that I have been encouraged in this hope by the perusal of the second preface, which is all I have yet looked into. Such a piece of barbarous writing I have not often seen. It contains scarce one sentence decently written. I am surprised to find such gross faults in a writer, who has had so much practice in composition.[26]

J. R. MacGillivray's observation that "This is not the language of devotion"[27] expresses the view of those critics who regard this adverse comment as proof that Wordsworth had cast off the spell of Godwin's fallacious arguments. Finally, the perverse rationalism consistently expressed by Oswald, the villain of *The Borderers,* seems to be echoed in passages in *The Prelude* which critics believe to be descriptive of Wordsworth's understanding of Godwin's ideas. The *Prelude* passages ridicule the philosophy they express; Oswald, the exponent of Godwinism is a villain, and is destroyed for

---

[26] *The Early Letters,* p. 156.
[27] "The Date of Composition of *The Borderers,*" *Modern Language Notes,* XLIX (1934), 110.

THE BORDERERS

his villainy in the last act of the play; hence, the critics contend, it is clear that *The Borderers* represents Wordsworth's repudiation of Godwinism.

All but the last of these three arguments may be quickly disposed of. We have seen already what *The Borderers* bears out still further—that the moral crisis which Wordsworth claimed to have experienced at Racedown had no real existence outside the pages of *The Prelude*. Obviously, then, since he had no moral crisis caused by Godwinism from which to recover, it was unnecessary for him to repudiate Godwinism to regain a moral composure he had never lost. Close scrutiny of the letter to Mathews reveals, moreover, that it is almost worthless as evidence of Wordsworth's regard for Godwin's philosophy. He informs Mathews that he has read no more than the "second preface" of the second edition; his comments are confined to the weaknesses of Godwin's literary style, not of his thought. So far as we can tell from this letter, it was Godwin's sentences rather than his syllogisms with which Wordsworth found fault. His hope to find *Political Justice* "much improved," his possession of the second edition within a few weeks of its publication, and his disappointment with the composition of the preface prove, if anything, that Wordsworth's interest in Godwin's work was unusually keen. Certainly there is nothing in the letter to Mathews to indicate that Wordsworth already had repudiated whatever influence Godwin was exerting upon him.

There remain to be considered the various passages in *The Borderers* that are believed to represent simultaneously Wordsworth's expression and repudiation of Godwinism. All of these passages slip from the tongue of the supersubtle Oswald, who is supposed to be Wordsworth's portrayal of the pure exponent of the radical rationalism set forth by William Godwin in *Political Justice*.

Oswald reveals, at the beginning of the second act, that he has ceased to be perplexed by the traditional rivalry of reason and emotion. He has cast his lot with reason, and holds those who feel in high contempt. "These fools of feeling," he muses,

>   are mere birds of winter
> That haunt some barren island of the north,
> Where, if a famishing man stretch forth his hand,
> They think it is to feed them.[28]

Feeling, he is convinced, is worthless, save to frustrate justice, but fortunately—in Oswald's opinion—he, Marmaduke, and the outlaw band

>   rank not . . .
> With those who take the spirit of their rule
> From that soft class of devotees who feel
> Reverence for life so deeply, that they spare
> The verminous brood, and cherish what they spare
> While feeding on their bodies.[29]

Most fortunate are they, he says,

> Who live in these disputed tracts, that own
> No law but what each man makes for himself;
> Here justice has indeed a field of triumph.[30]

But Oswald has occasion a little later on to doubt whether Marmaduke and his companions are not after all to be numbered among the "fools of feeling." Marmaduke hesitates to destroy Herbert for the heinous crime which Oswald insists he is about to commit; Lacy's lust for vengeance on the criminal diminishes when he learns that Herbert is blind; and Oswald, fearful lest weak emotion interfere with abstract reason's execution of justice, delivers an impassioned utterance upon the theme:

>   Are we Men,
> Or own we baby Spirits? Genuine courage
> Is not an accidental quality,
> A thing dependent for its casual birth
> On opposition and impediment.
> Wisdom, if Justice speak the word, beats down
> The giant's strength; and, at the voice of Justice,

---

[28] *The Borderers*, Act II, vv. 8-11.

[29] *Ibid.*, vv. 33-38. This passage, added in 1842, helps to confirm Wordsworth's statement that in his revision of the play he made "not the slightest alteration . . . in the . . . composition of the characters . . . ." This and the other additions and changes made in 1842 merely clarify points of character and plot that were somewhat obscure in the earlier versions of the play.

[30] *Ibid.*, vv. 46-48.

THE BORDERERS

> Spares not the worm. The giant and the worm—
> She weighs them in one scale. The wiles of woman,
> And craft of age, seducing reason, first
> Made weakness a protection, and obscured
> The moral shapes of things. His tender cries
> And helpless innocence—do they protect
> The infant lamb? and shall the infirmities,
> Which have enabled this enormous Culprit
> To perpetrate his crimes, serve as a Sanctuary
> To cover him from punishment? Shame!—Justice,
> Admitting no resistance, bends alike
> The feeble and the strong. She needs not here
> Her bonds and chains, which make the mighty feeble.
> —We recognize in this old Man a victim
> Prepared already for the sacrifice.[31]

But Oswald utters his most philosophic disquisition upon justice in the third act, when he congratulates Marmaduke for having, as he mistakenly supposes, destroyed Herbert. This noble action, according to Oswald, insures for Marmaduke a foremost place in the ranks of those who follow reason's guiding light: "They who would be just must seek the rule," Oswald declaims,

> By diving for it in their own bosoms.
> Today you have thrown off a tyranny
> That lives but in the torpid acquiescence
> Of our emasculated souls, the tyranny
> Of the world's masters, with the musty rules
> By which they uphold their craft from age to age:
> You have obeyed the only law that sense
> Submits to recognize; the immediate law
> From the clear light of circumstances, flashed
> Upon an independent Intellect.[32]

These passages, and others equally sensational but less weighty in substance,[33] have given rise to the conjecture that Oswald was Wordsworth's conception of a full-fledged devotee of William Godwin's philosophy. Legouis, in particular, argues with tantalizing plausibility that Oswald is a God-

---

[31] *Ibid.*, vv. 522–543. [32] *Ibid.*, Act III, vv. 352–362.
[33] For these see Legouis (*op cit*, pp. 272–275), who quotes and comments upon almost every speech uttered by Oswald that bears the faintest trace of Godwinism.

winian meant to portray the shocking consequences of radical rationalism.[84] Firm in the belief that it was his knowledge of Robespierre's Reign of Terror "which gave birth to Wordsworth's tragedy,"[85] Legouis invites us to "Imagine Godwin's argument for the necessity of extirpating all the human feelings read in the lurid light of '93; conceive his condemnation of all traditional rules of conduct interpreted by aid of the wholesale executions decreed by the Mountain in the name of public welfare, or, in other words, of the greatest amount of general happiness . . . ."[86] If we do this, Legouis continues, we shall perceive that *The Borderers* acquires profound meaning; we shall see at once that Oswald's code of ethics and behavior has been borrowed from Godwin;[87] and we shall recognize Oswald as a *"Montagnard . . .* surrounded by weak and virtuous *Girondins."*[88]

Now Legouis certainly has reason for his opinion that *The Borderers* takes on increased significance if the reader brings to it an intimate knowledge of the events of the early years of the French Revolution, especially of the Terror under Robespierre; Wordsworth himself suggests as much in the Fenwick note to the play. He tells us there that simultaneously with the composition of the tragedy he wrote a

> short essay illustrative of that constitution and those tendencies of human nature which make the apparently *motiveless* actions of bad men intelligible to careful observers. This was partly done with reference to the character of Oswald, and his persevering endeavour to lead the man he disliked into so heinous a crime; but still more to preserve in my distinct remembrance what I had observed of transition in character, and the reflections I had been led to make during the time I was a witness of the changes through which the French Revolution passed.

This makes it clear that Wordsworth regarded the play as a study of various extraordinary aspects of revolutionary psychology, and justifies Legouis's wish that we read *The Borderers* in the "lurid light of '93." But the Fenwick note and the essay which Wordsworth wrote as a preface to the play

---

[84] *Op. cit.,* pp. 270, 275.
[85] *Ibid.,* p. 270.
[86] *Ibid.*
[87] *Ibid.,* pp. 273, 275.
[88] *Ibid.,* p. 276.

THE BORDERERS

give no sanction whatever to the contention that Oswald was created in the image of William Godwin.

At first glance, it is true, Oswald appears to have torn a few pages from Godwin's *Enquiry concerning Political Justice,* a book in which much is written of "Reason" and of "Justice." Like Oswald, Godwin seems to exalt reason at the expense of the human emotions and affections. Like Oswald, Godwin insists that feelings, precedents, and prejudice must not be permitted to interfere with the dictates of reason in the administration of justice. Justice, he asserts, must be " 'no respecter of persons.' "[39] If the house is on fire, he argues, and the philosopher Fénelon and his valet are trapped within, it behooves me as a reasonable being to do all in my power to rescue Fénelon, even though the valet be my father or my brother. Fénelon is the more valuable of the two, the one more likely to contribute in the future to the welfare of society. Reason and justice demand that he be saved, my feelings and prejudices in favor of my father or my brother to the contrary notwithstanding. "What magic is there in the pronoun 'my,' " inquires Godwin in a brilliant passage, "to overturn the decisions of impartial truth? My brother or my father may be a fool or a profligate, malicious, lying or dishonest. If they be, of what consequence is it that they are mine?"[40] And again like Oswald, Godwin demands that all those who pretend to live by reason forego making decisions by facile reference to precedent or the general laws of conventional morality and render judgment only after cold reason has been permitted to play freely over the circumstances relevant to the immediate question. "I ought," he says,

as far as lies in my power, to examine every thing upon its own grounds, and decide concerning it upon its own merits. To rest in general rules is sometimes a necessity which our imperfection imposes upon us, and sometimes the refuge of our indolence; but the true dignity of human reason is, as much as we are able to go beyond them, to have our faculties in act upon every occasion that occurs, and to conduct ourselves accordingly.[41]

[39] *Enquiry concerning Political Justice, and Its Influence on Morals and Happiness* (London, 1796), I, 127. [40] *Ibid.*, p. 129. [41] *Ibid.*, p. 347.

Finally, Godwin resembles Oswald in his eagerness "to enlarge Man's intellectual empire." But this is as far as the correspondences between Oswald and Godwin may properly be carried. A further inquiry into Godwin's *Political Justice* reveals that any similarity between Oswald and Godwin is purely superficial, and that injustice is done the once famous philosopher by those who liken him to Wordsworth's villain.

Godwin was primarily interested in disseminating what he sincerely thought to be the truth. He was encouraged in his task by the belief that truth in the long run must triumph over falsehood. His great hopes for the human race were based upon the assumption that man is a rational being, capable of recognizing and assimilating the truth whenever it is presented to him clearly. There was nothing in the world more hateful to Godwin than falsehood and duplicity, save possibly force, which, in his opinion, worked with more dire results to the same ends as falsehood and duplicity. Truthful persuasion alone is necessary to influence and educate men. "Man is a rational being," Godwin asserts:

If there be any man, who is incapable of making inferences for himself, or understanding, when stated in the most explicit terms, the inferences of another, him we consider as an abortive production, and not in strictness belonging to the human species. It is absurd therefore to say that sound reasoning and truth cannot be communicated by one man to another. Whenever in any case he fails, it is that he is not sufficiently laborious, patient and clear. We suppose of course the person who undertakes to communicate the truth, really to possess it, and be master of his subject; for it is scarcely worth an observation to say, that that which he has not himself, he cannot communicate to another.[42]

Readers of *The Borderers* will agree that Marmaduke is as reasonable a being as most men; certainly we should not consider him "as an abortive production." If, then, Oswald has any profound truths concerning the superior worth of reason and the proper methods of dispensing justice which he wishes to impart to Marmaduke, he should—if he is a true disciple of Godwin—reason with Marmaduke "in the most explicit terms." If Oswald is in firm possession of the

[42] *Op. cit.*, I, 89.

truths which he desires to communicate, he cannot fail—according to Godwin—because truth is ever triumphant with reasonable creatures, and Marmaduke is a reasonable creature. But Oswald, who is not really a disciple of Godwin, does not employ mere reason in his effort to work what he calls Marmaduke's "liberation"; he resorts instead to falsehood, bribery, and distortion. By these extrarational means he succeeds in making an evil thing of Marmaduke's faculty of reason. Such machinations as Oswald's Godwin loathed.

A clear understanding of Godwin's definition of "virtue" and "duty" is indispensable to any accurate understanding of Godwin's doctrine, particularly as it relates to the problem presented by Oswald's character. "I would define virtue," writes Godwin, "to be any action or actions of an intelligent being, proceeding from kind and benevolent intention, and having a tendency to contribute to general happiness."[43] And lest there be any doubt as to whether Oswald's actions would have been deemed virtuous or vicious by Godwin, let us read his description of virtuous action:

An action, however pure may be the intention of the actor, the tendency of which is mischievous, or which shall merely be nugatory and useless in its character, is not a virtuous action. Were it otherwise, we should be obliged to concede the appellation of virtue to the most nefarious deeds of bigots, persecutors and religious assassins, and to the weakest observances of a deluded superstition. Still less does an action, the consequences of which shall be supposed to be in the highest degree beneficial, but which proceeds from a mean, corrupt and degrading motive, deserve the appellation of virtue. A virtuous action is that, of which both the motive and the tendency concur to excite our approbation.[44]

This makes it plain that Godwin would have condemned Oswald's actions as utterly vicious on both heads: his compelling motive was selfish and corrupt; the tendency of his plot was mischievous. In the light of Godwin's philosophy, Oswald is not a devotee, but a perverted criminal.

Such is the verdict, too, if we approach the case from Godwin's definition of "duty." Duty he describes as "that mode of action on the part of the individual, which constitutes the best possible application of his capacity to the

[43] *Ibid.*, p. 150.   [44] *Ibid.*

general benefit."[45] He goes on to point out by way of illustration that Everard Digby's attempt to blow up King James and Parliament can by no interpretation of the facts be considered an act of duty. It was Digby's duty, in Godwin's judgment, "to entertain a sincere and ardent desire for the improvement and happiness of others. With this duty he probably complied. But it was not his duty to apply that desire to a purpose, dreadful and pregnant with inexhaustible mischief."[46] If Everard Digby's action, motivated as it was by the virtuous desire to bring about the greatest good of the greatest number, cannot—because of its mischievous tendency—be approved by straight thinkers, what can be said for Oswald's behavior, motivated as it was by pride and selfishness?[47]

The truth seems to be that the tradition which connects the villainous Oswald with the philosophic Godwin rests upon a serious misunderstanding of *Political Justice*. R. A. Preston pointed out several years ago that the bulk of adverse criticism of Godwin's most famous work had been leveled at the man, not at his book.[48] As Preston remarks in his review of previous estimates of *Political Justice*,[49] Godwin has been ridiculed for assuming that man is capable of omniscience, or perfection. But Godwin argued only that man was capable of " 'indefinite progress towards perfection.' "[50] The history of the nineteenth century has been invoked as proof of Godwin's naïveté in believing that truth can triumph over error. But Godwin did not write that man was perfect, nor

---

[45] *Op. cit.*, I, 157.
[46] *Ibid.*, p. 158.
[47] Professor de Selincourt, following Legouis, remarks in his "Wordsworth's Preface to *The Borderers*": "And so Oswald becomes at once a mouthpiece and an exposure of Godwinism" (p. 171). He goes on, however, to qualify this somewhat by noting, quite properly, that Oswald "is not, indeed, the perfect Godwinian, for he is using the doctrines of Godwin, not to promote the general good, but to justify his own evil passions" (*ibid.*). Despite the fact, however, that this acknowledged difference between Oswald and a Godwinian is radical, Professor de Selincourt insists that the example presented by Oswald is sufficient to reveal the inadequacy of Godwinism.
[48] *An Enquiry concerning Political Justice and Its Influence on General Virtue and Happiness*, ed. by R. A. Preston (New York, 1926), I, xxiii.
[49] *Ibid.*, pp. xxiii–xxix.   [50] *Ibid.*, p. xxiv.

THE BORDERERS

that all error would be quickly driven from the world of men; he contended merely that as the years marched on error might be steadily diminished if man chose to use his ability to reason. It has been urged, furthermore, that Godwin " 'would expunge every vestige of tradition from the tablet of the human mind ... raze to the ground the whole structure of political and religious belief, and substitute a new order of things in which the sole binding force should be derived from pure abstract reasoning.' "[51] But—and this is written large on almost every page of *Political Justice*—Godwin insisted that the new order must be the result of evolution, not of revolution; that it could come only after the slow progress of many years, after men had been educated to understand that kings and priests, precedents and traditions, were evils necessary only so long as man chose not to employ with highest efficiency his natural powers of reason. Godwin merely looked forward hopefully to the day when man would emerge from the darkness of political, economic, and religious superstition to gaze at last upon the sun. Finally—and this is the allegation with which students of *The Borderers* are particularly concerned—it has been repeatedly argued that Godwin would cut man loose from the influence of the emotions, or the affections, so that reason alone might be his guide. It is this charge which has caused students of Wordsworth erroneously to associate Oswald with the author of *Political Justice*.

In *The Enquirer*, 1797, Godwin wrote a sentence which suggests that his reputation as a very radical rationalist has been somewhat exaggerated—"Man has not only an understanding to reason, but a heart to feel."[52] This clear admission that man is more than a "clear, cold, logic engine" was not a concession to those of Godwin's contemporaries who were offended by the emphasis he was accustomed to place on abstract reason; indeed, it was not even an indication of a fundamental change in Godwin's philosophy. Godwin had

---

[51] *Ibid.*, p. xxv. Preston here is quoting from Leslie Stephen's *English Thought in the Eighteenth Century*.

[52] Cited by Preston, *op. cit.*, p. xxvi.

already expressed the same idea in the tenth and eleventh chapters of the fourth book of the second edition (1796) of *Political Justice*—the version of the work which Wordsworth had before him when he began to write *The Borderers*. These chapters, entitled "Of Self-Love and Benevolence" and "Of Good and Evil," throw much-needed light on the true nature of Godwin's system, and provide us with the key to an understanding of *The Borderers*.

In these chapters Godwin opines that of all passions—and a passion to Godwin is "a permanent and habitual tendency towards a certain course of action"[53]—that of benevolence, or disinterestedness, is the most desirable for man to attain. He divides mankind into three classes, and comments upon the several types. The peasant's "contemptible insensibility of an oyster" he deplores;[54] he has a few words of faint praise for the man of taste, who "sits up late in scenes of gay resort"[55] when he is not amusing himself in athletic exercise, the appreciation of nature, science, and the arts, or enjoying the pleasures of solitude and study. But "Study," according to Godwin,

is cold, if it be not enlivened with the idea of the happiness to arise to mankind from the cultivation and improvement of sciences. The sublime and pathetic are barren, unless it be the sublime of true virtue and the pathos of true sympathy. The pleasures of the mere man of taste and refinement "play round the head, but come not to the heart." There is no true joy but in the spectacle and contemplation of happiness. There is no delightful melancholy but in pitying distress. The man who has once performed an act of exalted generosity, knows that there is no sensation of corporeal or intellectual taste to be compared with this. The man who has fought to benefit nations, rises above the mechanical ideas of barter and exchange. He asks no gratitude. To see that they are benefited, or to believe that they will be so, is its own reward. He ascends to the highest of human pleasures, the pleasures of disinterestedness.[56]

Many and wonderful are the virtues of disinterestedness, the ruling passion of the man of benevolence, who alone is worthy of receiving Godwin's unqualified praise. "When

[53] *Political Justice* (1796 ed.), I, 425.
[54] *Ibid.*, p. 446.
[55] *Ibid.*, p. 445.
[56] *Ibid.*, p. 447.

once we have entered into so auspicious a path as that of disinterestedness," Godwin writes,

> reflection confirms our choice, in a sense in which it never can confirm any of the factitious passions [avarice, drunkenness, lechery, and the like] .... We find by observation that we are surrounded by beings of the same nature with ourselves. They have the same senses, are susceptible of the same pleasures and pains, capable of being raised to the same excellence, and employed in the same usefulness. We are able in imagination to go out of ourselves, and become impartial spectators of the system of which we are a part. We can then make an appraisement of our intrinsic and absolute value; and detect the imposition of that self-regard which would represent our own interest as of as much value as that of all the world beside. The delusion being thus sapped, we can, from time to time at least, fall back in idea into our proper post, and cultivate those views and affections which must be most familiar to the most perfect intelligence.[57]

> The man, who vigilantly conforms his affections to the standard of impartial justice, who loses the view of personal regards in the greater objects that engross his attention, who from motives of benevolence sits loose to life and all its pleasures,[58] and is ready without a sigh to sacrifice them to the public good, has an uncommonly exquisite source of happiness. When he looks back, he applauds the state of his own affections; and, when he looks out of himself, his sensations are refined in proportion to the comprehensiveness of his sentiments. He is filled with harmony within; and the state of his thoughts is uncommonly favorable to what we may venture to style the sublime emotions of tranquillity.[59]

If Godwin had been no more than the exponent of "pure abstract reasoning" and the derider of the affections and the feelings, it would be startling thus to find him preferring the pleasures of the heart to those of the head and recommending the man of benevolence for emulation. There is no trace here of the radical rationalist whom Wordsworth supposedly repudiated in *The Borderers*. On the contrary, these chapters make it apparent that Godwin was as much a sentimental-

[57] *Ibid.*, p. 428.
[58] Godwin here seems to echo the advice of James Thomson in *Alfred: A Masque*, Act I, sc. v:
> Attach thee firmly to the virtuous deeds
> And offices of life: to life itself,
> And all its transient joys, sit loose—

[59] *Political Justice*, I, 430–431.

ist as a rationalist.[60] In the passages just quoted we find him endorsing a mode of behavior for the individual that presupposes not only a high degree of philosophic self-consciousness, but also the conviction that the enlightened man will be guided in his actions by a comprehensive faculty and perception which transcends mere reason, or mere emotion, and includes them both. The failure of commentators to recognize the important fact that Godwin in his wisest moments was capable of fusing reason and emotion thus may be attributed, I think, to Godwin's rather exhibitionistic use of the terminology of rationalism for his purposes of exposition. *Political Justice* for the most part is written in the jargon of the eighteenth-century dichotomy of reason and emotion. Godwin, however, was sufficiently advanced in philosophy to be able to cut through this arbitrary distinction in important places;[61] it was his ability to do so that enabled him to be of positive assistance to Wordsworth in 1796–97.

Wordsworth's chief philosophical preoccupation in the

[60] For a more detailed account of the evidence of Godwin's basic sentimentalism see B. Sprague Allen's excellent study, "William Godwin as a Sentimentalist," *Publications of the Modern Language Association*, XXXIII (1918), 1–29. Allen reveals that all of Godwin's novels were cast in the popular sentimental mode of the period. To prove his point that "The rationalistic structure of Godwin's philosophy disintegrated . . . under the influence of ideas and emotional tendencies that he had assimilated from Rousseauism" (pp. 28–29), he emphasizes the sentimentalism of the tenth chapter of the fourth book of *Political Justice*, "the inmost shrine of his philosophy," which, he concludes, "might be entered by way of either the reason or the feelings" (p. 29).

Allen, curiously enough, missed the implications of his thesis for *The Borderers* and supported the traditional belief that Wordsworth there "employs the convention of the noble robber to expose Godwinian fallacies" (*ibid.*, p. 12 n.).

[61] In the third act of *The Borderers* Wordsworth gives us an example of the tormenting philosophical confusion suffered by those thinkers who conceive of reason and emotion as distinct and antipathetic powers. It is Oswald, the perverse rationalist, whose speculations in terms of the old dichotomy find no end, "in wand'ring mazes lost": "Methinks," he says,

> It were a pleasant pastime to construct
> A scale and table of belief—as thus—
> Two columns, one for passion, one for proof;
> Each rises as the other falls: and first,
> Passion a unit and *against* us—proof—
> Nay, we must travel in another path,

early months of 1797, when he was busy with the composition of *The Borderers*,[62] was with the conflict of benevolence and its opposite—self-love, or pride. Just before the completion of his tragedy Wordsworth finished the composition of "Lines Left upon a Seat in a Yew-Tree,"[63] the poem, it is worth noting, in which Professor Harper discovers the first trace of Wordsworth's mature poetic style.[64] In this short blank-verse poem, in some respects an anticipation of Shelley's *Alastor*, Wordsworth describes a man of great talent and education who, because the world neglected him, lived his brief life in impotence and unhappiness. Nourished by the "food of pride," he would gaze upon the lovely forms of nature till they became

> Far lovelier, and his heart could not sustain
> The beauty still more beauteous. Nor, that time,
> Would he forget those beings, to whose minds,
> Warm from the labours of benevolence,
> The world, and man himself, appeared a scene
> Of kindred loveliness: then he would sigh
> With mournful joy, to think that others felt
> What he must never feel: and so, lost man!
> (Vv. 33–40)

The life of this sad egocentric has been of no apparent benefit to the world; his only monument is a seat of moss and stone beneath the yew tree. But from his example Wordsworth

---

> Or we're stuck fast for ever;—passion, then,
> Shall be a unit *for* us; proof—no, passion!
> (Vv. 11–19)

[62] In the Fenwick note Wordsworth asserted that *The Borderers* was the work of 1795–96. It has been recently established, however, that it was begun in the fall of 1796 and completed in 1797, probably in June. For the very interesting history of the dating of the play see de Selincourt in *The Early Letters*, pp. 156–157 n., MacGillivray, *op. cit.*, pp. 104–111, and de Selincourt in *The Letters of William and Dorothy Wordsworth: The Later Years*, III, 1388.

[63] Wordsworth tells us that the poem was begun at Hawkshead, probably in 1787, and completed in 1795. But Professor de Selincourt, writing with Wordsworth's early notebooks at hand, states that "it is very doubtful whether much of it was written as early as 1787, and almost certain that none of it was then in blank verse, whilst it was not finished before the early months of 1797, when Mary Hutchinson was at Racedown, and copied it into a note-book" (*The Early Wordsworth*, p. 27).

[64] *Op. cit.*, p. 180.

draws a moral of deep significance for all those who tend to follow in the dead man's lonely path:

> If thou be one whose heart the holy forms
> Of young imagination have kept pure,
> Stranger! henceforth be warned; and know, that pride,
> Howe'er disguised in its own majesty,
> Is littleness; that he, who feels contempt
> For any living thing, hath faculties
> Which he has never used; that thought with him
> Is in its infancy. The man, whose eye
> Is ever on himself, doth look on one,
> The least of nature's works, one who might move
> The wise man to that scorn which wisdom holds
> Unlawful, ever. O, be wiser thou!
> Instructed that true knowledge leads to love,
> True dignity abides with him alone
> Who, in the silent hour of inward thought,
> Can still suspect, and still revere himself,
> In lowliness of heart.   (Vv. 44–60)

It is true that the comprehensive humanitarianism of the wise man here recommended represents no advance beyond the philosophy expressed by Wordsworth in 1794 at Windy Brow which advised us to remain "evermore awake To feeling for all forms that life can take"; and it is true that the general love of every living thing here urged upon us is at least as old as Christian doctrine. Yet the focus of the poem, the pointed contrasting of the proud and self-centered mode of life with the self-forgetful and benevolent manner of living, suggests irresistibly the powerful contributory influence of the chapters on "Self-Love and Benevolence" and "Good and Evil" in William Godwin's *Political Justice*.

We shall now see that Wordsworth took this same subject of pride and benevolence for the central theme of *The Borderers*, and that *The Borderers*, far from being the record of Wordsworth's rejection of Godwin, is in reality the record of his acceptance and amplification of Godwin's explicit recommendations for the conduct of the enlightened individual in society. When we approach the tragedy from the point of view afforded by "Lines Left upon a Seat in a Yew-Tree," we immediately recognize Oswald and Marmaduke as personifications of pride and benevolence; the action of the play we perceive to be a conflict between these two "passions," or modes of life, and the conclusion little more than a revelation of the evil consequences of pride, and the blessings of disinterestedness and benevolence.

That Wordsworth conceived of Oswald as a personification of pride and self-regard is evident from his Preface to *The Borderers*—a rather tedious exposition of the psychology of pride, particularly as it applies to Oswald—and from numerous speeches uttered by Oswald and the supporting characters. In the opening sentence of the Preface, Wordsworth describes Oswald as "a young man of great intellectual powers, yet without any solid principles of genuine benevolence. His master passions are pride and the love of distinction."[65] Later on, when he is discussing the question of Oswald's motives for attempting the ruin of Marmaduke, Wordsworth writes: "they are founded chiefly on the very constitution of his character; in his pride which borders even upon madness . . . ."[66] Early in the first act Wilfred warns Marmaduke against Oswald by reminding him that Oswald owes him gratitude, and that "gratitude's a heavy burden To a proud Soul."[67] When Lacy remarks further on that Oswald holds human law in contempt and scorns the Christian faith, Lennox observes that Oswald's "pride has built Some uncouth superstition of its own."[68] And in the same discussion of Oswald's religious eccentricities, Wallace reveals his understanding of Oswald's nature and of the characteristics peculiar to the type:

> A most subtle doctor
> Were that man, who could draw the line that parts
> Pride and her daughter, Cruelty, from Madness,
> That should be scourged, not pitied. Restless Minds,
> Such Minds as find amid their fellow-men
> No heart that loves them, none that they can love,
> Will turn perforce and seek for sympathy
> In dim relation to imagined Beings.[69]

---

[65] *The Poetical Works*, p. 345.
[66] *Ibid.*, p. 348.
[67] *The Borderers*, vv. 30–31.
[68] *Ibid.*, Act III, vv. 306–307.
[69] *Ibid.*, vv. 314–321.

Finally, believing that Marmaduke has murdered Herbert and is ready, because of the suffering he endures, to receive with profit the great truths that are the fruit of Oswald's criminal experience, Oswald clearly reveals his own character:

> Compassion!—pity!—pride can do without them;
> . . . .
> He is a puny soul who, feeling pain,
> Finds ease because another feels it too.
> If e'er I open out this heart of mine
> It shall be for a nobler end—to teach
> And not to purchase puling sympathy.[70]

Indeed, Oswald's actions and remarks throughout the play are those of the proud egoist who holds the world and his fellow creatures in deep contempt. So great is his pride that he makes a show of suppressing even his hatred of humanity, deeming it an emotion unworthy of such as he. Concerning Marmaduke's election to the head of the outlaw band, he sneers:

> They chose *him* for their Chief!—what covert part
> He, in the preference, modest Youth, might take,
> I neither know nor care. The insult bred
> More of contempt than hatred; both are flown;
> That either e'er existed is my shame:
> 'Twas a dull spark—a most unnatural fire
> That died the moment the air breathed upon it.[71]

Injured pride causes him to hate Marmaduke, who has saved his life: "The Villains rose in mutiny to destroy me," he confides—

> I could have quelled the Cowards, but this Stripling
> Must needs step in, and save my life. The look
> With which he gave the boon—I see it now!
> The same that tempted me to loathe the gift.[72]

The neglect which he has suffered from the world as a result of his crime, moreover, has led Oswald in his vanity to scorn the praise of men—even, in fact, to welcome their disdain. "I had been nourished," he tells Marmaduke,

---

[70] *The Borderers*, Act III, vv. 419–425.
[71] *Ibid.*, Act II, vv. 1–7.   [72] *Ibid.*, vv. 367–371.

THE BORDERERS

> by the sickly food
> Of popular applause. I now perceived
> That we are praised, only as men in us
> Do recognize some image of themselves,
> An abject counterpart of what they are,
> Or the empty thing that they would wish to be.
> I felt that merit has no surer test
> Than obloquy; that, if we wish to serve
> The world in substance, not deceive by show,
> We must become obnoxious to its hate,
> Or fear disguised in simulated scorn.[73]

And a moment later Oswald admits to Marmaduke not only that he has no love for his fellow men, but also that he is grateful to the traitors who led him into crime: it was their action that began the sequence of events which ultimately purged him of the base, benevolent emotion of love:

> I had been,
> And in that dream had left my native land,
> One of Love's simple bondsmen—the soft chain
> Was off forever; and the men, from whom
> This liberation came, you would destroy:
> Join me in thanks for their blind services.[74]

Wordsworth clarifies and emphasizes this aspect of Oswald's character when he writes in the Preface: "The *mild* effusions of thought, the milk of human reason are unknown to him."[75]

It is clear then from the Preface, from the comments of Wilfred, Lacy, Lennox, and Wallace, and from Oswald's words of self-revelation, that Wordsworth intended Oswald to represent pride and self-love. And though the Preface—which is devoted exclusively to a discussion of Oswald's abnormal psychology—throws no light on Wordsworth's conception of Marmaduke, except to describe him as an "amiable young man,"[76] a glance at the play itself reveals that Marmaduke's character is in deliberate contrast to that of Oswald; Marmaduke, in fact, is nothing if not an embodiment of those principles of benevolence which Wordsworth first ap-

---

[73] *Ibid.*, Act IV, vv. 171–181.
[74] *Ibid.*, vv. 189–194.
[75] *The Poetical Works*, p. 346.
[76] *Ibid.*, p. 347.

proved at length in "Lines Left upon a Seat in a Yew-Tree" and to which he subscribed for the remainder of his life.

Early in the first act, when Oswald remarks that Herbert is prejudiced unreasonably against Marmaduke, the latter's reply betrays his chief characteristic: "Ne'er may I own the heart That cannot feel for one, helpless as he is."[77] And in the very next scene we learn through Idonea's efforts to mitigate her father's aversion for Marmaduke that the young chieftain is the very soul of virtue and benevolence. "O could you hear his voice," she exclaims:

> Alas! you do not know him. He is one
> (I wot not what ill tongue has wronged him with you)
> All gentleness and love. His face bespeaks
> A deep and simple meekness: and that Soul,
> Which with the motion of a virtuous act
> Flashes a look of terror upon guilt,
> Is, after conflict, quiet as the ocean,
> By a miraculous finger, stilled at once.[78]

The later lines of this character sketch have special significance, for they remind us that this gentle hero can be roused to dreadful action in the cause of virtue; justice having been done, however, his soul immediately regains the tranquility which distinguishes the man of benevolence. Marmaduke has the broad view that rises from the passion of disinterestedness; his actions, unlike those of Oswald, spring from his feeling of responsibility to society and humanity, not from a selfish desire to feed his pride.

"I have loved To be the friend and father of the oppressed, A comforter of sorrow,"[79] Marmaduke admits to Oswald. So highly developed is Marmaduke's benign sensibility, moreover, that his feelings embrace even the lowly members of the animal kingdom. When Herbert is being conducted to the dungeon of the ruined castle his old dog, Leader by name, slips from a narrow plank and falls to certain death in the torrent below. Marmaduke's response to this pathetic mishap is wholly admirable, as we learn later

---

[77] *The Borderers*, Act I, vv. 67–68.
[78] *Ibid.*, vv. 165–173.
[79] *Ibid.*, Act II, vv. 83–85.

THE BORDERERS

from Herbert, when he professes a high regard for his custodian:

> You will forgive me, but my heart runs over.
> When my old Leader slipped into the flood
> And perished, what a piercing outcry you
> Sent after him. I have loved you ever since.[80]

One might suppose that Marmaduke would take pride in the conscious possession of so much benevolence and tender feeling as he exhibits throughout the play. But there is not a trace of pride in his exemplary soul. With all his great virtue, Marmaduke is modest and humble; by his own admission he is "The weakest of God's creatures."[81] There can be no doubt that Marmaduke possesses that "lowliness of heart" which Wordsworth recommends at the close of "Lines Left upon a Seat in a Yew-Tree." Marmaduke is one well aware of the wisdom of Wordsworth's warning to the reader in that poem:

> he, who feels contempt
> For any living thing, hath faculties
> Which he has never used . . . thought with him
> Is in its infancy. The man, whose eye
> Is ever on himself, doth look on one,
> The least of nature's works . . . .

The dramatic interest of *The Borderers* is focused not on the fate of Herbert, where one might expect it to be, but on the character of Marmaduke. Oswald's malignant desire to remake Marmaduke in his own image provides the disturbing force, and whatever suspense is generated in the play's tedious five acts springs from the reader's anxiety for Marmaduke's integrity in particular, and for the outcome of the clash between pride and benevolence in general. Benevolence triumphs, of course, and the most important consequence of the action is the increase of Marmaduke's benevolence in proportion to the wisdom he acquires from his experience as Oswald's chosen victim.

For a while it appears that Oswald, or pride, will be successful in the conflict of rival modes of life. Marmaduke,

[80] *Ibid.*, vv. 283-286.
[81] *Ibid.*, Act III, v. 384. This line was added to the play in 1842.

whose faith in the innate goodness of man has been hitherto unshaken, begins to lose confidence in the world and in human nature under the pressure of Oswald's cunning plot. So shaken is he by the evidence against Herbert, by the realization that man could conceive so base a scheme as that attributed by Oswald to Herbert, that he is driven to the expression of extreme pessimism. In a moment of despair he exclaims to Wallace, Lacy, and Oswald:

> we look
> But at the surfaces of things; we hear
> Of towns in flames, fields ravaged, young and old
> Driven out in troops to want and nakedness;
> Then grasp our swords and rush upon a cure
> That flatters us, because it asks not thought:
> The deeper malady is better hid;
> The world is poisoned at the heart.[82]

So convinced does he become of the overwhelming preponderance of evil in the world and in the heart of man that he considers the destruction of infants the kindest act possible for their parents to perform: "Now for the cornerstone of my philosophy," he complains to Oswald:

> I would not give a denier for the man
> Who, on such provocation as this earth
> Yields, could not chuck his babe beneath the chin,
> And send it with a fillip to its grave.[83]

Finally, when Oswald has confessed the murder which he himself committed and has told Marmaduke of the "hellish mockery" and laughter with which his companions greeted the doomed man's cries for help, Marmaduke voices utter despair: "We all are of one blood," he cries, "our veins are filled At the same poisonous fountain!"[84] Believing this to be essential truth, Marmaduke laments the lot of "wretched Humankind," and envies

> The worm, that, underneath a stone whose weight
> Would crush the lion's paw with mortal anguish,
> Doth lodge, and feed, and coil, and sleep, in safety.[85]

---

[82] *The Borderers*, Act II, vv. 479–486.
[83] *Ibid.*, Act III, vv. 106–110.
[84] *Ibid.*, Act IV, vv. 89–90.
[85] *Ibid.*, vv. 145, 147–149. This passage was added in 1842.

THE BORDERERS

Critics have long insisted that the hopelessness expressed by Marmaduke in these speeches proves that *The Borderers* is a pessimistic play, and that Marmaduke's intense depression is merely a reflection of Wordsworth's state of mind at Racedown. Legouis regards Marmaduke's gloomy pronouncements as evidence of Wordsworth's discovery that "the causes of crime were less simple than he had supposed, that its sources were far more difficult to exhaust. Evil was inherent in man's limited and imperfect nature. Not only was it entrenched, beyond the reach of every attempt at reform, within the most secret recesses of the human heart; it could also enlist the services of the intellect."[86] Like Marmaduke, according to Legouis, "Wordsworth . . . was at that time unable to find any answer to Oswald's cynical philosophy. He might abominate it; he could not refute it. Before the depths of depravity, now for the first time revealed, his spirit shuddered, powerless."[87] De Selincourt is in complete agreement with Legouis, for he, too, asserts that "pessimism . . . is the dominating note of *The Borderers*," and that Wordsworth, when he wrote the play, "saw for the time no answer" to Marmaduke's "despairing cry."[88]

We have seen already that Wordsworth was in no pessimistic frame of mind when he wrote *The Borderers*, and we have discovered that as early as 1794 he possessed most of the ideas contained in his mature philosophy. Legouis and de Selincourt suppose, however, that Wordsworth found a satisfactory reply to Oswald's "cynical philosophy" only after he had completed *The Borderers*. Close scrutiny of the play —with special attention to the development of Marmaduke's character—reveals that their interpretation of the tragedy represents a misunderstanding of Marmaduke's experience and of Wordsworth's intentions, that *The Borderers* is not pessimistic, and that Wordsworth expressed therein as complete an answer to Oswald's cynicism as he was ever to express.

---

[86] *Op. cit.,* p. 277.
[87] *Ibid.,* p. 276.
[88] "Wordsworth's Preface to *The Borderers*," p. 172.

There can be no doubt that Marmaduke is the mouthpiece of pessimism during the interval in which he believes in Herbert's guilt. But it must be remembered that this pessimism is caused, not by a clear view of mankind or the world as they are in reality, but by the distorted picture of both held before Marmaduke's trusting eyes by Oswald. We must note, moreover, that even when the delusion conjured up in Marmaduke's mind is most potent, almost at the very moment when Marmaduke's reflections are most bitter, the young man's instinct for good remains undisturbed and presumably indestructible. Just prior to his desertion of Herbert on the moor Marmaduke sheds tears at his discovery of a resemblance to the voice of Idonea in that of Herbert. This unmistakable sign of benevolence, at the height of his spiritual torment, causes Marmaduke to deliver the following pathetic speech:

> these tears—
> I did not think that aught was left in me
> Of what I have been—yes, I thank thee, Heaven!
> One happy thought has passed across my mind.
> —It may not be—I am cut off from man;
> No more shall I be man—no more shall I
> Have human feelings![89]

But Marmaduke is mistaken, and his fears are without foundation. The texture of his moral fiber sustains him, and prevents him from losing his essential strength in the presence of evil. The basic virtue of his character is obviously incorruptible, for, at the climax of his temptation, Marmaduke, instead of killing Herbert, chooses to leave him before the bar of Providence. This is proof that, despite the apparently unshakable evidence on which he bases his pessimistic convictions that man and the world are evil, Marmaduke's store of tender feelings has by no means been exhausted.

The crowning significance of Marmaduke's character and the conclusive proof that Wordsworth had no intention of casting him in the rôle of a confirmed pessimist are not discernible before the ending of the play. Oswald has hoped

[89] *The Borderers*, Act III, vv. 189-195.

THE BORDERERS

that Marmaduke's discovery of evil in man would cause him deliberately to stifle any further impulse to love humanity and to accept gladly the passion of pride as a defense against those pangs of remorse which must inevitably follow his realization that he has murdered an innocent man. In such a way had Oswald reacted to the experience of his own crime. But Marmaduke is made of sterner stuff than Oswald: when he discovers that Oswald has betrayed him, Marmaduke tries to rescue Herbert; when he finds that Herbert is dead, instead of attempting to repress his remorse, Marmaduke welcomes it as an unmistakable sign of the healthy condition of his soul. So deep are his sympathies for humanity and his confidence in mankind, even in the face of this catastrophe, that he accepts with eagerness not only his own guilt, but also that of Eldred the peasant, whose natural benevolence has collapsed before the onslaught of narrow self-interest provoked by the situation which Marmaduke's action has created. Marmaduke's sorest distress is caused by his knowledge that his own misdeed has sullied the soul of Eldred: "I am deserted At my worst need," he cries out plaintively in the last act, "my crimes have in a net Entangled this poor man."[90] So great is his benevolence, never stronger than at the end of the play, and so far is he from accepting the conclusions of the pessimistic premises from which he has argued earlier in the play, that he endeavors in the final scene to save even Oswald, his betrayer, from the dreadful consequences of a life dedicated to pride, tainted by scorn, and divorced from human sympathy. Instead of slaying Oswald in revenge for his treachery, Marmaduke—conscious of the advisability of loving all and hating none—vouchsafes the following words of wisdom in the interest of Oswald's soul:

> Thy office, thy ambition, be henceforth
> To feed remorse, to welcome every sting
> Of penitential anguish, yea with tears.
> When seas and continents shall lie between us—
> The wider space the better—we may find
> In such a course fit links of sympathy,

[90] *Ibid.*, vv. 76-78.

> An incommunicable rivalship
> Maintained, for peaceful ends beyond our view.[91]

Oswald of course scorns repentance and cherishes his sinful pride to the end, when he dies at the hand of Wallace, while Marmaduke devotes the remainder of his life to the penitential pursuit of salutary remorse; Marmaduke's is a heroic effort to atone for the sin of having presumed to judge a fellow man[92] and for having dared to suspect that the world and man—God's best creation—were evil.

So far then from being a pessimistic play, *The Borderers,* when viewed in this light, ceases almost to be a tragedy; certainly it is not so stark and gloomy a performance as critics have hitherto supposed it to be. Professors Campbell and Mueschke, believing that Marmaduke has studiously endeavored throughout the play to stifle his natural feelings by a judicious application of Godwin's rationalistic doctrines, argue that "Marmaduke's tragedy lies not so much in the hideous nature of the attempted remedy as in the persistence of the remorse."[93] But they mistake for the heart of the tragedy what Wordsworth clearly intended to be the catharsis. Marmaduke's tragedy lies in his temporary alienation from man; the remorse which he feels as a result of his unpardonable sin is the very sign and hallmark of his salvation. He makes no effort to escape from remorse. He gives it the highest recommendation in his address to Oswald. He regards it as the only force capable of effecting his complete moral and spiritual regeneration. Instead of adopting Os-

---

[91] *The Borderers,* Act III, vv. 287-294. In the 1797 version Marmaduke merely "forgives" Oswald (see *The Poetical Works,* p. 223). When he revised the play in 1842 Wordsworth added this passage, apparently as a partial explanation for Marmaduke's generous action.

[92] The precise nature of Marmaduke's sin was left rather obscure in the 1797 text of *The Borderers*. In 1842, however, Wordsworth threw ample light on the matter by having Marmaduke make the following confession:

> I am the man,
> . . . .
> Presumptuous above all that ever breathed,
> Who, casting as I thought a guilty Person
> Upon Heaven's righteous judgment, did become
> An instrument of Fiends. (Act V, vv. 193-198)

[93] "*The Borderers . . . ,*" p. 472.

THE BORDERERS

wald's method of escape from remorse by mounting "from action up to action,"[94] the wise and virtuous Marmaduke isolates himself from mankind and the possibility of action in order that he may suffer the pangs of his remorse more keenly. He devotes the remainder of his life to the assiduous cultivation of remorse, believing that only thus will "anger be appeased in Heaven, and Mercy give him leave to die."[95]

One may well wonder why it is necessary for Marmaduke to go to such extremes in his effort to achieve forgiveness for his contribution to the general tragedy. Has his sin been so great, after all, that he must cut himself off from the presence of men to secure adequate punishment? Nothing could be harder for Marmaduke to endure, and he admits in his concluding speech that he must now loathe life. Surely any impartial judge would agree that the painful destiny which Marmaduke willingly embraces is undeserved. Like Othello, Marmaduke put his trust in a friend who proved a villain. Indeed, the evidence presented to Marmaduke by Oswald is far more convincing than that with which Iago destroys the Moor. And it would be vain to argue that Marmaduke is not more disinterested than Othello in his effort to see justice done. Marmaduke's innocence is less dubious than Othello's, and his crime is not so great. What is there, then, that hinders Marmaduke from continuing his active, benevolent life as a guardian of the poor and innocent "Along the confines of the Esk and Tweed?" Why, one is even tempted to ask, does Marmaduke not compensate the affectionate and faithful Idonea for the loss of her father by marrying her and endeavoring to make felicitous the remaining years of her life?

The answer to these questions might be merely that Wordsworth wanted *The Borderers* to end like a tragedy. Perhaps he felt, quite properly, that any other ending would have made the play little more than a five-act psychological experiment at Herbert's expense. It may be, on the other hand, that Wordsworth was keeping his eye firmly fixed upon

---
[94] *The Borderers*, Act IV, vv. 138-139.
[95] *Ibid.*, Act V, 336-337.

the ending of Schiller's *The Robbers,* which he certainly had in mind when he wrote his play. In *The Robbers,* Charles Moor, the leader of the outlaw band, gives up his office at the end of the play and—after destroying his sweetheart to save her from further suffering in this rough world—announces his intention of spending the rest of his life in penitent solitude.[96] But the most satisfactory explanation for Wordsworth's conclusion is that Marmaduke's guilt and his consciousness of guilt are much more profound than a casual study of his character and crime would suggest.

The extreme punishment which Marmaduke inflicts upon himself at the end of the play is the consequence of his conviction that his part in the death of Herbert was inexcusable. It is true that the case against Herbert presented by Oswald seems at first glance to be ironclad, and that even a close reading of the play reveals little substantial evidence in Herbert's favor which might have influenced Marmaduke to follow a different course of action from the one he chose. But a more careful review of *The Borderers* discloses irresistible evidence of the old man's innocence. Once the truth is out, Marmaduke perceives in retrospect the value of that evidence and concludes, in effect, that he has been a blind and blundering fool for whom no punishment is too severe.

The history of Marmaduke's undoing is the history of the conflict between the perverse reasoning and falsified evidence presented by Oswald and the subtle messages and valid testimony emanating from three unimpeachable sources: Marmaduke's sympathetic heart, the innocent voice and features of Herbert, and the visible world of nature. Marmaduke's sin, in Wordsworth's view, is his almost complete rejection of the evidence of the feelings and of nature. In an ignorant person such a sin might be venial; in Marmaduke, it is unforgivable. Marmaduke, in his essential and proper character, is a man of benevolence who has long known that the best

---

[96] The possibility that Wordsworth merely borrowed Schiller's conclusion is suggested not only by the obvious similarity of the endings of the two plays, but also by the circumstance that in the 1797 version of *The Borderers* Marmaduke's final resolution, like that of Schiller's outlaw, is inadequately accounted for.

actions are those prompted not only by the head but also by the heart. That he was aware of this great truth when he chose to abandon Herbert on the moor is obvious from his chiding remark to Oswald in the fourth act, when the latter has confessed his original crime:

> The proofs—you ought to have seen
> The guilt—have touched it—felt it at your heart—
> As I have done.[97]

But an investigation of the evidence proves that Marmaduke in truth had not felt Herbert's guilt at his heart. His heart, on the contrary, exerted its most potent influence, even up to the very moment of the tragic decision, to restrain Marmaduke from injuring an innocent man.

Marmaduke's earliest warning that Herbert is innocent and Oswald a traitor comes when he first lays eyes upon the old man: "I would fain hope that we deceive ourselves," he admits to Oswald:

> When first I saw him sitting there, alone,
> It struck upon my heart I know not how.[98]

But it is not until the second act, after the loss of Leader and the gaining of the dungeon, that the power of innocence begins to marshal its forces in earnest and lay siege to Marmaduke's susceptible heart. Marmaduke reports that Herbert, when he had learned of his dog's death,

> was troubled
> Even to the shedding of some natural tears
> Into the torrent over which he hung,
> Listening in vain.[99]

This evidence of tenderness in the old man, along with his assertion that "there's a Providence for them who walk In helplessness, when innocence is with them,"[100] gives Marma-

---

[97] *The Borderers*, Act V, vv. 119-121. Although Marmaduke thinks he has "touched" Herbert's guilt in the 1797 version of the play, only in the text of 1842 does he claim to have "felt it at his heart."

[98] *Ibid.*, Act I, vv. 375-377.

[99] *Ibid.*, vv. 211-214. In the 1797 version the dog is named Tray, and is thrown off the bridge by Oswald, much to Marmaduke's dismay.

[100] *Ibid.*, vv. 241-242.

duke pause and provokes the curious psychological state described in the following passage:

> These drowsy shiverings,
> This mortal stupor which is creeping over me,
> What do they mean? were this my single body
> Opposed to armies, not a nerve would tremble:
> Why do I tremble now?—Is not the depth
> Of this Man's crimes beyond the reach of thought?
> And yet, in plumbing the abyss for judgment,
> Something I strike upon which turns my mind
> Back on herself, I think, again—my breast
> Concentres all the terrors of the Universe:
> I look at him and tremble like a child.[101]

A further conversation with Herbert—during Oswald's temporary absence from the scene—in which the old man's remarks are full of an exemplary piety, destroys Marmaduke's confidence in the case against him so completely that he warns Oswald not to lay a finger upon Herbert, and flings away his own sword after muttering:

> Fallen should I be indeed—
> Murder—perhaps asleep, blind, old, alone,
> Betrayed, in darkness! Here to strike the blow—
> Away! away![102]

Thus does Marmaduke first resist temptation and repulse Oswald's diabolical attack upon his immortal soul.

Oswald, however, refuses to be thus easily thwarted. His sarcastic words of scorn revive in Marmaduke the conviction that Herbert is guilty and must die. Marmaduke retrieves his sword and descends into the dungeon with murder in his heart. But once again the guardians of innocence rally successfully, and Marmaduke returns to Oswald with his sword unstained and with an account of the inscrutable intervention of extraordinary forces.

Marmaduke wonders why Oswald has come into the dungeon and prevented the blow which would have sent Herbert to his just reward. He accuses Oswald of grasping his arm: "Scarcely, by groping, had I reached the Spot," he claims,

---

[101] *The Borderers*, Act I, vv. 226-236.
[102] *Ibid.*, vv. 350-353. In the 1797 version Herbert has been drugged.

THE BORDERERS

> When round my wrist I felt a cord drawn tight,
> As if the blind Man's dog were pulling at it.[103]

Oswald of course has been nowhere near the scene, and the mysterious power that stayed the murderous stroke has been engendered in Marmaduke's imagination by the tutelary forces that preserve the innocent from harm. When Oswald asks what happened after that, Marmaduke replies that his second effort to kill Herbert was brought to nought by his discovery that "The features of Idonea Lurked in his face"[104] —"Yes, her very look, Smiling in sleep."[105] The effect of this discovery upon Marmaduke's already shaken senses was apparently enhanced by a kind of supernatural light suffusing the old man's face, for Marmaduke informs us that it was "dark as the grave,"[106] and we know that he was forced to grope his way to the spot where Herbert lay, and that it was dark enough for him to be unable to ascertain whether it was Oswald or something else that held his arm.

Marmaduke's intention to destroy Herbert in the dungeon is not completely dissipated, however, by the intervention of the secret paralyzing force, and by the hereditary resemblance between Herbert and Idonea. His final decision not to murder the old man is effected by a natural object—by a single star. The recognition of "Idonea's filial countenance" in Herbert's features, he explains,

> put me to my prayers.
> Upwards I cast my eyes, and, through a crevice,
> Beheld a star twinkling above my head,
> And, by the living God, I could not do it.[107]

The momentous significance of these curious signs and prodigies is not entirely wasted on Marmaduke. Their mute warnings suffice to prevent him from murdering Herbert in the dungeon. For the moment even Oswald seems to be

---

[103] Ibid., vv. 414–416. See also vv. 407–412. Originally this scene was written in prose. Wordsworth put it into blank verse in 1842.
[104] Ibid., vv. 417–418.
[105] Ibid., vv. 421–422.
[106] Ibid., v. 434. In the 1797 version it was "dark as hell!"
[107] Ibid., vv. 436–440.

impressed by the singular occurrences which Marmaduke describes, for he observes:

> Plain it is that Heaven
> Has marked out this foul Wretch as one whose crimes
> Must never come before a mortal judgment-seat,
> Or be chastised by mortal instruments.[108]

That this is an expression of the inference drawn by Marmaduke from his experience is made clear by his reply: "A thought that's worth a thousand worlds!"[109]

Had Marmaduke had to contend with a less subtle and resourceful villain than Oswald, he would no doubt have understood the record of innocence written indelibly on Herbert's face and interpreted correctly the evidence afforded him by his own sensibility and the gentle agency of the twinkling star. His experience in the dungeon would have instructed him not only that Herbert, if guilty, was to be judged only by God, but that Herbert was not guilty at all. Oswald, however, diminishes the influence of the various forces enlisted by innocence to work on Marmaduke's sympathetic heart by repeating in lewd terms, and at greater length, the tale of Herbert's guilt. His presentation of the case is compelling, and Marmaduke, in a state of mind bordering on insanity,[110] determines once and for all to commit Herbert to the "Ordeal." But once again the innocence of Herbert proclaims itself in terms which Marmaduke, in retrospect at the end of the play, doubtless recognized as unmistakable. Marmaduke sheds tears in the old man's presence, and listens in bewilderment to his fund of wisdom. "Learn, young Man," Herbert advises him,

---

[108] *The Borderers*, Act I, vv. 449–452. Presumably Oswald himself has felt the benign influence of nature in the past. Before he committed his crime he had been "for many days, On a dead sea under a burning sky . . . deserted by man and nature;—if a breeze had blown," he tells Marmaduke, "It might have found its way into my heart" (*ibid.*, Act IV, vv. 47–51).

[109] *Ibid.*, Act II, v. 453.

[110] Marmaduke's behavior and speech from the third act on, but especially in the third act, frequently suggest the feigned madness of Hamlet. The influence of Shakespeare is particularly noticeable in the 1797 text of *The Borderers*.

THE BORDERERS

> To fear the virtuous, and reverence misery,
> Whether too much for patience, or, like mine,
> Softened till it becomes a gift of mercy.[111]

These and many other lines pregnant with benign sentiment and Christian wisdom, all calculated to thaw the coldest heart, Herbert speaks to Marmaduke, the man of benevolence. But the fate of both is sealed. Herbert is abandoned despite the overwhelming testimony to his innocence, and Marmaduke is destined to a long and joyless life of expiation.

The conclusion of *The Borderers* is Wordsworth's answer to Oswald's cynical philosophy and to all those philosophers who follow the head and forget the heart. It is at once his proclamation of the dominant importance of the individual's social responsibilities, his indication of the gravity of the consequences if those responsibilities be shirked or wrongly met, and his formula for the regeneration of any human being whose pride has caused him—either consciously, as in Oswald's case, or unconsciously, as in Marmaduke's—too greatly to presume. As Wordsworth sees it, the primary duty of the individual is to love his fellow man and every other living thing. No man, no matter what the circumstances, may harbor within his breast scorn for another; neither may he pass judgment upon the actions of any but himself.[112] By presuming to the extent of committing Herbert to the "Ordeal," Marmaduke performs an act proper to God alone.

---

[111] *The Borderers*, Act III, vv. 203–206.

[112] Soon after Wordsworth read *The Borderers* and "Lines Left upon a Seat in a Yew-Tree" to Coleridge in June, 1797, the latter wrote the following to Southey: "I am as much a Pangloss as ever, only less contemptuous than I used to be when I argue how unwise it is to feel contempt for anything" (cited by de Selincourt, *The Poetical Works*, p. 329). The strength of the impression which Wordsworth's philosophy of love made upon Coleridge may be approximately estimated when we observe that Coleridge expressed the same philosophy in *Osorio*, and in "The Rime of the Ancyent Marinere," where, it will be remembered, the wedding-guest receives this good advice:

> He prayeth well who loveth well,
> Both man and bird and beast.

> He prayeth best who loveth best,
> All things both great and small:
> For the dear God, who loveth us,
> He made and loveth all.

Marmaduke, therefore, is guilty of *hubris*. Anyone so unfortunate as to be guilty of this sin must, like Marmaduke, pay a heavy penalty: either he must devote his life to the cultivation of remorse, as Marmaduke does, or he must be content to pass his days in wretched divorce from human sympathy. The latter fate is that of the solitary described in "Lines Left upon a Seat in a Yew-Tree." Wordsworth strongly recommends remorse. Both ways are painful: one leads to possible salvation and happiness in heaven, the other to everlasting misery.

Wordsworth's interest in the responsibility of the individual toward his fellows in a border society where there is no formal administration of law to govern conduct clearly reveals for the first time his belief in a transcendent ethical principle whose existence and value are independent of prevailing institutions and modes of government. Whether one lives under the British Constitution of the 1790's or in the anarchy of the border regions in the reign of Henry III, he must live in accord with the principle of self-effacing love. No man need look far to discover this principle; its lodging is the human heart, and it is everywhere in nature. Its presence in *The Borderers* proves, incidentally, that nature, to Wordsworth, was "the nurse, The guide, the guardian of my heart, and soul Of all my moral being," long before he wrote "Tintern Abbey."

We have already seen, as a matter of fact, that this ethical principle, which involves faith in a high moral perception where the feelings unite with and direct the power of reason and confidence in external nature as a norm of conduct, is implicit in the verses written by Wordsworth at Windy Brow in 1794. Therein, we remember, Wordsworth told us that the heart must feel "for all forms that life can take"; it will be conscious of the presence of a "secret power" that endears all forms of nature; it will not be deaf to the "social accents" emanating from these forms; and it will act in harmony with a mind that approaches nature "in a calm angelic mood Of happy wisdom meditating love." But Wordsworth, in 1794, was rather vague and abstract in his reference to this power or principle which is found in nature. It is only in *The Borderers*, when Marmaduke's attempt to murder Herbert in the dungeon is baffled by a twinkling star, that Wordsworth first suggests to us in the vivid manner of his later work the benign efficacy of natural objects as guides to right conduct.

A glance at the genesis of the dungeon scene, wherein the star saves Marmaduke from doing wrong, gives us a clear idea of the development of Wordsworth's ability to express his new philosophy concretely, and to rid his poetry of the cheap tricks and properties of the popular Gothic school. The attempted murder in the dungeon evidently was a subject that had appealed to Wordsworth's creative fancy long before he undertook the composition of a full-length tragedy. At some indeterminable date, according to Professor de Selincourt, writing from his knowledge of Wordsworth's early notebooks,

> he perpetrated a romantic narrative in pseudo-Spenserian stanzas. On a wild tempestuous night a youth guides a blind old man and his dog over rough precipitous ground to a ruined castle, and together they take refuge in its dungeon underground. The old man is pitifully grateful to his guide, who, however, is all the while meditating his murder. But before he can do the deed, he is checked by several typically Gothic portents—two sinister figures bearing a white burden, and a third with spade and crowbar, then a grim phantom, and a hand of fleshly hue; and when, not to be denied, he lifts his murderous aim, a rumbling noise is heard, passing into a sound of uncouth horror, which is echoed by a rending peal of fearful and mysterious import. The noise awakens his would-be victim, and here the fragment breaks off.[113]

Comparison of this lurid business with the dungeon scene of *The Borderers* shows that Wordsworth's taste was sufficiently improved by the spring of 1797 for him to realize that the horrendous Gothic machinery of which he had been fond in earlier years was not a satisfactory deterrent from crime. In place of the "sinister figures bearing a white burden," and

---

[113] *The Early Wordsworth*, pp. 11-12. It is significant that in the "Fragment of a 'Gothic' Tale" (see *The Poetical Works*, pp. 287-292), which de Selincourt here describes, the star fills the would-be murderer's heart with "a momentary dread" (p. 291), but does not check permanently his criminal intentions.

the "grim phantom" with "hand of fleshly hue," we have the more subtle restraints imposed by Marmaduke's imagination; instead of the dreadful "rumbling noise," and the "rending peal of fearful and mysterious import," we have merely a twinkling star.[114]

To conclude this study of *The Borderers* as a document wherein Wordsworth first expressed concretely—however ineptly—the nature philosophy which he is supposed to have evolved only after the tragedy was written, we must take note of one more passage—a short conversation between Idonea and Herbert. Herbert has become weary from the labors of the road, is depressed and full of dark thoughts. Idonea attempts successfully to restore his better spirits:

> Believe me, honoured Sire!
> 'Tis weariness that breeds these gloomy fancies,
> And you mistake the cause: you hear the woods
> Resound with music, could you see the sun,
> And look upon the pleasant face of Nature—
>
> Herbert: I comprehend thee—I should be as cheerful
> As if we two were twins; two songsters bred
> In the same nest, my spring-time one with thine.[115]

Through Idonea and Herbert Wordsworth here expresses the conception—basic in his best known and most successful poems—of nature as an agent and minister of pleasure ever ready to remind disheartened and misguided men that joy is their proper emotion. This completes Wordsworth's answer to Oswald's cynical philosophy and our survey of the evidence opposed to the belief that *The Borderers* is a morbid, pessimistic play.

III

The position occupied by *The Borderers* in the evolution of Wordsworth's concern for the evils of society remains to

---

[114] This specimen of Wordsworth's early work and Wordsworth's significant alteration of it in *The Borderers* constitute a complete confirmation of the argument of Professors Campbell and Mueschke that Wordsworth in *The Borderers* took a great step in the direction of his mature aesthetic practice by purging himself of much of his concern with the paraphernalia of the Gothic school of terror ("The Borderers . . . ," passim).

[115] *The Borderers*, Act I, vv. 144-151.

THE BORDERERS

be considered. Legouis pointed out years ago that the play marked a significant change in Wordsworth's attitude toward society and its evils.[116] He called attention to the fact that Wordsworth in *Guilt and Sorrow* was disposed to place all the blame for the evil in this world upon social and political institutions. By the time he wrote *The Borderers*, however, Wordsworth had thought more deeply about the sources of evil, and had carefully observed the unpromising direction events had taken under Robespierre in republican France. He concluded finally that

> The deeper malady is better hid;
> The world is poisoned at the heart,

and that "Evil was inherent in man's limited and imperfect nature."[117] This discovery, Legouis continues, caused Wordsworth to despair of reforming society. Subsequent critics, who have concerned themselves with Wordsworth's interest in the evils of society, have agreed with Legouis and have repeated his contention that Wordsworth made no effort in *The Borderers* to strike at the social and political wrongs which he had attacked bitterly several years before in *Guilt and Sorrow*.[118] To these critics, in short, *Guilt and Sorrow* and *The Borderers* bear no relationship to one another so far as Wordsworth's attitude toward society is concerned.

It is true that Wordsworth made a conscious effort in *The Borderers* to avoid the outspoken and exaggerated social criticism that we find in *Guilt and Sorrow*. The events described in the earlier poem take place in the England which Wordsworth knew; the action of *The Borderers* is so remote in time that whatever the play contains of social comment seems to lack applicability to the England of the 1790's. In the Fenwick note to *The Borderers* Wordsworth declared: "As to the scene and period of action, little more was required for my purpose than the absence of established Law and Government; so that the agents might be at liberty to act on their own impulses . . . ." This certainly suggests, as Legouis

---

[116] *Op. cit.*, pp. 276–277.   [117] *Ibid.*, p. 277.
[118] See, for example, de Selincourt, "Wordsworth's Preface to *The Borderers*," pp. 171–172.

contends, that Wordsworth had progressed beyond the stage of *Guilt and Sorrow* in which he held the naïve opinion that evil and distress would vanish if England would follow the enlightened French and introduce sweeping political change. Robespierre, the Terror, and French aggression no doubt did much to shatter Wordsworth's faith in the political panacea and to lead him to the wise conclusion that old wrongs are not righted over night. This realization, in turn, doubtless caused him to probe the mind and heart of man in his search for a solution to the mystery of evil and for the means of its correction. The results of this search, however, were quite different from those described by Legouis. Some evil Wordsworth may have found; but he found also, as we have just observed, an antidote for evil, a potent force for good existing in the heart of man and in the world of nature. The emphasis of *The Borderers,* to be sure, falls upon Wordsworth's newly discovered ethical principle and the duty of the individual to live according to its dictates, not upon the inalienable right of the individual to receive just treatment from his government. It is a mistake, however, to believe that *The Borderers* was Wordsworth's farewell to reform. Despite his shift of emphasis from the rights to the responsibilities of the individual, and despite his effort to detach the action of his tragedy from the events of his own day by making it remote in point of time, Wordsworth had by no means absolved British social and political institutions from their share of blame for the wrongs and dislocations which he saw about him. He continued to describe in *The Borderers* many of the social evils which he had criticized in his *Letter to the Bishop of Llandaff* and in *Guilt and Sorrow—* evils, that is, which we associate not with the England of Henry III, but with Wordsworth's own experience in the England of the 1790's.

There is, first of all, the situation of Idonea and Herbert. Herbert's property has been unlawfully seized, and there is apparently nothing he can do to get it back. His only chance is to gain the favor of the Baron Clifford, whose great power and influence render all things possible to him.

THE BORDERERS

These circumstances compel the old man to pass his later days in pain and wretchedness and destroy Idonea's chances for future happiness. Were it not for her father's poverty and dependence upon her, Idonea would be free to marry Marmaduke. But duty forbids, and when Idonea at last is released from the filial responsibilities which have thwarted her hopes for domestic bliss, marriage with Marmaduke is no longer a possibility. The similarity between these misfortunes and those experienced by Wordsworth is of course close and clear.

Even more striking than the effects of injustice upon Herbert and Idonea is Wordsworth's description in *The Borderers* of the extremes of poverty and wealth, and of the moral consequences of the inequitable distribution of economic power. The Baron Clifford, who represents the nobility, is degenerate and tyrannical. He is an inveterate lecher who lives in a great castle, where—aided by his ability to play upon a minstrel's harp with irresistible charm—he ensnares the innocent maidens of the neighborhood and leads them to their ruin. His senses, blunted with excess, clamor for novelty; no sooner does he gain his vicious end with one than he casts her off in favor of another. The consequences of his depravity are vividly described by Wordsworth in a passage, spoken by Oswald, which all students of *Lyrical Ballads* will immediately recognize as a crude first draft of "The Thorn":

> You marked a Cottage,
> That ragged Dwelling, close beneath a rock
> By the brook-side: it is the abode of One,
> A Maiden innocent till ensnared by Clifford,
> Who soon grew weary of her; but, alas!
> What she had seen and suffered turned her brain.
> Cast off by her Betrayer, she dwells alone,
> Nor moves her hands to any needful work:
> She eats her food which every day the peasants
> Bring to her hut; and so the Wretch has lived
> Ten years; and no one ever heard her voice;
> But every night at the first stroke of twelve
> She quits her house, and, in the neighbouring Church-
>   yard
> Upon the self-same spot, in rain or storm,

> She paces out the hour 'twixt twelve and one—
> She paces round and round an Infant's grave,
> And in the Churchyard sod her feet have worn
> A hollow ring; they say it is knee-deep.[119]

In sharp contrast to this picture of the nobility is Wordsworth's description of the lower classes, presented to us in the speeches of the female beggar whom Oswald has suborned. This woman's situation is remarkably similar to that of the soldier's widow in *An Evening Walk*. She has a child, and must beg to keep herself and the child alive. When the child cries for bread she attempts to divert his attention from hunger by giving him flowers to play with. Once, however, the remedy proves worse than the evil it is meant to cure: a bee, lurking in the blossom of a foxglove which her son has pressed to his ear, stings the child so horribly that he turns black as if about to die. The memory of this dreadful accident and her consciousness of the utter hopelessness of her situation cause the beggar to wish that she might "rather be A stone than what I am."[120] "O sir," she cries,

> How would you like to travel on whole hours
> As I have done, my eyes upon the ground,
> Expecting still, I knew not how, to find
> A piece of money glittering through the dust.[121]

And then, commenting upon the inhumanity of her fellow beings, the beggar speaks in a vein reminiscent of the female vagrant:

> Well! they might turn a beggar from their doors,
> But there are Mothers who can see the Babe
> Here at my breast, and ask me where I bought it.[122]

Wretched and precarious as lower-class life is, however, throughout the irksome five acts of *The Borderers* it is plain that the heart of each peasant who appears upon the scene is in reality a little citadel of virtue and benevolence. Early in the play Herbert and Idonea, after a long walk, encounter an anonymous peasant. Perceiving at once that they are

[119] *The Borderers*, Act I, vv. 378–395.
[120] *Ibid.*, vv. 421–422.
[121] *Ibid.*, vv. 431–435.
[122] *Ibid.*, vv. 439–441.

strangers in the district and noticing Herbert's fatigue, the kind fellow offers to guide them and to lend old Herbert the support of his shoulder. Herbert refuses aid, however, and the peasant, after directing them to a hostel a short distance down the road, politely takes his leave with a "God speed you both."[123] The host, at whose inn Idonea and Herbert find shelter and rest, is the soul of generosity and solicitude. His anxiety for the welfare of his guests is arresting: when he learns that Idonea is to proceed on foot and leaving Herbert behind to rest his aged bones, he offers to let her take a palfrey and a groom—

> the lad
> Shall squire you . . . .
> And for less fee than I would let him run
> For any lady I have seen this twelvemonth.[124]

Such an offer as this is of course clear proof that the host is sensitive to the appeal of innocence and is, accordingly, a man to whom the principles of benevolence are dear. Further evidence of the goodness of the lower classes is the fact that the wretched female whom the wealthy Clifford has cast off is kept alive by the neighborhood peasants, who pity her and give her food. And finally, when Idonea finds shelter from a stormy night in the lowly cot of Eldred and Eleanor, and when Eldred, discovering the exhausted Herbert alone upon the moor, offers immediately to take him to his hut near-by, we see again what virtuous and benevolent impulses emanate from the peasant heart.

Only money and the most unjust and vicious treatment can pervert the innate virtue of these peasants. It is true that the beggar woman becomes the tool of Oswald and lies elaborately and with dire results for a handful of gold, and it is true that Eldred, in the hour of Herbert's greatest need, forsakes the highest principles of humanity and leaves the old man to perish on the moor. But in each case there were extenuating circumstances. The beggar's need was great and she was ignorant of Oswald's murderous design. It seems, in fact, that she bore false witness believing that only

---

[123] *Ibid.*, v. 222.   [124] *Ibid.*, vv. 311-314.

thus could Idonea be saved from the fate that awaited her in the castle of the Baron Clifford.[125] Here the end clearly justified the means. And of Eldred's defection Wordsworth gives us an explanation that proclaims once again his abiding dissatisfaction with the perverse justice meted out in the British courts of law.

Eldred is the only peasant in the play whose motives and psychology Wordsworth troubles to present at any length. One night long ago, according to the account of Eleanor, his wife, Eldred was

> Dragged from his bed . . . cast into a dungeon,
> Where, hid from me, he counted many years,
> A criminal in no one's eyes but theirs—
> Not even in theirs—whose brutal violence
> So dealt with him.[126]

This harrowing experience has left a scar: "Good Eldred," says Eleanor,

> Has a kind heart; but his imprisonment
> Has made him fearful, and he'll never be
> The man he was.[127]

Eleanor's words prove to be prophetic. No sooner has she spoken them than Eldred enters, paralyzed with fear, his frock besmeared with Herbert's blood. To his frightened wife he relates the details of his night's adventure. He tells her how he came upon the old man and raised him up to carry him to their cottage for shelter and restoration. By the light of the moon he saw the blood upon his garments and was afraid. He realized that Herbert, suffering from cold and hunger and a gash in the head, had no wish to live. He was convinced, he says, that Herbert was too far gone to be saved by human hands; so he left him upon the moor —helpless, dying, and alone. The good Eleanor is naturally distressed by this account of her husband's inhumanity and reproaches him for failing to do all in his power to sustain

---

[125] In the second act (v. 402), the beggar declares unequivocally that Oswald's money was not the cause of her informing Marmaduke that Idonea was her daughter, purchased from her by Herbert.

[126] *The Borderers*, Act IV, vv. 242-246.

[127] *Ibid.*, vv. 249-252.

THE BORDERERS

and comfort the little life remaining in the old man's body. But Eldred, for the moment unregenerate, reminds her of their past suffering and conjures up for her benefit a vision of what the future would hold in store for them should Herbert die in their custody.

Eldred's defense of his behavior reveals that his naturally tender heart has been hardened by the injustice which he has suffered in the past. He has spent years in a dungeon for a crime committed by another.[128] It is his fear of a repetition of such injustice that thwarts his benevolent instincts and causes him to refuse humane treatment to the dying Herbert. Were it not for this expectation of injustice, Eldred would be quick to aid the unfortunate old man; he would gladly shelter him in his cottage and nourish him from his own scanty resources. As it is, Eldred's humanity is destroyed by the terror engendered by the injustice prevalent in the society in which he lives. It is society, not Eldred, that is to blame for his shameful action; it is society that has taught him to put self-interest above benevolence, to desert a fellow being in distress, and to slink away from human duty under cover of night. Just as society was responsible in *Guilt and Sorrow* for the sailor's murder of his son and for the moral delinquency of the female vagrant, so is it responsible here for Eldred's crime against humanity. To assume that Wordsworth had abandoned his criticism of social institutions before he wrote *The Borderers* is to ignore this obvious fact.

It is equally plain, however, that Wordsworth's emphasis in *The Borderers* was not upon the cause of Eldred's iniquity. Wordsworth failed, to be sure, to resist entirely the temptation to suggest that Eldred's natural virtue had been corrupted by the evils of society and that the beggar woman's honesty had been destroyed by Oswald's bribery. But Wordsworth did not wish to stress the fall from virtue of these two lowly people; the important thing was that both the beggar woman and Eldred were basically good. Despite their temporary deviation from the path of strict righteousness and humanity,

[128] In the 1797 version of the play we learn that Eldred has been placed upon the rack by his persecutors (*The Poetical Works,* p. 206).

we see clearly before the end of the play that their essential virtue is indestructible. The beggar, in the last act, rushes onto the stage in a veritable fit of remorse and penitential anguish. "God is my judge," she cries, for the benefit of Idonea—

> I thought there was no harm: but that bad Man,
> He bribed me with his gold, and looked so fierce.
> Mercy! I said I know not what—oh pity me—
> I said, sweet Lady, you were not his Daughter—
> Pity me, I am haunted;—thrice this day
> My conscience made me wish to be struck blind;
> And then I would have prayed, and had no voice.[129]

And Eldred, too, repents immediately after he has confessed his inhumanity to Eleanor. When Idonea appears and reveals that it is her father whom Eldred has deserted, the good peasant, deeply moved by the sight of innocence in distress, regains his natural benevolence, guides Idonea to her father, and conducts himself admirably throughout the rest of the play.

The Borderers does, then, record a change in Wordsworth's attitude toward the evils of English society which he castigated in his earlier work. He has not lost sight of these evils, but his point of view has changed. Here Wordsworth refrains from underscoring the causes of the reprehensible actions of the beggar woman and Eldred and makes no attempt to account for the glaring inequality in the distribution of wealth between the degenerate nobility and the virtuous peasantry. In the *Letter to the Bishop of Llandaff* and *Guilt and Sorrow* Wordsworth was certain that monarchy was responsible for all such evils and economic discrepancies. In *The Borderers*, however, there is scarcely a trace remaining of his hatred of monarchy and his zeal for a democratic form of government. He was content, in his later work, to let the reader believe that Clifford was rich and a villain, Eldred poor but essentially noble, simply because Providence —whose ways are inscrutable—had so decreed. This did not mean that Wordsworth had lost faith in reform or that he was

---

[129] *The Borderers*, Act V, vv. 228-235.

ready to accept things as they were. The fact that he made such a pointed distinction between Eldred and the Baron Clifford and the fact that he bothered to explain Eldred's inhumane behavior are proof that he had lost neither social consciousness nor social conscience. His shift of emphasis from the evil caused by monarchical institutions to the good that resides in the hearts of common men merely reflects his adoption of a new method of reform, a method more likely to succeed than the one he had used in his earlier, more obviously provocative work. This new method, destined to become fixed and basic in *Lyrical Ballads* and subsequent productions, we shall study and describe in the following chapter. We shall see that Wordsworth's desire to remake the world according to his own ideal continued unabated; it was only his manner of attack that changed.

CHAPTER VI

The Naturalism of 1798

I

OF THE various poems written by Wordsworth in 1797 and 1798 none shows more clearly than *The Ruined Cottage* the elements, both old and new, of which *Lyrical Ballads* and much of his later poetry were composed. From the spring of 1794, when he had finished the first draft of *Guilt and Sorrow* and made significant additions to *An Evening Walk* at Windy Brow, until the spring of 1797, when he completed *The Borderers,* Wordsworth's interest was divided between his desire to castigate the evils of monarchical society, from which he had suffered, and his wish to celebrate the joy and benevolence which, his reading and experience assured him, reward the student of external nature. Both of these impulses, as we have seen, received unmistakable expression in *The Borderers,* where Wordsworth for the first time since his return from France, in a poem of any length, subordinated his concern for social ills to his faith in the moral power of nature and the innate goodness of the common man. In *The Borderers,* however, Wordsworth's social sympathy and philosophical love of nature were crudely juxtaposed, not artistically fused. It was not until he wrote *The Ruined Cottage* that he achieved his characteristic synthesis of these basic elements of his best poetry.

Critics have long recognized the unusual importance of *The Ruined Cottage* in the history of Wordsworth's development. Legouis, for example, remarks that "Between the poems which betray the effect of his moral crisis on the one

THE NATURALISM OF 1798

hand, and *The Recluse* and the *Lyrical Ballads* . . . on the other, *The Ruined Cottage* occupies a unique position . . . ."[1] Herbert Read observes that the poem marks a great advance over Wordsworth's earlier work "in the direction of simplicity and realism"—so great an advance, in fact, "that it really contains the germ of all his subsequent development."[2] And Professors Campbell and Mueschke discover in *The Ruined Cottage* "the first indication of a revolution in Wordsworth's aesthetic practice."[3] But because facts now available concerning the composition of the poem were unknown before 1935 and because these critics have approached *The Ruined Cottage* with an incomplete understanding of Wordsworth's earlier work, their accounts of the significance of *The Ruined Cottage* in the evolution of Wordsworth's poetry are necessarily lacking in precision.

In his old age Wordsworth associated the composition of *The Ruined Cottage* with that of *The Borderers*. In the Fenwick note to *The Excursion*, in whose first book *The Ruined Cottage* was later incorporated, Wordsworth declared that the lines "beginning, 'Nine tedious years,' and ending, 'Last human tenant of these ruined walls' " were "composed in '95 at Racedown . . . ."[4] It would seem, however, that he was mistaken in attributing these lines to the year 1795, just as he was mistaken in his belief that he had begun to write *The Borderers* in the same year, for in her letter to Mary Hutchinson in June, 1797, Dorothy asserts that "The first thing that was read after he [Coleridge] came was William's new poem *The Ruined Cottage* . . . ."[5] It is unlikely

---

[1] Émile Legouis, *The Early Life of William Wordsworth, 1770–1798*, tr. by J. W. Matthews (New York, 1918), p. 355.

[2] *Wordsworth: The Clark Lectures, 1929–1930* (New York, 1931), p. 133.

[3] O. J. Campbell and P. Mueschke, "Wordsworth's Aesthetic Development, 1795–1802," *Essays and Studies in English and Comparative Literature*, University of Michigan Publications, Language and Literature, X (Ann Arbor, 1933), 15.

[4] Wordsworth here refers to vv. 871–916 of the first book of *The Excursion*.

[5] *The Early Letters of William and Dorothy Wordsworth (1787–1805)*, ed. by Ernest de Selincourt (Oxford, 1935) (hereafter referred to as *The Early Letters*), p. 169.

that Dorothy would have described as a "new poem" verses which her brother had composed almost two years before, and it is now certain that the only part of *The Ruined Cottage* which Wordsworth could have read to Coleridge in June, 1797, consisted of those lines which he later claimed to have written in 1795.

On March 5, 1798, Dorothy answered Mary Hutchinson's request for a copy of the poem that had been "new" a year before by announcing that it had "grown to the length of 900 lines," by remarking that "The Pedlar's character now makes a very, certainly the *most*, considerable part of the Poem," and by transcribing approximately four hundred lines that were "immediately and solely connected with the Cottage."[6] Dorothy's description of the entire poem, the lines she copies, and her remark at the end of her letter—"You have the rest to the end of Margaret's story. There is much more about the Pedlar"[7]—establish clearly that Mary Hutchinson already knew the lines which later became verses 871–916 of the first book of *The Excursion*, that no more than these lines had been written before late May or early June, 1797, when Mary Hutchinson left Racedown, and that the poem was all but complete by March 5, 1798.[8] *The Ruined Cottage* must therefore be regarded as the work of late 1797 and early 1798.

To the student of Wordsworth's early poetry it is readily apparent that *The Ruined Cottage* is similar in narrative detail to the story of the female vagrant in *Guilt and Sorrow*. Margaret and Robert, her husband, were industrious English

---

[6] *The Early Letters*, p. 176. This letter was printed for the first time in 1935 by Professor de Selincourt.
[7] *Ibid.*, p. 187.
[8] The final version of the poem—the first book of *The Excursion*—contains only 970 lines, and the concluding fifty-four of these serve primarily to connect *The Ruined Cottage* with the following books of the longer poem. They probably were composed at a much later date.

It may be that Wordsworth, when he dated *The Ruined Cottage* verses as of 1795, confused them with a fragment entitled "Incipient Madness," which seems to be a crude first draft of the longer poem. Professor de Selincourt published this fragment for the first time in 1940 and attributes it to 1795 or 1796 (*The Poetical Works of William Wordsworth: Poems Written in Youth, Poems Referring to the Period of Childhood*, ed. by Ernest de Selincourt [Oxford, 1940] [hereafter referred to as *The Poetical Works*], pp. 314–316, 375).

THE NATURALISM OF 1798

peasants who lived happily in a cottage with their two children until the nation was oppressed with bad harvests, war, and economic depression. Although rich people were impoverished and many of those already poor died, presumably of starvation, Margaret and Robert struggled hopefully on until Robert was stricken with a fever. When he had recovered from his long illness, Robert found that the family savings were exhausted and that no employment was available in England. He took temporary pleasure in performing odd jobs about the house and garden, but before long his spirit drooped and "poverty brought on a petted mood And a sore temper." One moment he would play merrily with his children; the next, "he would speak lightly of his babes And with a cruel tongue." Then, he was wont to leave his home and wander idly through the fields and into town. Finally, he disappeared and for two days was unheard of. On the third day, however, Margaret discovered a purse of gold inside her window, and shortly thereafter was told by a messenger sent by Robert that he had gone to fight with the army in a distant land. This information Robert had not dared to deliver himself for fear that Margaret and the children would follow and be exposed to the horrors of war.

Nine long years Margaret waited in vain for her husband's return. For a few months, aided by the purse of gold and what little she could earn by spinning, she kept her family together. But by the end of the first summer she was obliged to let her elder son be "Apprenticed by the parish." Meanwhile, she had fallen into the habit of strolling aimlessly about the countryside, neglecting her cottage, her garden, and her baby. There is a suggestion that she either suffered a psychological collapse like that experienced by Robert, or, like the female vagrant, was driven by need to prostitution. These seem at least to be the most satisfactory explanations of her curious confession to the Pedlar:

> I am changed,
> And to myself . . . have done much wrong,
> And to this helpless infant.[9]

---

[9] Professors Campbell and Mueschke suggest that these lines are another furtive manifestation of Wordsworth's remorse for his desertion of Annette

Before the end of autumn, in any case, Margaret's cottage and garden had fallen into complete disorder: her few books lay scattered in confusion; her baby was dead. For seven or eight years more, nourished by the futile hope that Robert would return, she continued to exist. At length, however, the decay of the cottage was so extreme that the winter winds would shake her ragged clothes as she huddled before her fire, and "the nightly damps Did chill her breast." After nine sad years of widowhood, Margaret—"Last human tenant of these ruined walls"—was dead.

Clearly the suffering of Margaret in *The Ruined Cottage* resembles closely that of the female vagrant in *Guilt and Sorrow*. Both women experience the various hardships of war and economic depression. The two poems, nevertheless, are worlds apart. In *Guilt and Sorrow*, as we have seen, Wordsworth placed the responsibility for war, for depression—and their attendant ills—upon the monarchical form of government sustained by the British Constitution. But in *The Ruined Cottage* there is no suggestion that monarchy, or any other man-made institution, is to blame for Margaret's tragedy. In 1797 and 1798, in describing how a poor harvest and "the plague of war" combined to destroy the happiness of Margaret and Robert, Wordsworth explained the disasters as acts of God—"It pleased heaven," he wrote, "to add a worse affliction in the plague of war." Since most of the distress that befell Margaret, Robert, and their children was the direct and unmistakable result of war, it is obvious that Wordsworth in *The Ruined Cottage* chose to regard human suffering as a "chastisement of Providence," rather than as the work of selfish and misguided men.

This fundamental shift in Wordsworth's view of the causes of domestic catastrophe calls attention to the fact that in *The Ruined Cottage*, as in *The Borderers*, he preferred to stress, not the evil implicit in monarchical institutions, but the comfort and joy available to man in nature and the inexhaustible good emanating from the heart of common humanity. A

Vallon (*op. cit.*, p. 14). This theory, however, is no more tenable in regard to *The Ruined Cottage* than it is in connection with *Guilt and Sorrow*.

THE NATURALISM OF 1798

study of the narrative method used in *The Ruined Cottage* shows that Wordsworth's immediate object here was quite different from that which prompted the composition of *Guilt and Sorrow*. In *Guilt and Sorrow* Wordsworth, with his pointed descriptions of social injustice, plainly attempted to arouse his readers to action; in *The Ruined Cottage* he made an obvious effort to cushion them against the full impact of the emotional disquietude and shock likely to result from the tale of undeserved suffering which he invited them to contemplate. Wordsworth wished to plunge the readers of *Guilt and Sorrow* into a state of feverish indignation; the readers of *The Ruined Cottage* he hoped to leave in a lush condition of benevolent tranquility.

To prevent the painful situation described in the poem from disturbing the reader by seeming to reflect too closely conditions of the day, Wordsworth set his narrative back ten years in time and told it indirectly through the Pedlar. And, what is more important, the Pedlar tells the story of Margaret, not for its own sake, but only incidentally, as an apt illustration of certain metaphysical observations which he, in his own character, feels obliged to make. "I see around me Things which you cannot see," he announces to his companion, who has just slaked his thirst at a spring near the ruined cottage—

>   We die, my Friend,
> Nor we alone but that which each man loved
> And prized in his peculiar nook of earth
> Dies with him, or is changed; and very soon
> Even of the good is no memorial left.
> The waters of that spring, if they could feel,
> Might mourn. They are not as they were, the bond
> Of brotherhood is broken; time has been
> When every day the touch of human hand
> Disturbed their stillness, and they ministered
> To human comfort. As I stooped to drink,
> Few minutes gone, at that deserted well
> What feelings came to me! A spider's web
> Across its mouth hung to the water's edge,
> And on the wet and slimy footstone lay
> The useless fragment of a wooden bowl.
> It moved my very heart. The time has been

> When I could never pass this way but She
> Who lived within these walls, when I appeared
> A daughter's welcome gave me, and I loved her
> As my own child. Oh Sir! the good die first,
> And they whose hearts are dry as summer dust
> Burn to the socket. Many a passenger
> Has blessed poor Margaret for her gentle looks
> When she upheld the cool refreshment drawn
> From that forsaken well, and no one came
> But he was welcome, no one went away
> But that it seemed she loved him. She is dead,
> The worm is on her cheek, and this poor hut
> Stripped of its outward garb of household flowers,
> Of rose and woodbine, offers to the wind
> A cold bare wall whose earthy top is tricked
> With weeds and the rank spear-grass. She is dead
> And nettles rot, and adders sun themselves
> Where we have sate together, while she nursed
> Her infant at her bosom. The wild colt,
> The unstalled heifer, and the Potter's ass
> Find shelter now within the chimney wall
> Where I have seen her evening hearth-stone blaze,
> And, through the window, spread upon the road
> Its chearful light.[10]

To the Pedlar, in other words, the ruined cottage and the various objects which surround it are significant as symbols of mutability, and it is to illuminate the nature of change and decay rather than to suggest the need for social reform that he proceeds with the history of Margaret. This is obviously what Professors Campbell and Mueschke have in mind when they point out that "Wordsworth was clearly at pains to make the sorrows of Margaret unrelated to the actual life of either the *raconteur* or his companion. The Wanderer [the Pedlar] takes the attitude of a sympathetic observer ... who has attained a philosophical disinterestedness."[11]

The Pedlar interrupts his distressing tale from time to time with lyrical descriptions of external nature. These are clearly designed to confer a share of the Pedlar's philosophic

---

[10] Quotations from *The Ruined Cottage*, unless otherwise indicated, are taken from the version of 1798 as it was recorded by Dorothy for Mary Hutchinson (*The Early Letters,* pp. 176–187).

[11] *Op. cit.,* p. 11.

detachment upon the reader, and to relieve the intensity of the latter's reaction to the sufferings of Margaret. Typical of these sedative digressions is the passage in which the Pedlar describes his travels through the enduring world of nature in the interval between Robert's disappearance and the day when Margaret informed him that she had parted with her elder son:

> I roved o'er many a hill and many a dale
> With this my weary load, in heat and cold,
> Through many a wood and many an open ground
> In sunshine, or in shade, in wet or fair,
> Now blithe, now drooping, as it might befal;
> My best companions now the driving winds
> And now the "trotting" brooks, and whispering trees,
> And now the music of my own sad steps
> With many a short-lived thought that past between
> And disappeared.

By means of these digressions and, as Professors Campbell and Mueschke observe, by having the Pedlar frequently invoke "the peace inherent in the natural objects which surround her deserted cottage,"[12] Wordsworth employed "the central peace of Nature . . . to raise the mind of the observer above the endless agitation of human action,"[13] and succeeded in giving to the story of Margaret "psychic distance and universal significance."[14]

Finally, the concluding lines of the poem—the lines first written by Wordsworth, and read to Coleridge at Racedown, in June, 1797—focus the reader's attention, not upon the manifold ills which Margaret has experienced, but upon the unusual patience and fortitude, the inexhaustible hope with which she endured the last years of her pathetic existence:[15]

---

[12] *Ibid.*, p. 15.   [13] *Ibid.*, pp. 15–16.   [14] *Ibid.*, p. 15.

[15] Oscar James Campbell (in his "Sentimental Morality in Wordsworth's Narrative Poetry," *Studies by Members of the Department of English*, Series No. 2, University of Wisconsin Studies in Language and Literature, No. 11 [Madison, 1920], 21–57) denies that Wordsworth intended to exhibit peasant strength of character in his account of Margaret: ". . . it is hard to see," he observes, "how the wretched woman's actions after the loss of her husband can be considered essentially courageous or in any deep sense admirable. She seems to be unnerved and fairly possessed by her uncertainty and grief. She wanders disconsolately about the country-side; she neglects her infant; she

Nine tedious years;
From their first separation, nine long years,
She lingered in unquiet widowhood;
A Wife and Widow. Needs must it have been
A sore heart-wasting! I have heard, my Friend,
That in yon arbour oftentimes she sate
Alone, through half the vacant Sabbath-day,
And if a dog passed by she still would quit
The shade, and look abroad. On this old Bench
For hours she sate; and evermore her eye
Was busy in the distance, shaping things
That made her heart beat quick. You see that path,
Now faint,—the grass has crept o'er its grey line;
There, to and fro, she paced through many a day
Of the warm summer, from a belt of hemp
That girt her waist, spinning the long drawn thread
With backward steps. Yet ever as there pass'd
A man whose garments shewed the Soldiers red,
Or crippled Mendicant in Sailor's garb,
The little Child who sate to turn the wheel
Ceas'd from his task; and she with faultering voice
Made many a fond enquiry; and when they,
Whose presence gave no comfort, were gone by,
Her heart was still more sad. And by yon gate,
That bars the Traveller's road, she often stood,
And when a stranger Horseman came the latch
Would lift, and in his face look wistfully;
Most happy, if, from aught discovered there
Of tender feeling, she might dare repeat
The same sad question. Meanwhile her poor Hut
Sank to decay: for he was gone—whose hand,
At the first nipping of October frost,

---

allows her garden to become choked with weeds and to show first 'the sleepy hand of negligence' and then actual decay. After her babe dies, 'she lingers in unquiet widowhood nine tedious years, until she, too, dies in the ruins of her home.' This woman, who allows all her natural duties to be swallowed up in grief, can hardly have been presented as a splendid example of the robust fortitude of the peasants" (*op. cit.*, pp. 34–35).

It is true that Margaret neglects her "natural duties" for a year or two following her husband's disappearance. The fact remains, however, that the lines descriptive of her behavior during her last years emphasize the strength and courage with which she meets her fate. There seems to be a clear distinction between the instability which Margaret displays immediately following the initial shock of her bereavement, and the persistent hope which characterizes by far the greater part of her widowhood.

THE NATURALISM OF 1798

>   Closed up each chink, and with fresh bands of straw
>   Chequered the green-grown thatch. And so she lived
>   Through the long winter, reckless and alone;
>   Until her House by frost, and thaw, and rain,
>   Was sapped; and while she slept the nightly damps
>   Did chill her breast; and in the stormy day
>   Her tattered clothes were ruffled by the wind;
>   Even at the side of her own fire. Yet still
>   She loved this wretched spot, nor would for worlds
>   Have parted hence; and still that length of road,
>   And this rude bench, one torturing hope endeared,
>   Fast rooted at her heart: and here, my Friend,
>   In sickness she remained; and here she died,
>   Last human Tenant of these ruined Walls.[16]

We must now attempt to explain Wordsworth's purpose in writing *The Ruined Cottage*. Why in this poem, as in *The Borderers*, after again describing in detail many of the evils which he attributed solely to monarchy in the *Letter to the Bishop of Llandaff* and in *Guilt and Sorrow*, did he choose to absolve the government of England from blame and to hold "heaven" responsible for human suffering? Why, to put it another way, was he now content to write of famine, war, unemployment, crime, and the disintegration of families without attempting to persuade us that these unwholesome aspects of English life might be eliminated by the adoption of a republican form of government? Why did Wordsworth now find it sufficient to invoke the calm of nature and to emphasize only the virtues of humanity when he obviously knew that England had done little if anything to ameliorate the misery of the people?

The best answers thus far provided for these questions have been written by Professor Campbell, who suggests that Wordsworth, after rejecting Godwin's radical rationalism,

began to write a kind of poetry which he had not attempted before.[17] He retained his interest in the common man, but he no longer pre-

---

[16] Because Mary Hutchinson was already familiar with these lines, Dorothy did not transcribe them in her letter of March, 1798. The text followed here is that of the first edition of *The Excursion*, 1814.

[17] The more recent studies of the evolution of Wordsworth's aesthetic practice by Professor Campbell in collaboration with Paul Mueschke ("*Guilt*

sented his condition as one to invite the reforms of rational humanitarians. He made him the object of compassion by showing him enduring with fortitude undeserved suffering; he gave the reader authentic instances of the reformation of erring human beings by the sight of virtue in distress. In embodying these ideas in poetic tales he felt that he was not merely indulging his temperament, but softening human hearts into virtue by evoking the tender emotion of pity.[18]

Professor Campbell bases his argument soundly upon those verses of *The Ruined Cottage* which contain the Pedlar's excuse for telling a tale of sorrow at an hour of the day when nature is full of joy:

> It were wantonness, and would demand
> Severe reproof, if we were men whose hearts
> Could hold vain dalliance with the misery
> Even of the dead; contented thence to draw
> A momentary pleasure, never marked
> By reason, barren of all future good;
> But we have known that there is often found
> In mournful thoughts, and always might be found,
> A power to virtue friendly.[19]

Wordsworth, according to this critic, found a sanction for these sentimental tales in the literature of the eighteenth century, particularly in the "moral system" of David Hartley, in which "a central place [was] given to compassion for undeserved human suffering."[20]

This description of the new direction taken by Wordsworth's poetry, though sound in its general outline, is nevertheless unsatisfactory in several important details. It assumes, for example, that Wordsworth "rejected" Godwin and that the influence of David Hartley was essentially antipathetic to that of Godwin, whereas Hartley, as will soon appear, probably reinforced strongly the influence of his disciple. It

---

and Sorrow: A Study in the Genesis of Wordsworth's Aesthetic," *Modern Philology*, XXIII [1926], 293–306; "*The Borderers* as a Document in the History of Wordsworth's Aesthetic Development," *ibid.*, XXIII [1926], 465–482) correct this mistaken assertion that Wordsworth "began to write a kind of poetry which he had not attempted before" when he turned to poetic tales of sentimental morality. We have already seen that Wordsworth incorporated at least one such tale in *An Evening Walk*, his earliest significant composition.

[18] "Sentimental Morality in Wordsworth's Narrative Poetry," pp. 24–25.
[19] *Ibid.*, pp. 25–26.   [20] *Ibid.*, p. 57; but see also pp. 52–56.

THE NATURALISM OF 1798

maintains, furthermore, that Wordsworth in the period of his maturity devoted himself to making "morally better men"[21] of his readers by providing them with various stimuli to virtue, but it fails to distinguish the kind of virtue Wordsworth attempted to generate, or precisely how and for what specific purpose he hoped to increase the moral strength of his readers. It suggests, finally, that Wordsworth, after 1796 and 1797, lost interest in humanitarian reform, when, in reality, his interest in reform continued unabated, although his method of working for the betterment of society was radically changed.

The key to an explanation of Wordsworth's purpose not only in *The Ruined Cottage,* but also in *Lyrical Ballads* and most of the poetry he wrote after 1797, is to be found, I believe, in a letter written in April, 1798, by Samuel Taylor Coleridge to his brother George. This letter contains a remarkably complete statement of the principles for which both Coleridge and Wordsworth were striving in the year in which they collaborated on *Lyrical Ballads*. Since it has been generally neglected by the critics of both poets, we must subject it to the closest scrutiny.[22]

In this letter Coleridge defines his political position in clear and unequivocal terms:

I collect from your letter that our opinions and feelings on political subjects are more nearly alike than you imagine them to be. Equally with you (and perhaps with a deeper conviction, for my belief is founded on actual experience), equally with you I deprecate the moral and intellectual habits of those men, both in England and France, who have modestly assumed to themselves the exclusive title of Philosophers and Friends of Freedom. I think them at least *as* distant from greatness as from goodness. If I know my own opinions, they are utterly untainted with French metaphysics, French politics, French ethics, and French theology. As to *the Rulers* of France, I see in their views, speeches, and actions nothing that distinguishes them to their advantage from other animals of the same species. History has taught me that rulers are much the same in all ages, and under all forms of government; they are as bad as they dare to be. The vanity of ruin and the curse of blindness

---

[21] *Ibid.,* p. 26.
[22] Lawrence Hanson quotes this letter almost in entirety in his recent biography of Coleridge (*The Life of S. T. Coleridge* [New York: Oxford University Press, 1939], pp. 272–276), but fails to recognize the unusually clear light it throws upon *Lyrical Ballads*.

have clung to them like an hereditary leprosy. Of the French Revolution I can give my thoughts most adequately in the words of Scripture: "A great and strong wind rent the mountains, and brake in pieces the rocks before the Lord; but the Lord was not in the wind; and after the wind an earthquake; and after the earthquake a fire; and the Lord was not in the fire;" and now (believing that no calamities are permitted but as the means of good) I wrap my face in my mantle and wait, with a subdued and patient thought, expecting to hear "the still small voice" which is of God. In America (I have received my information from unquestionable authority) the morals and domestic habits of the people are daily deteriorating; and one good consequence which I expect from revolution is that individuals will see the necessity of individual effort; that they will act as good Christians, rather than as citizens and electors; and so by degrees will purge off . . . the error of attributing to governments a talismanic influence over our virtues and our happiness, as if governments were not rather effects than causes. It is true that all effects react and become causes, and so it must be in some degree with governments; but there are other agents which act more powerfully because by a nigher and more continuous agency, and it remains true that governments are more the *effect* than the cause of that which we are. . . . Of guilt I say nothing, but I believe most steadfastly in original sin; that from our mothers' wombs our understandings are darkened; and even where our understandings are in the light, that our organization is depraved and our volitions imperfect; and we sometimes see the good without wishing to attain it, and oftener *wish* it without the energy that wills and performs. And for this inherent depravity I believe that the *spirit* of the Gospel is the sole cure. . . .

You think, my brother, that there can be but two *parties* at present, for the Government and against the Government. It may be so. I am of no party. It is true I think the present Ministry weak and unprincipled men; but I would not with a safe conscience vote for their removal; I could point out no substitutes. . . . I am inclined to consider the aristocrats as the most respectable of our three factions, because they are more decorous. The Opposition and the Democrats are not only vicious, they wear the *filthy garments* of vice.

>   He that takes
> Deep in his soft credulity the stamp
> Design'd by loud declaimers on the part
> Of liberty, themselves the slaves of lust,
> Incurs derision for his easy faith
> And lack of knowledge, and with cause enough:
> For when was public virtue to be found
> Where private was not? Can he love the whole

THE NATURALISM OF 1798

> Who loves no part? He be a *nation's* friend,
> Who is, in truth, the friend of *no* man there?
> Can he be strenuous in his country's cause
> Who slights the charities, for whose dear sake
> That country, if at all, must be belov'd?
>   Cowper [*The Task*, Bk. V]

... I therefore consent to be deemed a Democrat and a Seditionist ... but I have snapped my squeaking baby-trumpet of sedition, and the fragments lie scattered in the lumber-room of penitence. I wish to be a good man and a Christian, but I am no Whig, no Reformist, no Republican, and because of the multitude of fiery and undisciplined spirits that lie in wait against the public quiet under these titles, because of them I chiefly accuse the present ministers, to whose folly I attribute, in a great measure, their increased and increasing numbers. You think differently, and if I were called upon by you to prove my assertions, although I imagine I could make them appear plausible, yet I should feel the insufficiency of my data. The Ministers may have had in their possession facts which alter the whole state of the argument, and make my syllogisms fall as flat as a baby's card-house. And feeling this, my brother! I have for some time past withdrawn myself totally from the consideration of *immediate causes*, which are infinitely complex and uncertain, to muse on fundamental and general causes the "causae causarum."[23]

Thus far the letter reveals that Coleridge's political views in the spring of 1798 differed in no important respect from those which Wordsworth had long held. If we except those phrases which seem to place Coleridge in a direct line of descent from Dr. Pangloss, we have as accurate a description of Wordsworth's political philosophy in 1798 as he himself could have written. Coleridge believes that existing governments are bad, but he does not advocate their overthrow by revolution. Revolution merely changes the form of government, and a government is an immediate, not a fundamental, cause of evil. The disappointing march of events in France, reports of the deterioration of habits and morals in the young American republic, and his consciousness of the presence of evil in the human heart have convinced Coleridge that revolution is good only in so far as it discloses the need for the purification of the individuals who constitute society. These were

[23] *Letters of Samuel Taylor Coleridge*, ed. by E. H. Coleridge (Boston, New York, 1895), I, 240-243.

views which Wordsworth had endorsed as early as 1793 and 1794. In his *Letter to the Bishop of Llandaff* Wordsworth suggested that revolution was futile unless it was supplemented by education and by strenuous efforts to cultivate not only the political but also the milder, social virtues of the people. In June, 1794, moreover, in a letter to his friend William Mathews, Wordsworth wrote: "I recoil from the bare idea of a Revolution";[24] then, a few sentences later, he exclaimed:

I deplore the miserable situation of the French; and think we can only be guarded from the same scourge by the undaunted efforts of good men in propagating with unremitting activity those doctrines, which long and severe meditation has taught them are essential to the welfare of mankind.... I severely condemn all inflammatory addresses to the passions of men, even when it is intended to direct those passions to a good purpose.[25]

Finally, in 1796 and 1797, as we have seen, Wordsworth dedicated his tragedy, *The Borderers,* not to social and political reform or to the generation of revolutionary passions, but to the reformation of the individual and the generation of the single, social passion of benevolence.[26] In the light of these facts it is safe to say that the authors of *Lyrical Ballads* were in virtually complete agreement over political issues in the spring of 1798.

These political sentiments are important to this study because of the literary program which they caused Coleridge and Wordsworth to adopt. In the culminating passage of his letter, the passage to which the discussion of politics serves merely as an introduction, Coleridge describes the objectives

[24] *The Early Letters,* p. 120.
[25] *Ibid.,* p. 121.
[26] It is worth noting here that Wordsworth as late as February, 1797, was collaborating with Francis Wrangham upon an imitation of Juvenal which was directed against the King, the Prince Regent, and various members of the British government and aristocracy. Although his part in the composition of this satire may be said to violate his scruples against "inflammatory addresses to the passions of men," the verses were never published, Wordsworth expressly forbidding Wrangham to publish them in 1806, declaring that he had "long since come to a fixed resolution to steer clear of personal satire" (cited by de Selincourt, *The Poetical Works,* p. 372). For the extant fragments of this satire see *ibid.,* pp. 302–306.

THE NATURALISM OF 1798

in poetry and prose that are the consequence of his political beliefs:

I devote myself to such works as encroach not on the anti-social passions—in poetry, to elevate the imagination and set the affections in right tune by the beauty of the inanimate impregnated as with a living soul by the presence of life—in prose to the seeking with patience and a slow, very slow mind, "Quid sumus, et quidnam victuri gignimus,"— what our faculties are and what they are capable of becoming. I love fields and woods and mountains with almost a visionary fondness. And because I have found benevolence and quietness growing within me as that fondness has increased, therefore I should wish to be the means of implanting it in others, and to destroy the bad passions not by combating them but by keeping them in inaction.[27]

Then by quoting eighteen lines of Wordsworth's blank verse to clinch and clarify these remarks, Coleridge shows unmistakably that this same program, these same literary aims, were Wordsworth's own:

> Not useless do I deem
> These shadowy sympathies with things that hold
> An inarticulate Language; for the Man—
> Once taught to love such objects as excite
> No morbid passions, no disquietude,
> No vengeance, and no hatred—needs must feel
> The joy of that pure principle of love
> So deeply, that, unsatisfied with aught
> Less pure and exquisite, he cannot choose
> But seek for objects of a kindred love
> In fellow-nature and a kindred joy.
> Accordingly he by degrees perceives
> His feelings of aversion softened down;
> A holy tenderness pervade his frame!
> His sanity of reason not impair'd,
> Say, rather, that his thoughts now flowing clear
> From a clear fountain flowing, he looks round,
> He seeks for good; and finds the good he seeks.[28]

The significance of this letter with its quotation from Wordsworth cannot be exaggerated. Unless I am greatly

---

[27] *Letters of Samuel Taylor Coleridge,* I, 243–244.

[28] *Ibid.,* p. 244. In the Fenwick note to *The Excursion,* in the fourth book of which these lines were incorporated, Wordsworth declared that this passage—after the lines of *The Ruined Cottage*—was "in order of time composed the next, either at Racedown or Alfoxden, I do not remember which."

mistaken, it gives us a precise and unusually lucid definition of the controlling purpose of almost everything Wordsworth wrote after 1797. Like Coleridge, Wordsworth designed his poetry to keep in abeyance the "anti-social passions," "to elevate the imagination and set the affections in right tune by the beauty of the inanimate impregnated as with a living soul by the presence of life." Like Coleridge, Wordsworth sought to discover "what our faculties are and what they are capable of becoming." Like Coleridge, finally, Wordsworth knew that "fields and woods and mountains" were productive of calm and benevolence; that sympathetic intercourse with natural objects would "destroy the bad passions not by combating them but by keeping them in inaction" and encouraging the growth of their opposites, the social affections. Such objects, speaking their "inarticulate Language," evoke feelings of love and joy, and contribute perforce to the decay of all that is evil in man. He who turns to nature for his education must eventually experience complete intellectual and spiritual purification: his "feelings of aversion" will tend to disappear; he will be pervaded by "A holy tenderness"; his "reason," unlike that of Oswald in *The Borderers,* will be enlisted in the cause of benevolence.

Here, then, is the explanation for Wordsworth's decision in *The Ruined Cottage* to hold "heaven" responsible for human suffering, and to stress, not the immediate cause of social evil—the existing form of government—but the serenity and benign influence of nature and the good which resides in the human heart. In 1798 Wordsworth had come to understand that vehement attacks on government and the champions of government, like his *Letter to the Bishop of Llandaff,* and stark revelation of the consequences of current social imperfections, the chief feature of the original *Guilt and Sorrow,* were likely to result in more harm than good. According to the psychology which he now accepted, such attacks and revelations could only irritate the reader, sharpen aversions already formed, and minister to the evil passions. This does not mean, however, that Wordsworth had lost his social consciousness or that he had abandoned his desire to

THE NATURALISM OF 1798

conquer evil and improve society. Convinced that true social reform depended upon the improvement of the individual, Wordsworth was not satisfied to stimulate mere abstract and isolated virtue; in the poetry of his great decade he stressed the lofty moral influence of nature and told carefully insulated tales of undeserved and unnecessary suffering bravely borne to cultivate in his readers those particular virtues which were certain to produce, in the end, a harmonious society founded on universal love.

II

Wordsworth did not borrow from Coleridge the psychology on which his best poetry is based. Just as he had reached independently the political philosophy which he shared with Coleridge in 1798, so, too, did he understand, at least a year before he met Coleridge, those principles of psychology which gave a definite purpose and direction to *Lyrical Ballads*. The interest in studying the mind of man, to see "what our faculties are and what they are capable of becoming," and the idea that the contemplation of natural objects tends to destroy the antisocial passions, set the affections in right tune, and generate benevolence and tranquility were both expressed clearly in the precocious additions which Wordsworth made at Windy Brow to *An Evening Walk*. In one of these, for example, Wordsworth specifies the value of wandering in nature, beside "the huddling rill":

> Its sober charms can chase with sweet controul
> Each idle thought and sanctify the soul,
> And on the morbid passions pouring balm
> Resistless breathe a melancholy calm.[29]

A few lines further on, in that extraordinary passage commented upon in the preceding chapter, Wordsworth advises the reader to approach nature with

> A heart that vibrates evermore, awake
> To feeling for all forms that Life can take,
> That wider still its sympathy extends
> And sees not any line where being ends;

[29] *The Poetical Works*, p. 9.

> Sees sense, through Nature's rudest forms betrayed,
> Tremble obscure in fountain rock and shade,
> And while a secret power those forms endears
> Their social accents never vainly hears.[30]

Then, in a later passage, Wordsworth suggests that of all the students of nature the particularly fortunate are those to whom "Science" has unlocked the "celestial stores" of psychology, those who have "That other eye" which "Explores the illimitable tracts of mind" and sees "Whatever man has been and man can be."[31]

Wordsworth's source for these ideas in 1794 cannot be determined with complete certainty from existing evidence. His enthusiasm for the insight of the psychologist suggests, however, that he had already made the acquaintance, either directly or at second hand, of David Hartley's *Observations on Man, His Frame, His Duty, and His Expectations*, 1749, a book whose title reveals that it is a study of what man is and what he is capable of becoming. Hartley's elaborate structure of Christian optimism was one of William Godwin's acknowledged sources for *Political Justice*, and it was probably Godwin who sent Wordsworth to Hartley's pages. There Wordsworth could find a scientifically defined mechanistic psychology that lent the strongest possible intellectual support to Godwin's recommendation of the man of benevolence as the highest social type.[32] There, too, he could find explicit

---

[30] *The Poetical Works*, p. 10.   [31] *Ibid.*, pp. 12-13.

[32] The closely interrelated influences of Hartley and Godwin on Wordsworth frequently defy precise definition. Although it is likely that Wordsworth read the first edition of *Political Justice* in 1793 and that he then turned directly to the *Observations on Man*, we cannot be sure that he ever read Hartley's original, and we know only that he had read Godwin's first edition sometime before March 21, 1796. It is possible that Wordsworth read Joseph Priestley's condensed version of Hartley's *Observations* (*Hartley's Theory of the Human Mind*), the second edition of which appeared in 1790, before he read Godwin, and it is also possible, though not probable, that his knowledge of Hartley was taken at second hand from Godwin. Whatever the facts may be, since Wordsworth and Godwin found a common source in Hartley, it is virtually impossible to tell when Wordsworth is following the one or the other. A further complication is the fact that Hartley's influence on Godwin seems to have been much more extensive than Godwin indicated; many of Godwin's most celebrated ideas were clearly anticipated by Hartley. But in spite of these many uncertainties, and partly because Wordsworth

instructions for strengthening the benevolent affections at the expense of the malevolent or "morbid" passions, as well as the best available philosophic sanction for the tempered optimism which distinguishes his finest poetry. A review of those passages from Hartley's *Observations* which almost certainly contributed to Wordsworth's inspiration at Windy Brow, and formed the basis of the poetic formula that he and Coleridge agreed upon in 1798, throws new light on Wordsworth's mature philosophy of nature and corrects the prevalent belief that Hartley's only significant influence on Wordsworth's poetry sprang from his somewhat fantastic lucubrations about vibratiuncles, the principle of association, and the "three ages of man."[33]

Hartley maintains in the First Part of his book that man can trace with almost mathematical precision the development of his mind and can break down into their component parts, "by reversing the steps of the associations which concur to form them," his various "affections and passions."[34] Our ability to analyze and account for our affections and passions is "of the utmost consequence to morality and religion," ac-

---

appears to have had a more detailed understanding of Hartley's system than he could have gained from Godwin or Priestley, I am inclined to believe that Godwin sent Wordsworth to the original Hartley, and that Hartley, with his quasi-scientific grounds for optimism, sent Wordsworth enthusiastically back to Godwin's arguments for disinterested benevolence.

[33] See *William Wordsworth, His Doctrine and Art in Their Historical Relations*, University of Wisconsin Studies in Language and Literature, No. 24 (Madison, 1927), by Professor Arthur Beatty, whose discovery of Wordsworth's knowledge of Hartley represents perhaps the most important single contribution ever made to the understanding of Wordsworth's poetry. In describing the Hartleian influence, however, Professor Beatty seems to give undue emphasis to the purely sensationalistic aspects of Hartley's psychology. Melvin M. Rader, among others, has shown that Wordsworth, in his great decade, was not completely satisfied with a conception of the mind that made thought a strictly mechanical operation (*Presiding Ideas in Wordsworth's Poetry*, University of Washington Publications in Language and Literature, Vol. VIII, No. 2 [Seattle, 1931]). And at least one of the additions made in 1794 to *An Evening Walk* proves that even then, when Hartley's system held for him all the charm of novelty, Wordsworth insisted that the mind drew experience not only from the world of the senses, but from "worlds beyond the reign of sense" (*The Poetical Works*, p. 9).

[34] *Observations on Man, His Frame, His Duty, and His Expectations* (London, 1834), p. 52.

cording to Hartley, "For thus we may learn how to cherish and improve good ones, check and root out such as are mischievous and immoral...."[35] If we take advantage of this power, there is virtually no limit to the amount of happiness which we may create for ourselves here upon earth.

Hartley's optimism rests upon his conviction that God is infinitely benevolent.[36] Evidence of His benevolence in this world becomes apparent when we consider the superiority of pleasure over pain. "It appears probable," Hartley explains,

> that there is an over-balance of happiness to the sentient beings of this visible world, considered both generally and particularly. For though disorder, pain, and death, do very much abound every where in the world, yet beauty, order, pleasure, life, and happiness, seem to superabound. This is indeed impossible to be ascertained by an exact computation. However, it is the general opinion of mankind, which is some kind of proof of the thing itself.[37]

It must be admitted that the present preponderance of pleasure over pain is not so great as might be expected, but fortunately the infinity of God's benevolence makes it possible for us indefinitely to increase our happiness while we diminish our misery. All we must do, apparently, to achieve such results is observe the laws of benevolence—this I take to be Hartley's meaning in the following passage:

> If we should lay down, that there is just as much misery as happiness in the world, (more can scarce be supposed by any one,) it will follow, that if the laws of benevolence were to take place in a greater degree than they do at present, misery would perpetually decrease, and happiness increase, till, at last, by the unlimited growth of benevolence, the state of mankind, in this world, would approach to a paradisiacal one. Now, this shews that our miseries are, in a great measure, owing to our want of benevolence, *i.e.* to our moral imperfections, and to that which, according to our present language, we do and must call *ourselves*. It is probable therefore, that, upon a more accurate examination and knowledge of this subject, we should find, that our miseries arose not only in great measure, but entirely from this source, from the imperfection of our benevolence....[38]

[35] *Observations on Man*, p. 52.
[36] See *ibid.*, pp. 330–340.
[37] *Ibid.*, p. 331.
[38] *Ibid.*, p. 332.

THE NATURALISM OF 1798

Clearly Hartley's position in regard to the desirability of the benevolence of the individual is strikingly similar to that held by both Godwin and Wordsworth.

Hartley explains specifically how we may increase and perfect benevolence. Benevolence, or the "Pleasures of Sympathy," as he sometimes describes it, should first of all be made our "primary Pursuit."[39] This studied quest of benevolence demands first of all

> that the pleasures of sense should be made entirely subservient to the health of the body and mind, that so each person may best fill his place in life, best perform the several relative duties of it, and prolong his days to their utmost period, free from great diseases and infirmities .... All gratifications therefore, which tend to produce diseases in the body, and disturbances in the mind, are forbidden by benevolence ....[40]

Then we must diligently

> practise all such acts of friendship, generosity, and compassion, as our abilities of any kind extend to; and rigorously ... refrain from all sallies of anger, resentment, envy, jealousy, &c. For though our affections are not directly and immediately subject to the voluntary power, yet our actions are; and consequently our affections also mediately. He that at first practises acts of benevolence by constraint, and continues to practise them, will at last have associated such a variety of pleasures with them, as to transfer a great instantaneous pleasure upon them, and beget in himself the affections from which they naturally flow. In like manner, if we abstain from malevolent actions, we shall dry up the ill passions, which are their sources.[41]

The last sentence of this passage recalls Coleridge's desire "to destroy the bad passions not by combating them but by keeping them in inaction," and Wordsworth's conviction that whoever loves "such objects as excite No morbid passions" will necessarily "feel The joy of that pure principle of love," will tend to lose his "feelings of aversion" and become imbued with a "holy tenderness." This sentence reminds us, more-

---

[39] In the sixty-eighth proposition of the Second Part of his book Hartley writes: "The Pleasures of Sympathy improve those of Sensation, Imagination, Ambition, and Self-Interest; and unite with those of Theopathy and the Moral Sense; they are self-consistent, and admit of an unlimited Extent: they may therefore be our primary Pursuit" (*ibid.*, p. 498).

[40] *Ibid.*, p. 457. [41] *Ibid.*, p. 503.

over, that Hartley offers specific directions not only for the stimulation of what he calls the "five grateful passions, love, desire, hope, joy, and pleasing recollection,"[42] but also for the course we are to follow if the "five ungrateful ones, hatred, aversion, fear, grief, and displeasing recollection,"[43] are to be forced into atrophy and decay. "As far as malevolence is allowed," Hartley observes,

benevolence must be destroyed; they are heat and cold, light and darkness, to each other. There is, however, this exception; that where wishing evil to some disposes us to be more benevolent upon the whole, as in the case of what is called a just indignation against vice, it may perhaps be tolerable in the more imperfect kinds of men, who have need of this direction and incitement to keep them from wandering out of the proper road, and to help them forward in it. But it is extremely dangerous to encourage such a disposition of mind by satire, invective, dispute, however unworthy the opponent may be, as these practices generally end in rank malevolence at last. *The wrath of man worketh not the righteousness of God.*[44]

These latter precepts have a special interest for students of Wordsworth's life and work, for there is good evidence suggesting that they exerted a considerable influence on his personal conduct as well as upon his choice of important details for his poetry. In May, 1798, for instance, Coleridge could write this description of Wordsworth to the Reverend J. P. Estlin: "It is his practice and almost his nature to convey all the truth he knows without any attack on what he supposes falsehood, if that falsehood be interwoven with virtues or happiness. He loves and venerates Christ and Christianity."[45] And a survey of Wordsworth's use of external nature in his poetry from *An Evening Walk* to *The Ruined Cottage* shows that by 1798 he was exercising as much care in the

---

[42] *Observations on Man*, p. 235.
[43] *Ibid.* [44] *Ibid.*, pp. 501–502.
[45] *Letters of Samuel Taylor Coleridge*, p. 246. Wordsworth's esteem for Christ was probably never great enough to give Coleridge complete peace of mind. Coleridge's admission here, however—when he had been very close to Wordsworth for almost a year—that Wordsworth loved and venerated Christ and Christianity, must carry more weight than his remark to Thelwall on May 13, 1796—when his acquaintance was superficial—that Wordsworth was "at least, a *semi*-atheist" (*ibid.*, p. 164). Critics have repeatedly quoted this earlier utterance and neglected the later, sounder one.

selection and rejection of natural objects and phenomena as he employed in his deliberate suppression of unpleasant facts regarding the condition of England. Such a survey shows, indeed, that Wordsworth had gone a long way toward accepting one of Hartley's more extreme opinions—"that the polite arts are scarce to be allowed, except when consecrated to religious purposes; but that ... their cultivation may be made an excellent means of awakening and alarming our affections, and transferring them upon their true objects."[46]

Before 1794 Wordsworth ordinarily conceived of nature as something full of sights and sounds which poets might describe. In *An Evening Walk*, nature is primarily decorative, impersonal, and devoid of special philosophic or moral significance. In one passage, however—that which describes the suffering of the female beggar and the freezing of her two children—Wordsworth suggests that nature becomes on occasion more than scenery. In *Descriptive Sketches*, nature again is usually placid and pretty, something to be eagerly approached with open eye and ear, but in Switzerland, as in England, she is sometimes the cause of catastrophe. In this poem Wordsworth tells the tale of a Grison gypsy caught out in a fierce Alpine storm.[47] After finding shelter in a "roof'd bridge" spanning the headwaters of the Rhine near the chasms of Viamala, she is swept to a violent death when the stream swells to a torrent and destroys the bridge. Here, too, we learn of a chamois hunter who, trapped by an avalanche, starves to death as an Alpine eagle circles overhead. Wordsworth, after commenting upon the futile hopes of the poor man's family, reveals his knowledge of the natural processes of decay by observing grotesquely that the hunter's child

> in fearful doubt may gaze,
> Passing his father's bones in future days,
> Start at the reliques of that very thigh,
> On which so oft he prattled when a boy.
> (Vv. 410–413)

In *Guilt and Sorrow* Wordsworth chose to emphasize nature's stormy moods, but here, as in the earlier poems, it might be

[46] Hartley, *op. cit.*, p. 481.   [47] *Descriptive Sketches*, vv. 184–214.

said that nature is merely background—sometimes cheerful, sometimes grim—were it not for one line which Wordsworth inserted in his account of the sailor's encounter with the criminal on the gibbet—"And, hovering round it often did a raven fly."

The 1794 additions to *An Evening Walk,* as we have seen, marked an important change in the conception of nature reflected in Wordsworth's poetry. In these verses Wordsworth first "Sees sense through Nature's rudest forms betrayed" and first announces his ability not only to discover in the apparently lifeless and trivial objects of nature "a secret power," but also to hear the "social accents" of what he later called their "inarticulate Language." This was the idea of nature that caused Wordsworth in *Peter Bell* to insist that "A primrose by a river's brim" is something more than a yellow primrose. To this philosophy of nature Wordsworth first gave dramatic expression in *The Borderers,* in which he illustrated the benign operations of nature's "secret power" by means of the twinkling star that deters Marmaduke from murder. But even in *The Borderers* nature is not entirely benevolent. Wordsworth had not yet completely purged his poetry of those elements—social and natural—which were likely to excite the reader's evil passions. In *The Borderers* Eldred's description of the discovery of Herbert's body stresses the same gruesome detail that attracted attention in *Guilt and Sorrow:*

>   there was a black tree,
> A single tree; she [Idonea] thought it was her Father.
>
> . . . .
>   The daylight dawned, and now—
> . . . .
> As we approached, a solitary crow
> Rose from the spot . . . .[48]

Not until he wrote *The Ruined Cottage* was Wordsworth able, in a poem of any length, to bring his understanding of nature under the consistent control of those principles of selection and emphasis with which he had been experimenting since the early months of 1794. Just as there are vestiges

[48] Act V, vv. 83–89.

THE NATURALISM OF 1798

in *The Ruined Cottage* of Wordsworth's earlier criticism of society, so are there traces of that destructive power in nature which seems to have had a morbid attraction for him in his youth. Margaret's death, like that of the unfortunate children in *An Evening Walk*, results from exposure—"the nightly damps Did chill her breast"; her cottage, moreover, presents an all too eloquent record of the irresistible forces of decay. Here, however, such evidence of what might be considered nature's unfriendliness is not a source of emotional disturbance for the reader. When he wrote *The Ruined Cottage* Wordsworth had learned that by emphasizing the beauty and the peace of nature, as well as her quiet collaboration with "mournful thoughts" in the generation of the benevolent affections, he could describe human suffering and yet leave his reader in a hopeful mood of philosophic calm.

This review of Wordsworth's use of nature in his poetry up to and including *The Ruined Cottage* enables us to answer those critics who suggest that the nature philosophy expressed in Wordsworth's best-known verse is invalid because it neglects those aspects of nature which seem unpleasant or unfriendly to man. Mr. Aldous Huxley, for instance, has opined that if Wordsworth had lived for a short time in the tropical jungles of Malaya or Borneo his conception of nature might have been more acceptable to modern readers who have kept abreast of nineteenth- and twentieth-century science.[49] In the tropics, Mr. Huxley observes, Wordsworth would have learned that "Nature, even in the temperate zone, is always alien and inhuman, and occasionally diabolic."[50]

Now it is true that Wordsworth did not know that nature is "always alien and inhuman"—he supposed, as do many contemporary men of science whose generalizations are less sweeping than Mr. Huxley's,[51] that man was nature's best

---

[49] "Wordsworth in the Tropics," *Do What You Will* (Garden City [New York]: Doubleday, Doran and Company, Inc., 1930), pp. 123–139.
[50] *Ibid.*, p. 127.
[51] For an evaluation of Wordsworth's nature philosophy in the light of modern science see Professor Ernest Bernbaum's excellent essay, "Is Wordsworth's Nature-Poetry Antiquated?" *A Journal of English Literary History*,

creation and therefore no stranger to her. But it is equally true that Wordsworth knew that nature was, or seemed to be, "occasionally diabolic"—the frozen bodies, bare bones, and carrion crows of his early poems are incontrovertible proof of this. Wordsworth's attention was called to nature's predatory ferocity in 1802 when one Isaac Chapel, a sail-maker, stopped at the Grasmere cottage and told a grisly tale of a slave ship on which "one man had been killed, a boy put to lodge with the pigs and was half eaten, set to watch in the hot sun till he dropped down dead."[52] According to Mr. Huxley's theory, such an example of "Nature, red in tooth and claw" should have wrought a revolution in Wordsworth's thought, but there is nothing to suggest that this alarming information caused the slightest alteration in Wordsworth's regard—in his poetry at least—for "Nature's holy plan." Consequently, it seems unlikely that a visit to Malaya or Borneo would have had much effect on the view of nature which Wordsworth expressed in his poetry after 1797.

Wordsworth was well aware of the fact that, so far as man is concerned, nature is a mixture of the good and the bad. Those stanzas of *Peter Bell* which account for Peter's immoral character show clearly Wordsworth's knowledge that nature could form vicious as well as virtuous characters:

> Though Nature could not touch his heart
> By lovely forms, and silent weather,
> And tender sounds, yet you might see

VII (1940), 333–340. Professor Bernbaum shows that modern science confirms rather than invalidates Wordsworth's sense of man's oneness with nature; his belief in the existence of a deep affinity between nature, typified by country as opposed to urban life, and the mind of man; his suspicion that the commonplace rather than the rare and unusual in nature is likely to prove of greatest significance to our understanding of the world we live in; his conviction that nature is purposeful and harmonious, rather than blind, chaotic, and haphazard; and his comfortable faith in the preëminent dignity of man. To prove that Wordsworth's teleological interpretation of nature is not at variance with the conclusions of modern natural philosophers, Professor Bernbaum mentions, among others, W. Macneile Dixon and Julian Huxley, who both suggest that man's extraordinary brain, itself the product of nature, is now capable of giving intelligent direction to evolution.

[52] *Journals of Dorothy Wordsworth*, ed. by William Knight (London, 1897), I, 100.

THE NATURALISM OF 1798

>At once, that Peter Bell and she
>Had often been together.
>
>A savage wildness round him hung
>As of a dweller out of doors;
>In his whole figure and his mien
>A savage character was seen
>Of mountains and of dreary moors.
>
>To all the unshaped half-human thoughts
>Which solitary Nature feeds
>'Mid summer storms or winter's ice,
>Had Peter joined whatever vice
>The cruel city breeds.

These lines prove that Wordsworth's assertion, made earlier in the poem, that "nature ne'er could find the way Into the heart of Peter Bell," was a half truth. What Wordsworth meant to say was that Peter, prior to his reformation, had been impervious to those emanations from nature which nourish the benevolent affections, for it is obvious that that side of nature which breeds evil in man—the mountains and the moors, the ice of winter and the summer storms—has joined forces with the wicked city and left her mark upon him.

It was Wordsworth's knowledge, not his ignorance, of nature, society, and the psychology of men, that caused him to stress in his poetry the serene rather than the turbulent in nature, the good rather than the evil in common humanity. It is important to remember that Wordsworth was writing, not laboratory reports on the physical world or objective descriptions of the squalor and misery endured by England's neglected masses, but poetry—poetry with a purpose that was well-defined. Virtually everything Wordsworth wrote after 1797 was brought into close accord with principles of selection and emphasis which he had formulated on the basis of his personal experience, the wisdom of his predecessors in poetry and philosophy, and the best that eighteenth-century England could offer in psychological and political theory. Following these principles with scrupulous care, Wordsworth celebrated only those aspects of nature and humanity most likely to encourage the development of the benevolent or social affections and to further the deterioration of the malevolent or antisocial passions. In his most successful verse Wordsworth deliberately curbed his youthful tendency to cry out against the more ugly and reprehensible features of English society[53] and consciously refrained from describing the savage violence and agitation which many of his modern successors have delighted to find in nature. He imposed these restraints upon himself not because he had become indifferent to the condition of England—he was never deaf to "the still, sad music of humanity"—or because he was innocent of the facts of life, but because he took very seriously his responsibility as a writer. As he understood it in 1798—and he had the support of Hartley, Godwin, and Coleridge, three of the best names in a great century—the whole truth about nature and the existing social

[53] An interesting example of the sort of thing Wordsworth put on paper under the initial impulse to create and later rejected under the influence of his selective principle is provided by four stanzas from an early, unpublished draft of *Peter Bell*. These stanzas, in no way inferior artistically to many of those remaining in the published version, fitted into the poem near the conclusion of the second part, where Peter Bell is disturbed by a crimson stain—"as of a drop of blood"—upon a stone:

> The dusty road is white as bone
> And Peter casting down his eyes
> Towards the moonlight now espies
> A drop of blood upon a stone.
>
> Peter has little power to move
> Upon the ass remain he must
> He travels on and now and then
> He sees that drop of blood again
> Upon a stone or in the dust.
>
> Did Peter e'er with club or stake
> Smite some poor traveller on the head
> Or beat his father in a rage
> And spill the blood of his old age
> Or kick a child till he was dead?
>
> Did Peter ever kill his man
> With pick or staff or single duel
> Or stab with some inhuman wound
> A soldier bleeding on the ground?
> No Peter never was so cruel.

These stanzas, the last two in particular, are reminiscent of the criminal violence described in *Guilt and Sorrow*, where Wordsworth attempted to make, not men of benevolence, but active revolutionists of his readers. In his later poetry he found no place for such provocative descriptions.

and political situation was not conducive, in poetry at least, to the most efficient generation of those virtues upon whose cultivation genuine social betterment depends. In other words, the whole truth about nature and society was not congenial to the educational and reformatory purpose to which Wordsworth chose to dedicate his verse.

III

Thus, by the spring of 1798, Wordsworth had formulated a philosophy of poetry that brought into focus his experience with nature, society, and the mind of man. With the successful realization of this philosophy in *The Ruined Cottage* Wordsworth's formative years may be said to have come to an end. The study of Wordsworth's early development may not be properly concluded, however, until some notice has been taken of the doubts and misgivings with which he held his new philosophy almost from the moment of its earliest significant expression. For nearly a decade after 1797 Wordsworth was consistently able to conjure up for the social and spiritual benefit of his readers the vision of a world beautiful and fair inhabited by creatures whose actions, almost without exception, spring from the purest compassion and love. But Wordsworth himself, ironically, could believe in such a world only after strenuous exertions of the intellect and will.

His difficulty in accepting, even temporarily, the optimistic view of the world which he expressed in his best poetry is evident in "Lines Written in Early Spring," one of his most successful contributions to *Lyrical Ballads*. Here he voices the popular eighteenth-century notion that nature is full of joy, observes that man is a part of nature, and then laments "What man has made of man." The perversity of man's social behavior, presumably, is the sole cause of the absence from his life of that preponderance of pleasure which is a fundamental principle of what Wordsworth later refers to as "Nature's holy plan." At first glance, the poem seems to be little more than a faintly melancholy reflection on those social imperfections which, according to Wordsworth's cheerful poetic faith, were virtually certain of ultimate correction.

Close study of the lines reveals, however, that Wordsworth was not sure of the real existence of the pleasure principle, one of the mainstays of his naturalistic optimism.

Wordsworth's awareness that the principle of pleasure, given great prominence by David Hartley, might be a fiction, the vain product of wishful thought, and his uncertainty as to whether the periwinkle, the birds, and budding twigs really experienced the joy which he wished to attribute to them are more than hinted at by the closing verses of the fifth stanza. The lines—

> And I *must think, do all I can,*
> *That there was pleasure there—*[54]

argue strongly that Wordsworth's faith "that every flower Enjoys the air it breathes" was never firmly established or easily held. This argument is supported, moreover, by the original conclusion of the poem, in which Wordsworth—saying nothing of "Nature's holy plan"[55]—suggests that he was forced to believe in the principle of pleasure because it was indispensable to the "creed" which he had chosen to adopt:

> If I these thoughts may not prevent,
> If such be of my creed the plan,
> Have I not reason to lament
> What man has made of man?

Even more impressive evidence of Wordsworth's inability to convince himself completely of the soundness of his philosophy is found where we might least expect to find it—in "Lines Written a Few Miles above Tintern Abbey," the poem usually thought to represent the high-water mark of his faith in nature. In this great meditative lyric Wordsworth utters his most enthusiastic and unequivocal vow of allegiance to nature:

> Therefore am I still
> A lover of the meadows and the woods,
> And mountains; and of all that we behold

---

[54] The italics are my own.
[55] Many discussions of "Lines Written in Early Spring" are vitiated by their authors' failure to distinguish between the text of 1798 and those of 1820 and 1837; see, for example, the otherwise admirable analysis of the poem by Joseph Warren Beach, *The Concept of Nature in Nineteenth-Century English Poetry* (New York, 1936), pp. 180–187.

THE NATURALISM OF 1798

> From this green earth; of all the mighty world
> Of eye and ear, both what they half-create,
> And what perceive; well pleased to recognize
> In nature and the language of the sense,
> The anchor of my purest thoughts, the nurse,
> The guide, the guardian of my heart, and soul
> Of all my moral being.

Yet even here, where he is most eager to affirm his faith, Wordsworth intimates that he is disturbed by doubt. Why does he feel obliged to insist that he is *"still* A lover of the meadows and the woods, And mountains"? Why should he, of all men, *not* be a lover of nature? Why, furthermore, does he find it necessary, in the presence of his sister Dorothy, to justify the continuation of his affection for nature?

Some of the earlier lines of the poem answer these questions by showing how Wordsworth's philosophy, based on nature, failed to give him complete satisfaction. After describing the landscape of which he is especially fond, Wordsworth asserts that often when he has been "in lonely rooms, and mid the din Of towns and cities," his memory of the beautiful valley of the Wye has dispelled whatever weariness he may have felt and produced in him an exalted mood of visionary tranquility—

> that blessed mood,
> In which the burthen of the mystery,
> In which the heavy and the weary weight
> Of all this unintelligible world
> Is lighten'd:—that serene and blessed mood,
> In which the affections gently lead us on,
> Until, the breath of this corporeal frame,
> And even the motion of our human blood
> Almost suspended, we are laid asleep
> In body, and become a living soul:
> While with an eye made quiet by the power
> Of harmony, and the deep power of joy,
> We see into the life of things.

Precisely what Wordsworth saw when, in his naturalistic trance, he saw "into the life of things" he does not explain. Whatever it was, it enabled him to escape from the dark thoughts evoked by the disquieting agitation of urban life, whose "fretful stir Unprofitable" suggested only too plainly that the world was neither harmonious nor remarkably joyful. We may suppose, accordingly, that in the mystical moods generated by his memory of nature's "beauteous forms," he had glimpses of that perfectly ordered, predominantly joyful society which man, according to Hartley and Godwin, must some day create.

That Wordsworth discovered such promise for the future in the visions in which his retrospective contemplation of nature sometimes culminated there can, I think, be no doubt; and his ability to do so is in itself a sufficient explanation for his close attachment to nature. But in the very passage wherein he praises his naturalistic insight Wordsworth reveals that he is not certain of its validity or significance. He admits that the world is not only "heavy" and "weary" but also "unintelligible," and, in the line which introduces the next passage of the poem—"If this Be but a vain belief"—he clearly acknowledges the possibility that his faith has been misplaced, that he may be the victim of a major delusion.

Having made these disturbing admissions, Wordsworth, with extraordinary honesty, vouchsafes still more evidence that might be used against the philosophy in which he wishes to believe. Reflecting on the development of his mind, he observes that the pleasures which he now derives from nature differ markedly from those he experienced in his youth. The joys he knew when he first came to Tintern Abbey have vanished; he can no longer feel the sensuous exultation which the colors and the forms of natural objects formerly aroused in him. This remembrance of things past and the consciousness of personal loss fill Wordsworth with "somewhat of a sad perplexity." He insists, however, that he does not mourn the change. Thanks to nature's power to lead us on "from joy to joy," increasing years have brought him new sources of pleasure, which are, he "would believe, Abundant recompense":

>   For I have learned
> To look on nature, not as in the hour
> Of thoughtless youth, but hearing oftentimes
> The still, sad music of humanity,

THE NATURALISM OF 1798

> Not harsh nor grating, though of ample power
> To chasten and subdue. And I have felt
> A presence that disturbs me with the joy
> Of elevated thoughts; a sense sublime
> Of something far more deeply interfused,
> Whose dwelling is the light of setting suns,
> And the round ocean, and the living air,
> And the blue sky, and in the mind of man,
> A motion and a spirit, that impels
> All thinking things, all objects of all thought,
> And rolls through all things.

In other words, it is because the lost joys of his youth have been replaced by sympathy, and philosophic power which enables him to remain moderately cheerful in the presence of human suffering, that Wordsworth can continue to believe in the principle of pleasure and proclaim himself "*still* A lover of the meadows and the woods, And mountains."

But in the lines which follow, just as in those which precede Wordsworth's affirmation of his love for nature, it seems that he is still uncertain and ill at ease. Despite his protestations to the contrary, he is not thoroughly convinced that his new pleasures—"By thought supplied"—are adequate compensation for his loss. This is not surprising when we remember his admission that his visionary power—the intuitive perception of a "something far more deeply interfused"—might be false and misleading. In any case, he is prompted to speak again of the "decay" of his "genial spirits," and to take what extra solace he can from the presence of Dorothy, in whom he sees what he once was.[56] Finally, with a curious mixture of faith and melancholy foreboding, Wordsworth anticipates the day when he and Dorothy may be separated—I think he means by death—and recommends his naturalism to her as an almost certain source of consolation for "solitude, or fear, or pain, or grief."

[56] When he tries to forget his personal loss the more to enjoy vicariously the youthful pleasures of his sister, Wordsworth comes very close to the position of Walt Whitman, Swinburne, and Meredith, the great naturalistic poets of the nineteenth century, who, possessing scientific knowledge not available to Wordsworth, learned to accept the fact of personal death by losing themselves "in the thought of nature's eternal life" (Beach, *op. cit.*, p. 473).

WORDSWORTH'S FORMATIVE YEARS

Readers of Wordsworth no doubt will disagree as to the significance of this sometimes bewildering but always impressive vacillation between conviction and doubt in "Tintern Abbey," the clearest and most memorable expression of his nature philosophy that Wordsworth ever achieved. Some perhaps will feel that they cannot accept Wordsworth's naturalism when even he failed to give it consistent support. They may choose to regard his frankly acknowledged uneasiness as proof that his nature poetry expresses an artificial and arbitrary creed in which he himself did not wholly believe, and that his poetry is therefore insincere and slight in value. Others, however, will discover in "Tintern Abbey" an authentic record of a resourceful and tenacious thinker who had the courage and the honesty to question, from the recognizable truth of his personal experience, the optimistic philosophy which he had constructed slowly and with great care—a philosophy whose basic validity neither time nor science has yet destroyed.

This latter view, I think, is the sound one. Within a few short years Wordsworth yielded to the demands of his experience, sought and found a new basis for his optimism, and built a new philosophy from the wreckage of the old. On July 13, 1798, when he wrote "Tintern Abbey," he had just begun to understand that mutability—nature's inexorable process of change and decay—would have its way with him even as with a peasant's cottage or the body of a hapless chamois hunter in the Alps. Consciousness of mortality, of decay and deterioration culminating in the single fact of personal death, Wordsworth could not long reconcile with the pleasure principle on which his naturalism was founded. In the summer of 1798, his formative years behind him, he could truthfully announce the continuation of his faith in nature; but the day was not far distant when, well along in the next stage of his development, Wordsworth would feel no more in nature the "sense sublime Of something far more deeply interfused," when he would lament the loss of his visionary power and plaintively ask, "Where is it now, the glory and the dream?"

Bibliography

I. Primary Sources

COLERIDGE, SAMUEL TAYLOR, *Letters of Samuel Taylor Coleridge,* two volumes, edited by Ernest Hartley Coleridge. Boston and New York: Houghton, Mifflin and Co., 1895.

—— *Unpublished Letters of Samuel Taylor Coleridge,* two volumes, edited by Earl Leslie Griggs. London: Constable Press, 1932; New Haven: Yale University Press, 1933.

—— AND WORDSWORTH, WILLIAM, *Lyrical Ballads, with a Few Other Poems.* Bristol: Printed by Biggs and Cottle, for T. N. Longman, 1798.

GODWIN, WILLIAM, *Enquiry concerning Political Justice, and Its Influence on Morals and Happiness,* two volumes. Second edition. London: Printed for G. G. and J. Robinson, 1796.

—— *An Enquiry concerning Political Justice and Its Influence on General Virtue and Happiness,* two volumes, edited and abridged by Raymond A. Preston. New York: Alfred A. Knopf, 1926.

HARTLEY, DAVID, *Observations on Man, His Frame, His Duty, and His Expectations.* Sixth edition. London: Printed for Thomas Tegg and Son, 1834.

WORDSWORTH, DOROTHY, *Journals of Dorothy Wordsworth,* two volumes, edited by William Knight. London and New York: Macmillan and Co., 1897.

WORDSWORTH, DOROTHY AND WILLIAM, *The Early Letters of William and Dorothy Wordsworth (1787–1805),* edited by Ernest de Selincourt. Oxford: At the Clarendon Press, 1935.

WORDSWORTH, WILLIAM, *The Excursion, Being a Portion of The Recluse, a Poem.* London: Printed for Longman, Hurst, Rees, Orme, and Brown, 1814.

—— *The Poetical Works of William Wordsworth: Poems Written in Youth, Poems Referring to the Period of Childhood,* edited by Ernest de Selincourt. Oxford: At the Clarendon Press, 1940.

—— *The Poetical Works of William Wordsworth,* eight volumes, edited by William Knight. London and New York: Macmillan and Co., 1896.

WORDSWORTH'S FORMATIVE YEARS

WORDSWORTH, WILLIAM, *The Prelude, or Growth of a Poet's Mind.* edited by Ernest de Selincourt. Oxford: At the Clarendon Press, 1926.

—— *The Prose Works of William Wordsworth,* three volumes, edited by Alexander B. Grosart. London: Edward Moxon, Son, and Co., 1876.

—— *Wordsworth: Representative Poems,* edited by Arthur Beatty. Garden City (New York): Doubleday, Doran and Company, Inc., 1937.

—— AND COLERIDGE, SAMUEL TAYLOR. See above under Coleridge.

II. SECONDARY MATERIALS

ALLEN, B. SPRAGUE, "William Godwin as a Sentimentalist," *Publications of the Modern Language Association of America,* XXXIII (1918), 1–29.

AUBIN, ROBERT ARNOLD, *Topographical Poetry in XVIII-Century England.* New York: The Modern Language Association of America, 1936.

BEACH, JOSEPH WARREN, *The Concept of Nature in Nineteenth-Century English Poetry.* New York: The Macmillan Company, 1936.

BEATTY, ARTHUR, "Joseph Fawcett: *The Art of War,* Its Relation to the Early Development of William Wordsworth," *Studies by Members of the Department of English,* University of Wisconsin Studies in Language and Literature, No. 2 (Madison, 1918), 224–269.

—— *William Wordsworth: His Doctrine and Art in Their Historical Relations,* University of Wisconsin Studies in Language and Literature, No. 24. Second edition. Madison, 1927.

BERNBAUM, ERNEST, "Is Wordsworth's Nature-Poetry Antiquated?" *A Journal of English Literary History,* VII (1940), 333–340.

CAMPBELL, OSCAR JAMES, "Sentimental Morality in Wordsworth's Narrative Poetry," *Studies by Members of the Department of English,* Series No. 2, University of Wisconsin Studies in Language and Literature, No. 11 (Madison, 1920), 21–57.

—— AND MUESCHKE, PAUL, "*The Borderers* as a Document in the History of Wordsworth's Aesthetic Development," *Modern Philology,* XXIII (1926), 465–482.

—— —— "*Guilt and Sorrow:* A study in the Genesis of Wordsworth's Aesthetic," *Modern Philology,* XXIII (1926), 293–306.

BIBLIOGAPHY

CAMPBELL, OSCAR JAMES, AND MUESCHKE, PAUL, "Wordsworth's Aesthetic Development, 1795–1802," *Essays and Studies in English and Comparative Literature,* University of Michigan Publications, Language and Literature, Vol. X (Ann Arbor: University of Michigan Press, 1933), 1–57.

DE SELINCOURT, ERNEST, *Dorothy Wordsworth: A Biography.* Oxford: At the Clarendon Press, 1933.

—— *The Early Wordsworth,* Presidential Address to the English Association. Oxford: Humphrey Milford, Oxford University Press, 1936.

—— "Wordsworth's Preface to *The Borderers,*" *Oxford Lectures on Poetry* (Oxford: At the Clarendon Press, 1934), pp. 157–179.

GARROD, H. W., *Wordsworth: Lectures and Essays.* Oxford: At the Clarendon Press, 1923.

HARPER, GEORGE MCLEAN, *William Wordsworth, His Life, Works, and Influence.* Third edition. New York: Charles Scribner's Sons, 1929.

LEGOUIS, ÉMILE, *The Early Life of William Wordsworth, 1770–1798,* translated by J. W. Matthews. New York: E. P. Dutton and Co., 1918.

—— *William Wordsworth and Annette Vallon.* London and Toronto: J. M. Dent and Sons Ltd.; New York: E. P. Dutton and Co., 1922.

LOVEJOY, ARTHUR O., *The Great Chain of Being: A Study of the History of an Idea.* Cambridge (Mass.): Harvard University Press, 1936.

MACGILLIVRAY, J. R., "The Date of Composition of *The Borderers,*" *Modern Language Notes,* XLIX (1934), 104–111.

MUESCHKE, PAUL. See above under Campbell.

RADER, MELVIN M., *Presiding Ideas in Wordsworth's Poetry,* University of Washington Publications in Language and Literature, Vol. VIII, No. 2. Seattle: University of Washington Press, 1931.

READ, HERBERT, *Wordsworth: The Clark Lectures, 1929–1930.* London and Toronto: Jonathan Cape, 1930.

WORDSWORTH, CHRISTOPHER, *Memoirs of William Wordsworth,* two volumes. London: Edward Moxon, 1851.

Index

(Numbers in italics indicate the principal references.)

Allen, B. Sprague, on William Godwin's sentimentalism and *The Borderers*, 188 n.
Annette (*see* Vallon)
Aubin, Robert Arnold: on *An Evening Walk;* 38, 54 n.; on *Descriptive Sketches*, 38

Beach, Joseph Warren: 250 n., 253 n.; on Wordsworth's naturalism, 168 n.
Beattie's *Minstrel*, 29
Beatty, Arthur: 54 n., 113 n.; on the influence of David Hartley, 48 n., 167-168 n., 239 n.; on the influence of Ramond de Carbonnières, 78-79, 82 n.
Beaupuy, Michel, his influence on Wordsworth's political philosophy, 79-82, 83, 84, 86, 89, 135
Bernbaum, Ernest, on Wordsworth's naturalism and modern science, 245-246 n.
Burke, Edmund, 103-104, 105, 117, 124
Burns's poems, *Chiefly in the Scottish Dialect*, 17

Calvert, Raisley: 29; nursed by Wordsworth, 31; leaves Wordsworth £900, 32, 32 n.; Wordsworth's tributes to, 35-36
Calvert, William: 29, 32 n.; travels with Wordsworth, 28, 136
Campbell, Oscar James, on *The Ruined Cottage*, 227-228 n., 229-230
Campbell, Oscar James, and Mueschke, Paul: 112, 165 n., 210 n., 229-230 n.; on *Guilt and Sorrow*, 111, 131, 140-141, 142; on *The Borderers*, 111, 174, 175, 200; on *The Ruined Cottage*, 221, 223-224 n., 226, 227
Chain of Being, The Great, 96-97, 98, 99, 104, 106, 142, 143, 144 n., 168 (*see* also Lovejoy, Arthur O.)
Coleridge, George, 231
Coleridge, Samuel Taylor: 3, 5, 35, 47, 48 n., 111, 141, 152, 207, 242, 248; on *Descriptive Sketches*, 39; meets Wordsworth, 166 n.; and the Racedown "crisis," 154, 155, 159-161, 163, 166, 167, 168 n.; and the Hartley influence, 167-168 n., 169-170 n., 239; *The Ruined Cottage* read to, 221-222, 227; shares political and poetic principles with Wordsworth, 231-237, 239, 241; on Wordsworth's Christianity, 242 n.; Wordsworth's influence on his *Osorio* and "The Rime of the Ancyent Marinere," 207 n.
Condorcet, 80
Cookson, Dorothy (Wordsworth's grandmother), 13, 15, 16
Cookson, William (Wordsworth's grandfather), 13
Cookson, William (Canon of

INDEX

Windsor, Wordsworth's Uncle William): 26, 29, 31; recommends the study of Oriental languages to Wordsworth, 22, 24; Dorothy lives with, 43, 49, 137, 138; ostracizes Wordsworth, 95, 102

Cowper, William: 39; quoted by Coleridge, 232-233

Coxe, William: 79; his letters on Switzerland translated by Ramond de Carbonnières, 78

Crackanthorpe, Christopher Cookson (Wordsworth's Uncle Kit): 9, 10, 15, 16; dislikes Wordsworth, 12, 13, 14

Crackanthorpe, Mrs. Christopher, Dorothy's Windy Brow letter to, 29-30

de Carbonnières, Ramond, influence of, 78-83

de Selincourt, Ernest: 16 n., 22, 22 n., 31, 33 n., 113 n., 153, 161, 161 n., 209, 209 n., 222 n.; on *An Evening Walk,* 47 n.; on the Windy Brow additions to *An Evening Walk,* 167, 169–170 n.; publishes the original version of *Guilt and Sorrow,* 112; on the Racedown "crisis," 156-157, 159-160; on *The Borderers,* 171, 172–173 n., 173–174 n., 174, 184 n., 189 n., 197; on "Lines Left upon a Seat in a Yew-Tree," 189 n.

Dixon, W. MacNeile, 246 n.

Enquirer, The, William Godwin's sentimentalism in, 185

Estlin, J. P., 242

Fenwick, Isabella, 38

Fenwick notes, The: to *An Evening Walk,* 38; to *Descriptive Sketches,* 69; to *The Borderers,* 180, 189 n., 211; to *The Excursion,* 235 n.

French Revolution, The, and Wordsworth's republicanism, 5–7, 11–12, 16, 20–21, 23, 63, 74, *79–87,* 88–90, *93–109,* 111, 112, 154, 180, 211, 212, 232–234

Garrod, H. W.: 110; on *Descriptive Sketches,* 40, 76; on the influence of the French Revolution, 89 n.; on *Guilt and Sorrow,* 111–112 n.; on the date of composition of the Racedown soliloquy, 161; on *Lyrical Ballads,* 111–112 n.; on *The Borderers,* 111–112 n., 171, 174

Godwin, William: 11, 12, 80, 89 n., 94, 248, 252; influence of his *Caleb Williams,* 134 n.; influence of his *Political Justice,* 111, 133-135, 154, 155, 156, 162, 167, *174–191,* 200, 230, 241; David Hartley's influence on, 238, 238–239 n., 241

Hanson, Lawrence, 231 n.

Harper, George McLean: 174; on the Lonsdale case, 9; on Wordsworth's tour of Switzerland, 17–18; on Wordsworth's residence in France, 23-24; on *Descriptive Sketches,* 40, 76; on the *Letter to the Bishop of Llandaff,* 101, 101 n.; on Dorothy's observation of natural objects, 154 n.; on the Racedown "crisis," 155-157; on "Lines Left upon a Seat in a Yew-Tree," 189

Hartley, David: 248, 250, 252; influence of his *Observations on Man . . .* on Wordsworth, 48, 48 n., 51 n., 167, 167–168 n., 169–170 n., 230, *238–243;* influence of his *Observations on Man . . .* on William Godwin, 238, 238–239 n., 241

Herford, C. H., 134 n.

INDEX

Hutchinson, Mary, 189 n., 221, 222, 226 n., 229 n.
Huxley, Aldous, on Wordsworth's naturalism, 245-246
Huxley, Julian, 246 n.

Johnson, Joseph (publisher of *An Evening Walk* and *Descriptive Sketches*), 93-94, 93 n., 94 n., 134 n.
Jones, Robert, 17, 19, 24, 65 n., 77, 136
Juvenal, Wordsworth imitates, 234 n.

Legouis, Émile: 54 n.; on Wordsworth's finances, 15; on *An Evening Walk* and *Descriptive Sketches*, 39-40; on Michel Beaupuy, 79-80, 81 n.; on the influence of Ramond de Carbonnières, 78, 82 n., 83 n.; on the *Letter to the Bishop of Llandaff*, 101, 101 n.; on *Guilt and Sorrow*, 151-152 n.; on *The Borderers*, 174, 179-180, 179 n., 184 n., 197, 211-212; on *The Ruined Cottage*, 220-221
Llandaff, The Bishop of (*see* Watson, Richard)
Lonsdale, Lord (Sir James Lowther), the Wordsworth case against, 8-11, 14, 15, 16, 31, 41, 92, 93, 94, 136 n., 139
Lovejoy, Arthur O., on the Great Chain of Being, 96 n., 97 n., 98 n.

MacGillivray, J. R., 176, 189 n.
Mackintosh, Sir James (author of *Vindiciae Gallicae*), 134
Marshall, Jane (nee Pollard), Dorothy's letters to, 9-10, 12-13, 14, 15, 16-17, 18-19, 22 n., 24, 27, 28-29, 29 n., 34 n., 41-42, 43-44, 47-48, 52, 56, 62, 68, 70, 70 n., 138, 138 n., 154 n.

Mathews, William, Wordsworth's letters to, 19-22, 23, 26, 27, 31, 32-33, 34, 37, 40, 90, 93, 93-94 n., 134 n., 176, 177, 234
Meredith, George, 253 n.
Milton, John: 39; Wordsworth a student of *Il Penseroso*, 53
Mueschke, Paul (*see* Campbell, Oscar James, and)

Napoleon, 76

Paine, Tom, 94, 119 n., 134
Philanthropist, The, a Monthly Miscellany (projected by Wordsworth and William Mathews), 32
Pinney, John Frederick, loans Wordsworth the cottage at Racedown, 34
Preston, Raymond A., on the critics of William Godwin, 184, 185, 185 n.
Price, Dr. Richard, 134
Priestley, Joseph, 94, 238-239 n.

Racedown "crisis," The, 111, *153-166*, 167, 169-170, 175, 177, 197
Rader, Melvin M., 239 n.
Rawson, Mrs. William (Wordsworth's aunt), 33
Read, Herbert, on *The Ruined Cottage*, 221
Robinson, John: 22 n.; offers Wordsworth a curacy, 22, 26
Rosset, P. F., Wordsworth imitates his *L'Agriculture* in *An Evening Walk*, 54, 54 n.
Rousseau, Jean Jacques, Wordsworth's knowledge of, 78-79, 80

Schiller's *The Robbers*, 141; influence on *The Borderers*, 201-202, 202 n.
Selective principle, The, of Wordsworth's naturalism, 247-249
Shakespeare, William: 141; influence on *The Borderers*, 172-173 n., 206 n.

INDEX

Shelley's *Alastor*, anticipated by "Lines Left upon a seat in a Yew-Tree," 189

Swinburne, Algernon Charles: 253 n.; on *The Borderers*, 170–171

Thomson, James, 39, 187 n.

Vallon, Annette; 7, 27, 28, 40, 88, 93, 102; her letters to Wordsworth and Dorothy, 90–91, 91 n.; Wordsworth's desire for a reunion with, 91–92, 94–95; Wordsworth's supposed remorse for, 131–132, 154, 162, 175, 223–224 n.; Wordsworth's separation from reflected in *Guilt and Sorrow*, 135, 139, 139–140 n.

Watson, Richard (Bishop of Llandaff): 112, 114, 117, 124, 128, 132, 142, 143; moves Wordsworth to defend the French Revolution and to criticize English society, 95–109

Whitman, Walt, 253 n.

Wordsworth, Anne (Wordsworth's mother), 5, 7

Wordsworth, Anne Caroline (daughter of Wordsworth and Annette Vallon), 27, 90, 91, 92, 93, 94, 95, 102

Wordsworth, Christopher (Wordsworth's brother), 12, 14, 19

Wordsworth, Dorothy (Wordsworth's sister): 4, 8, 11, 15, 16, 17, 18, 19, 22 n., 24, 25, 27, 28, 31, 33, 35, 45, 50, 53 n., 56, 56 n., 62, 63, 66, 68, 70, 70 n., 77, 79, 90, 91, 91 n., 92, 94, 95, 154 n., 226 n., 229 n., 251, 253; on the Lonsdale case, 9–10, 93 n.; unhappy with guardians, 11, 12–14, 41; with Wordsworth at Windy Brow, 29–30; her ideas of domestic bliss, 41–44, 46; her preference for evening walks, 47–49; *An Evening Walk* addressed to, 52, 61; her experiences reflected in *Guilt and Sorrow*, 137-138, 138 n., 139; and the Racedown "crisis," 34, 111, 154, 155, 156, 159–160, 161, 163, 166, 167; on *The Ruined Cottage*, 221–222

Wordsworth, John (Wordsworth's father): 7–8; consequences of his death, 8–9

Wordsworth, John (Wordsworth's brother), 12, 14, 34

Wordsworth, Richard (Wordsworth's uncle), 9

Wordsworth, Richard (Wordsworth's brother): 14, 15, 24, 25, 27, 92, 93, 136 n.; warns Wordsworth about expressing radical opinions, 31

Wordsworth, William: rationalizes his youthful experience, 4–5, 35; childhood experience, 5–7; consequences of the death of his parents, 7–9, 34; the Lonsdale case, 8–11 (*see* Lonsdale); unhappy with guardians, 11–14; youthful maladjustment, 14–15, 34; his finances, 15–16, 91, 92–95; refuses to choose a profession, 16–34; tour of Switzerland, 17–18, 24, 44–46, 62, 65 n., 66; with Dorothy at Forncett, 46–47; fails to work for Cambridge fellowship, 18–19; walking tour in Wales, 19, 22; intellectual indifference, 19–21; refuses to study Oriental languages and enter church, 22; residence in France, 23–25, 27; plans made for him to enter church, 22, 25–27; composes *An Evening Walk* and *Descriptive Sketches* (their style and character), 37–40, 62, 63, 148; his and Dorothy's conception of the ideal existence, 41–49; his and Dorothy's preference for

INDEX

Wordsworth—*continued*
evening walks, 47–48; his early understanding of the value of memory and association, 48–49, 73–74 n.; birth of Ann Caroline Wordsworth, 27, 90; return to England, 27, 88-95; crisis of 1793, 89–95; his desire for a reunion with Annette Vallon, 91–92, 94–95; publication of *An Evening Walk* and *Descriptive Sketches*, 27, 28, 92, 93; ostracized by Uncle William, 28–29, 95; writes *The Letter to the Bishop of Llandaff*, 95, 95 n.; tours western England with William Calvert, 28, 28 n.; composes first draft of *Guilt and Sorrow*, 113–114, 117; with Dorothy at Windy Brow, 29–30; his radicalism alarms his brother Richard, 31; Raisley Calvert's legacy makes him financially independent, 31–32, 35–36; desires employment, moves to London, 32–34; meets Coleridge, 166 n.; settles with Dorothy in the Pinney cottage at Racedown, 34, 34 n., 153, 154 n.; composes the Racedown soliloquy, 161; revises *Guilt and Sorrow*, 119–120, 120 n.; composes *The Borderers*, 153, 189 n.; completes "Lines Left upon a Seat in a Yew-Tree," 189, 189 n.; composes *The Ruined Cottage*, 221–222, 222 n.

Works of:
Borderers, The: 110, 126 n., 143 n., 153, *170–219*, 220, 221, 236; Preface to, 172 n., 180, 191, 193; summary of, 171–173; its date of composition, 189 n.; and the influence of William Godwin, 111, 154, *174–191*; not a pessimistic play, 197–210; naturalism in, 205, 206 n., 208–210, 244; social criticism in, 210–217, 220, 224, 229, 234

"The Complaint of a Forsaken Indian Woman," 144

"The Convict," 113 n.

Descriptive Sketches: 37–41, *62–87*, 91, 93–94 n., 112, 127, 140, 148, 149 n., 151, 154 n., 169; publication of, 27, 28, 92, 93; purpose in, 37, 62–64, 81; description of, 63–87; similarity to *An Evening Walk*, 65–70, 71, 81; expresses Wordsworth and Dorothy's conception of the ideal existence, 41, 63, 65–73, 84–87, 137, 138; expresses Wordsworth's republican enthusiasm, 16, 70–87, 101, 102, 118–119; and Wordsworth's reflections on the Golden Age, 73, 75, 79, 80, 83, 83 n., 86; anticipates the political sonnets, 73–77, 77 n.; anticipates Wordsworth's later preoccupation with mutability, 85 n.; view of nature in, 243

Evening Walk, An: 37–41, 47, *49–62*, 63, 83, 86, 90, 91, 93–94 n., 112, 140, 148, 149 n., 151, 154 n., 161, 214, 230 n., 242, 245; anticipated by early sonnet, 48; publication of, 27, 28, 92, 93; purpose in, 37, 52, 61; addressed to Dorothy, 52, 61; description of, 49–62; similarity to *Descriptive Sketches*, 65–70, 71, 81; expresses Wordsworth and Dorothy's conception of the ideal existence, 13, 41, 49, 55–57, 61–62, 137, 138; anticipates "Tintern

INDEX

Wordsworth—*continued*
Abbey," 50–52, 51 n.; anticipates *Guilt and Sorrow*, 58, 134; view of nature in, 243; Windy Brow (1794) additions to: 163, 176, 190, 208, 220, 239, 239 n.; mature naturalism in, 167–169, 168 n., 244; reveal Wordsworth's early interest in psychology and science, 169–170 n., 237–238
Excursion, The, 221, 221 n., 222, 222 n., 229 n., 235 n. (see *The Ruined Cottage*)
"Expostulation and Reply," 167–168 n.
"The Female Vagrant," 120 n., 149 n. (see *Guilt and Sorrow*)
"Fragment of a Gothic Tale," and *The Borderers*, 209, 209 n.
Guilt and Sorrow: 11, 16, 29, 58, 88, 101, 109, *110–152*, 153, 166, 169, 220, 223–224 n., 248 n.; purpose in, 112–114, 119, 123, 225; early versions of, 112, 113 n., 114–119, 120 n., 122–123 n.; summary of, 119–123; its relation to *The Letter to the Bishop of Llandaff*, 112, 118–119, 118–119 n., 124, 132, 134, 142; social criticism in, 114–119, 120, 123–133, 211–212, 217, 218, 229, 236; reflects Wordsworth's personal experience, 112, 135–139, 139–140 n.; artistic confusion in, 140–151; similarity to *The Ruined Cottage*, 222–224; view of nature in, 243–244
"Hartleap Well," 167
"Incipient Madness," a crude first draft of *The Ruined Cottage*, 222 n.
"Intimations of Immortality, Ode on," 85 n., 110
Juvenal, Imitation of (in collaboration with Frances Wrangham), 234 n.
Letter to the Bishop of Llandaff, The: 16, 21, 28, *95–109*, 111, 123, 142, 151; its date of composition, 95 n.; the Lonsdale case reflected in, 11, 100; expresses Wordsworth's republicanism, 88, 101–103, 104–106, 109; social criticism in, 101–103, 106–107, 109, 124, 212, 218, 229, 236; expresses Wordsworth's faith in education, 108–109, 234; similarity to *Descriptive Sketches*, 101–102; relation to *Guilt and Sorrow*, 112, 118–119, 118–119 n., 124, 132, 134, 142
"Lines Left upon a Seat in a Yew-Tree": 194, 195, 208; its date of composition, 189 n.; reflects the influence of William Godwin, 189–190; influences Coleridge, 207 n.
"Lines Written in Early Spring": 167, 250 n.; reveals the uncertainty of Wordsworth's naturalism, 249–250
Lyrical Ballads: 89, 111, 111–112 n., 120 n., 149 n., 152, 166, 174, 220, 221, 249; Prefaces to, 165; relation of *The Letter to the Bishop of Llandaff* to, 101; philosophy of anticipated in 1794 at Windy Brow, 167–168; anticipated in *The Borderers*, 176, 219; Coleridge's letter and the purpose in, 231–237

INDEX

Wordsworth—*continued*
"Michael," 48, 73–74 n.
Peter Bell: 144, 244; reveals Wordsworth's knowledge of the evil in nature, 246–247; unpublished stanzas from, 248
Prelude, The: 5–6, 7 n., 79, 80, 81, 136, 156, 176; its fallibility as a source for Wordsworth's biography, 3–5, 20 n., 23, 153, 157–161, 161 n., 177; the Racedown soliloquy (*Prelude*, I, 1–54), 161–166, 169; tribute to Raisley Calvert in, 35–36
Racedown soliloquy, The (*see The Prelude*)
Recluse, The, 164, 221
Ruined Cottage, The: 220–237, 242; its date of composition, 221–222, 222 n.; purpose in, 225, 226–227, 229–237; summary of, 222–224; similarity to *Guilt and Sorrow,* 222–224; social criticism in, 224–225, 229, 236–237; narrative technique in, 225–229; view of nature in, 226–227, 244–245; the first successful synthesis of the best elements of his poetry, 220–221, 249
Sonnets:
"Great Men Have Been among Us," 74–75
"It Is not to Be Thought of that the Flood," 75
"On Seeing Miss Helen Maria Williams Weep at a Tale of Distress," Wordsworth's first published poem, 37 n.
"Sweet Was the Walk along the Narrow Lane," *An Evening Walk* in miniature, 48
"To the Memory of Raisley Calvert," 36
"Two Voices Are There; One Is of the Sea," 75–76
"Thorn, The": 144; first draft of in *The Borderers,* 213–214
"Tintern Abbey, Lines Written a Few Miles above": 77 n., 110, 164–165, 169, 174–175, 208; anticipated in *An Evening Walk* and "The Vale of Esthwaite," 51–52, 51 n.; anticipated in the Racedown soliloquy, 164–165; anticipated in *The Borderers,* 208; reveals uncertainty of Wordsworth's naturalism, 250–254
"To My Sister," 110
"The Vale of Esthwaite": 14; records Wordsworth's reaction to his father's death, 7–8, 56 n.; anticipation of "Tintern Abbey" in, 51 n.
Windy Brow verses (*see An Evening Walk*)
Wrangham, Frances: 112–113, 113 n., 114; collaborates with Wordsworth on an imitation of Juvenal, 234 n.

Young's *Night Thoughts,* echoed in *An Evening Walk,* 60

UNIVERSITY OF MICHIGAN PUBLICATIONS

Orders and requests for detailed book lists should be directed to the University of Michigan Press.

SERIES IN LANGUAGE AND LITERATURE

Vol. I. STUDIES IN SHAKESPEARE, MILTON AND DONNE. By Member of the English Department. Pp. v + 232. $2.50.

Vol. II. ELIZABETHAN PROVERB LORE IN LYLY'S 'EUPHUES' AND IN PETTIE'S 'PETITE PALLACE,' WITH PARALLELS FROM SHAKESPEARE. By Morris P. Tilley. Pp. x + 461. $3.50.

Vol. III. THE SOCIAL MODE OF RESTORATION COMEDY. By Kathleen M. Lynch. Pp. xi + 242. $2.50.

Vol. IV. STUART POLITICS IN CHAPMAN'S 'TRAGEDY OF CHABOT.' By Norma D. Solve. Pp. x + 176. $2.50.

Vols. V-VI. EL LIBRO DEL CAUALLERO ZIFAR. By C. P. Wagner.
  Vol. V. PART I. TEXT. Pp. xviii + 532. With 9 plates. $5.00.
  Vol. VI. PART II. COMMENTARY. (*In preparation.*)

Vol. VII. STRINDBERG'S DRAMATIC EXPRESSIONISM. By C. E. W. L. Dahlström. Pp. xi + 242. $2.50.

Vol. VIII. ESSAYS AND STUDIES IN ENGLISH AND COMPARATIVE LITERATURE. By Members of the English Department. Pp. vii + 231. $2.50.

Vol. IX. TOWARD THE UNDERSTANDING OF SHELLEY. By Bennett Weaver. Pp. xii + 258. $2.50.

Vol. X. ESSAYS AND STUDIES IN ENGLISH AND COMPARATIVE LITERATURE. By Members of the English Department. Pp. vi + 278. $2.50.

Vol. XI. FRENCH MODAL SYNTAX IN THE SIXTEENTH CENTURY. By Newton S. Bement. Pp. xviii + 168. $2.50.

Vol. XII. THE INTELLECTUAL MILIEU OF JOHN DRYDEN. By Louis I. Bredvold. Pp. viii + 189. $2.50.

Vol. XIII. ESSAYS AND STUDIES IN ENGLISH AND COMPARATIVE LITERATURE. By Members of the English Department. Pp. vii + 328. $3.00.

Vols. XIV-XV. THREE CENTURIES OF FRENCH POETIC THEORY (1328-1630). By W. F. Patterson.
  Vol. XIV. PARTS I-II. Pp. xx + 978. $5.00.
  Vol. XV. PARTS III-IV. Pp. v + 523. $3.50.

Vol. XVI. THE SOURCES OF JOHN DRYDEN'S COMEDIES. By N. B. Allen. Pp. xviii + 298. $3.00.

SERIES IN LANGUAGE AND LITERATURE

VOL. XVII. ELIZABETHAN COMIC CHARACTER CONVENTIONS AS REVEALED IN THE COMEDIES OF GEORGE CHAPMAN. By P. V. Kreider. Pp. xi + 206. $2.50.

VOL. XVIII. THE AESTHETIC THEORY OF THOMAS HOBBES, WITH SPECIAL REFERENCE TO THE PSYCHOLOGICAL APPROACH IN ENGLISH LITERARY CRITICISM. By Clarence DeWitt Thorpe. Pp. ix + 339. $4.00.

VOL. XIX. THOMAS RE QUINCEY'S THEORY OF LITERATURE. By Sigmund K. Proctor. Pp. vii + 315. $3.50.

VOL. XX. WORDSWORTH'S FORMATIVE YEARS. George W. Meyer. Pp. vii + 265. $3.50.

www.ingramcontent.com/pod-product-compliance
Lightning Source LLC
Chambersburg PA
CBHW021138230426
43667CB00005B/167